AF575753

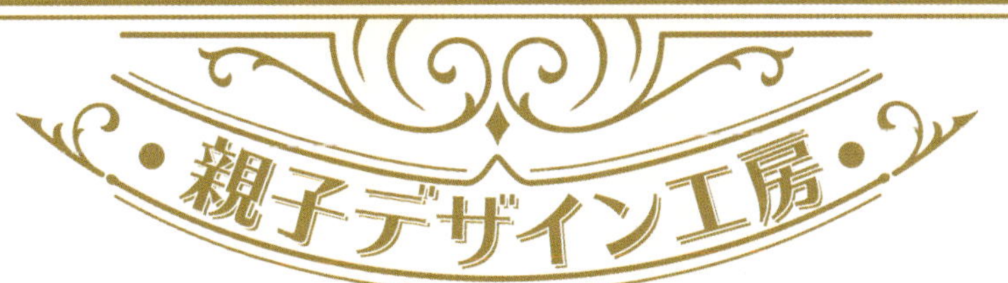

FAMILY TRAITS

The Fantastic Bestiary of a Father and his Sons

Itsuki, Ryunosuke & Thomas ROMAIN

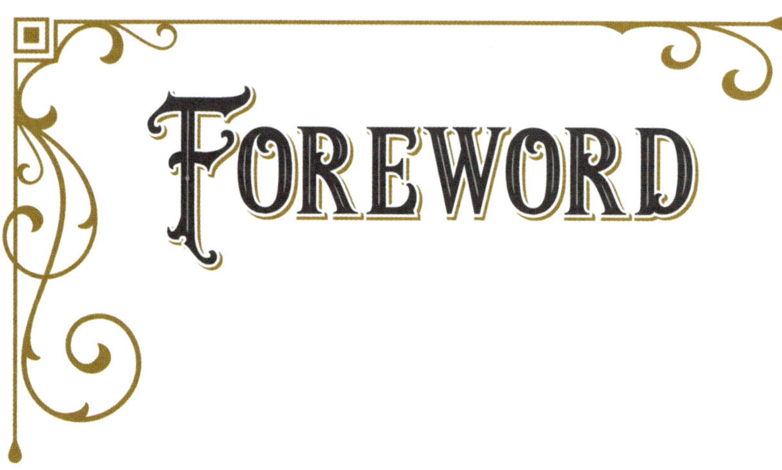

It is with immense pleasure and great pride that we welcome you inside the imagination of Itsuki and Ryunosuke, two Franco-Japanese boys aged 9 and 11 years old.

My name is Thomas Romain. I had the good fortune to grow up and study in the great country of freedom and culture that is France. But, like many children of my generation raised during the 80s and 90s, I was also nurtured by the icons of Japanese pop culture, from manga to anime to videogames. This influence was so strong that, at the beginning of my animation career, I decided to expatriate myself to Tokyo, to understand, learn, and immerse myself in this creative milieu and especially to work alongside the Japanese artists I so admired.

I've lived in Japan since 2003. I succeeded in making a place for myself within the world of Japanese animation, a sector as fascinating as it is hermetic. However, my pride and joy remains that of having two wonderful sons.

Although I've always wanted to transmit my passion for drawing to my children, I've never wished it to be against their wills. This desire must first and foremost come from them. I hope that seeing their dad drawing will influence them in that direction, but if drawing doesn't interest them, then so be it. Each child must be free to discover their own talent, whatever it may be.

About a year ago I began to detect something special in Itsuki and Ryunosuke's drawings. Certainly, my view was biased by them being my own sons - parents always believe that their children are the most extraordinary youngsters in the entire world - but, regardless of that, I also detected some potential in my role as a professional. The forms, the colors they used, their ideas, they all stimulated me. I simply had the urge to reinterpret their characters, out of curiosity, and for my own pleasure as an artist. I was certain that this would surprise, delight, and even evoke pride in them, seeing their dad interesting himself in their creations to the point of becoming inspired by them himself.

Such was the beginning of this project. However, it quickly took on some surprising proportions. I discovered their universal appeal when I shared them with the world across social media, from America to Russia, by way of Asia and the Middle East, not to mention the European countries. We've received some extraordinarily positive feedback. More than enough to motivate us to draw new characters week after week while filling up a universe in constant expansion. A dream then formed itself, one of publishing our drawings in the form of a beautiful book. Thanks to the support of all our fans and the confidence given to us by our publisher this dream has become a reality, and we haven't the kind words to thank you all.

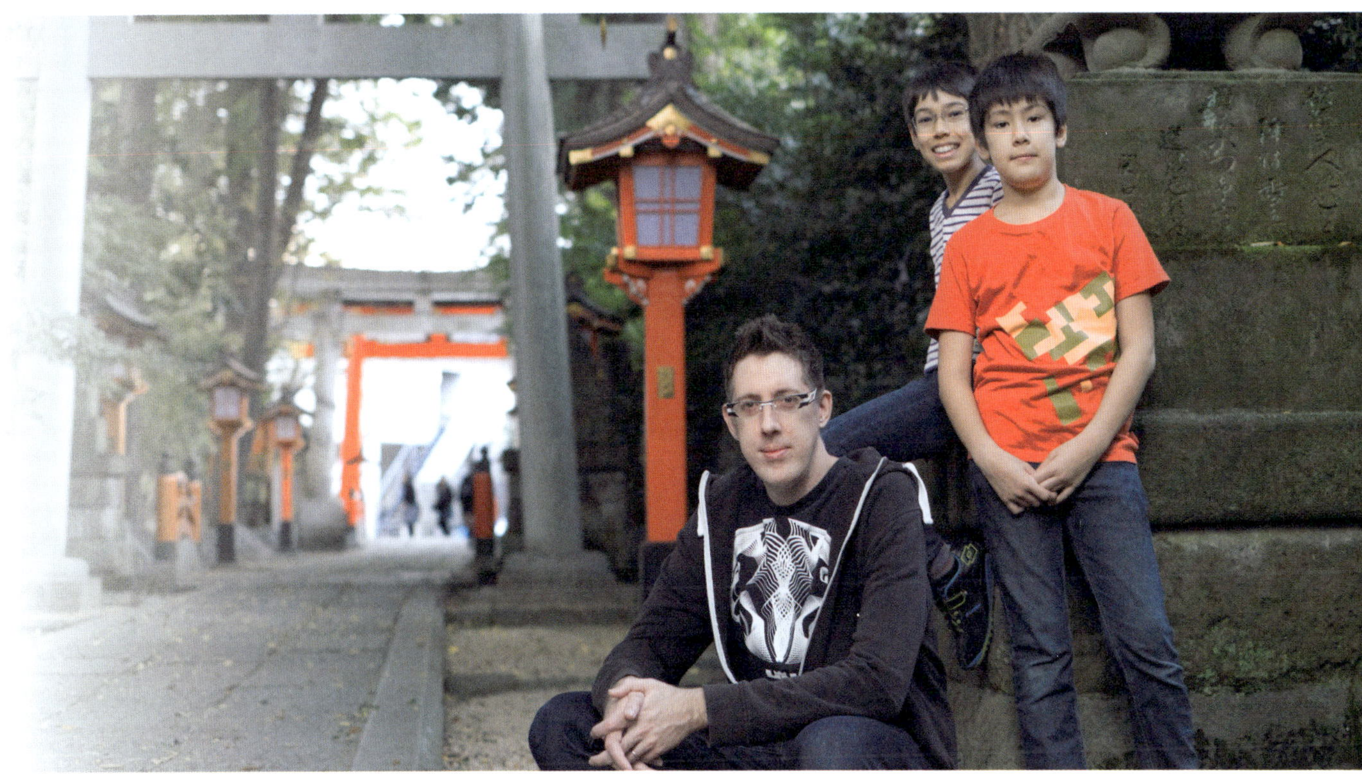

The texts that accompany the images will give you an idea of what was going through our heads during the creation of these drawings. These will sway between the inspirational anecdotes by Itsuki and Ryunosuke, impressions on both the original drawing as well as its interpretation, commentaries on the design process, and small incursions into our fantastic world. But I dare to hope that this creative project is clear enough to be appreciated on its visual aspect alone.

By working off my sons' imaginations in particular, I sought to show that all the children of the world have creative potential that just asks to be developed. I made every effort to put my experience as an artist at their service, to give them the initiative without imposing constraints. I have assisted them in this process, often contenting myself with giving a more polished form to the images that were freely born out of their imaginations. My role is that of a translator who interprets these children's drawings so that an untrained eye may appreciate their full flavor. Speaking as a creative type, the experience in incredibly enriching. Successfully pulling out a coherent illustration from the original drawing is a passionate exercise which pushes me to surpass myself, to find solutions to multiple graphical problems, and forces me to draw things that I would never have taken on myself, thus enlarging my own horizons. Of course, as a father, the bonds that tie me to my sons, our complicity, were all reinforced, drawing after drawing.

I hope that - beyond the newbie and professional artists, beyond the fans of pop-culture and art lovers - this book will simply succeed in gathering around it parents and children. Devour these few pages with great appetite, let yourselves be drawn in by its playful side - compare the images, choose your favorite characters, amuse yourselves by imagining other scenes, let your imaginations run wild! There are multiple ways to appreciate this work, but above all I hope that, like for us at the time of its creation, it will give you the occasion to share precious moments with your family.

Thomas Romain, January 2018

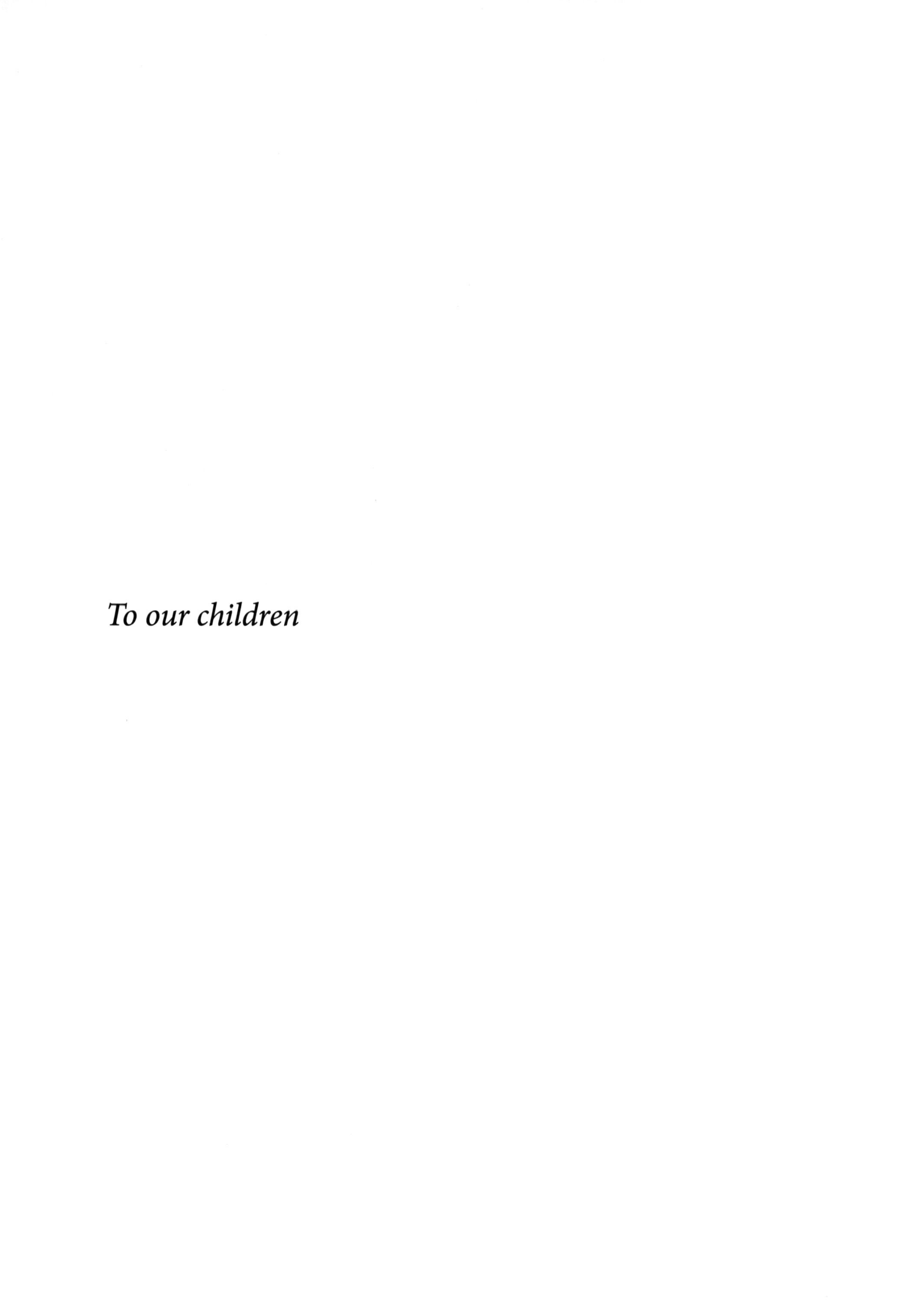

To our children

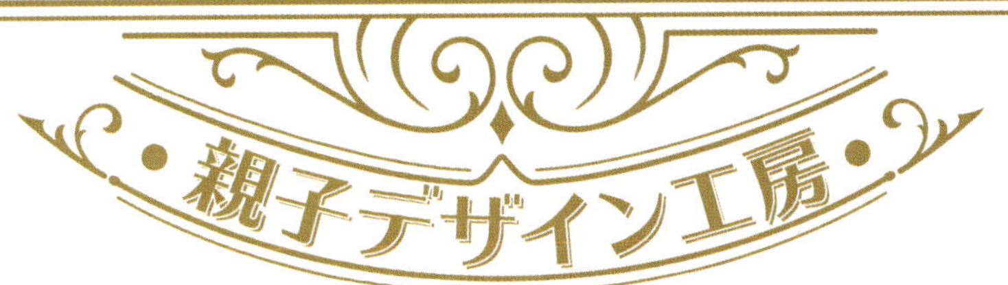

ILLUSTRATIONS

December 2016 ~ September 2017

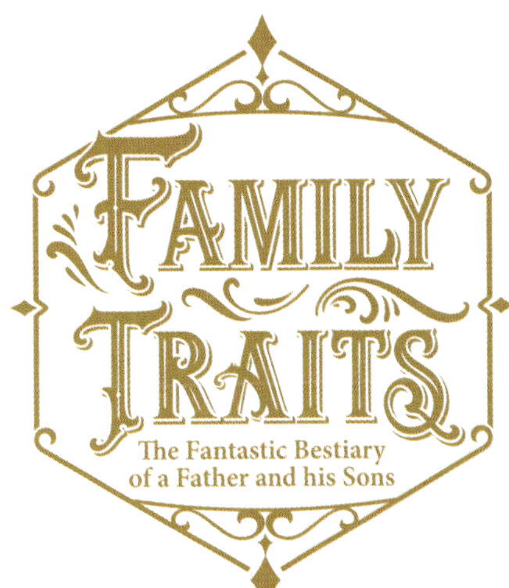

01

Saturn

The Champion Cyclops

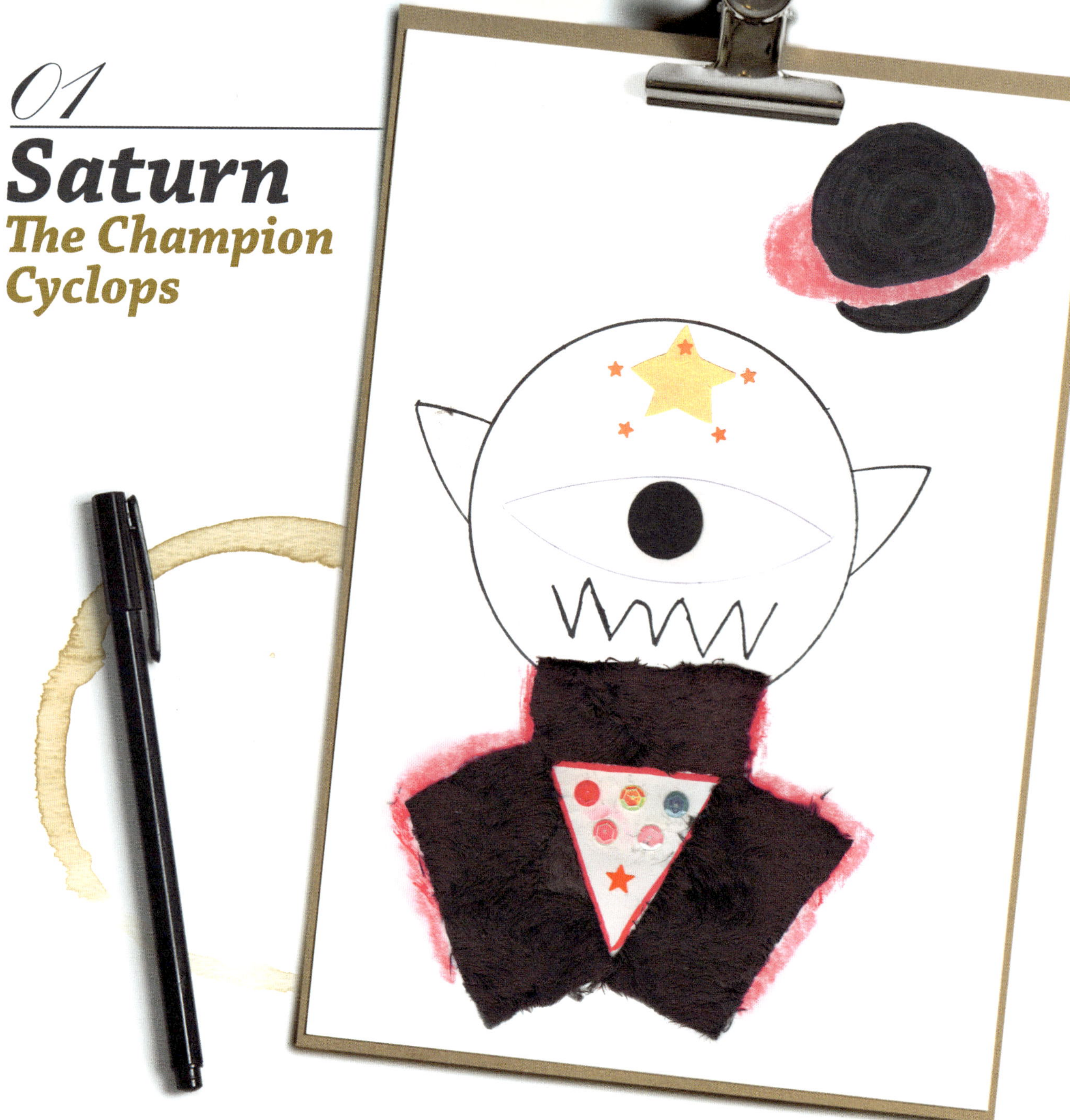

Thomas

This drawing by Ryunosuke is what started it all! He drew this at an art workshop organized by *Tokyo Sky Tree* that we stumbled upon randomly during one of our outings. He was a little shy at first, not wishing to participate, but then thankfully he jumped right in. I found his drawing to be very balanced; simple, but with little details both cool and original. I simply had the urge to redraw it! The result is slightly different than the other illustrations as I started to ink the drawings with a marker from the second artwork. Saturn is an alien wrestler in a class of his own, one of the most feared in the intergalactic wrestling league.

Ryunosuke

Dad surprised me by redrawing my character on Christmas Night. I wasn't expecting it at all. I was happy because that meant that he really liked my drawing. I think it's so cool the way he added shadows. It gives the character some volume and makes him feel more real.

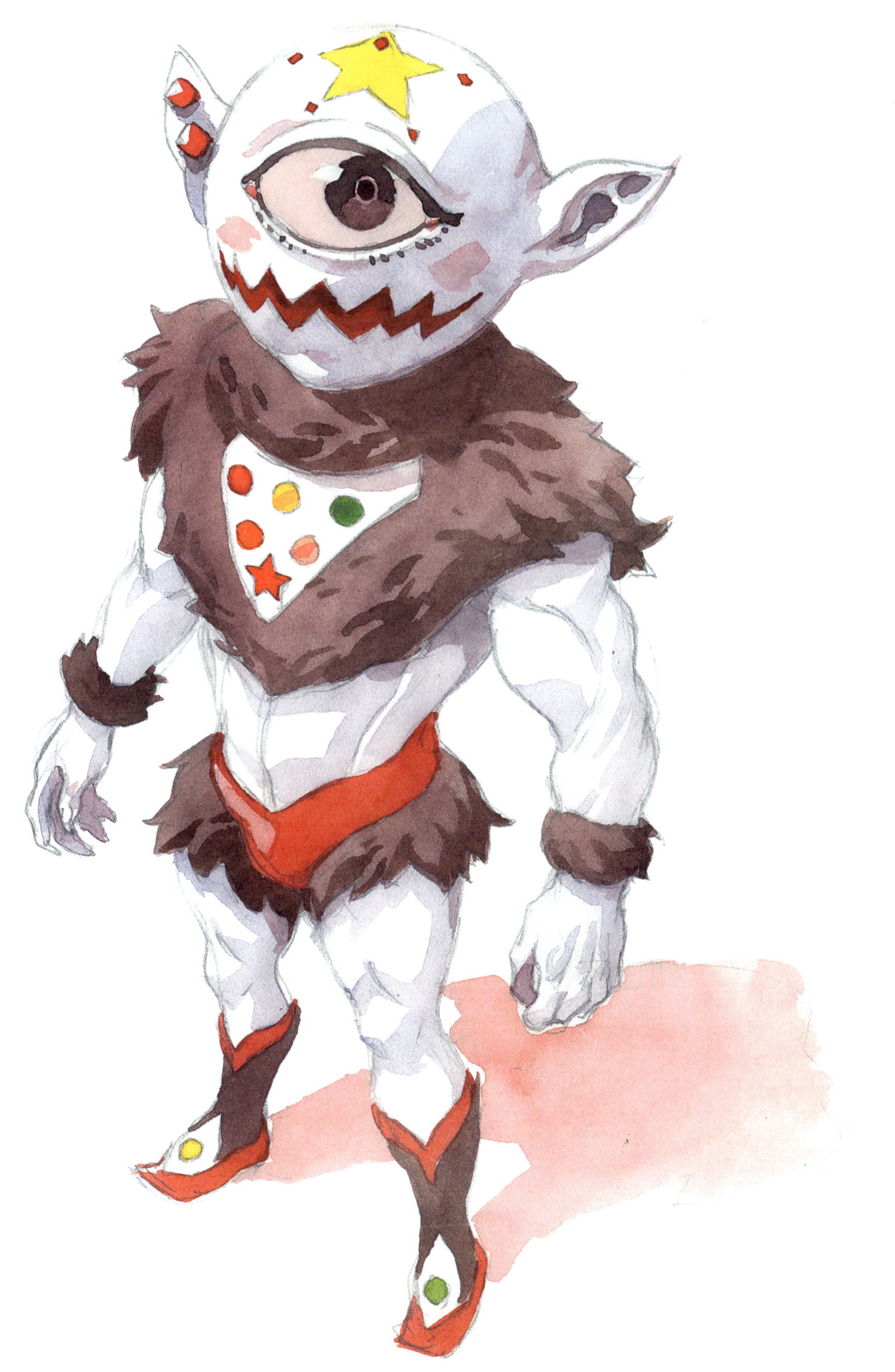

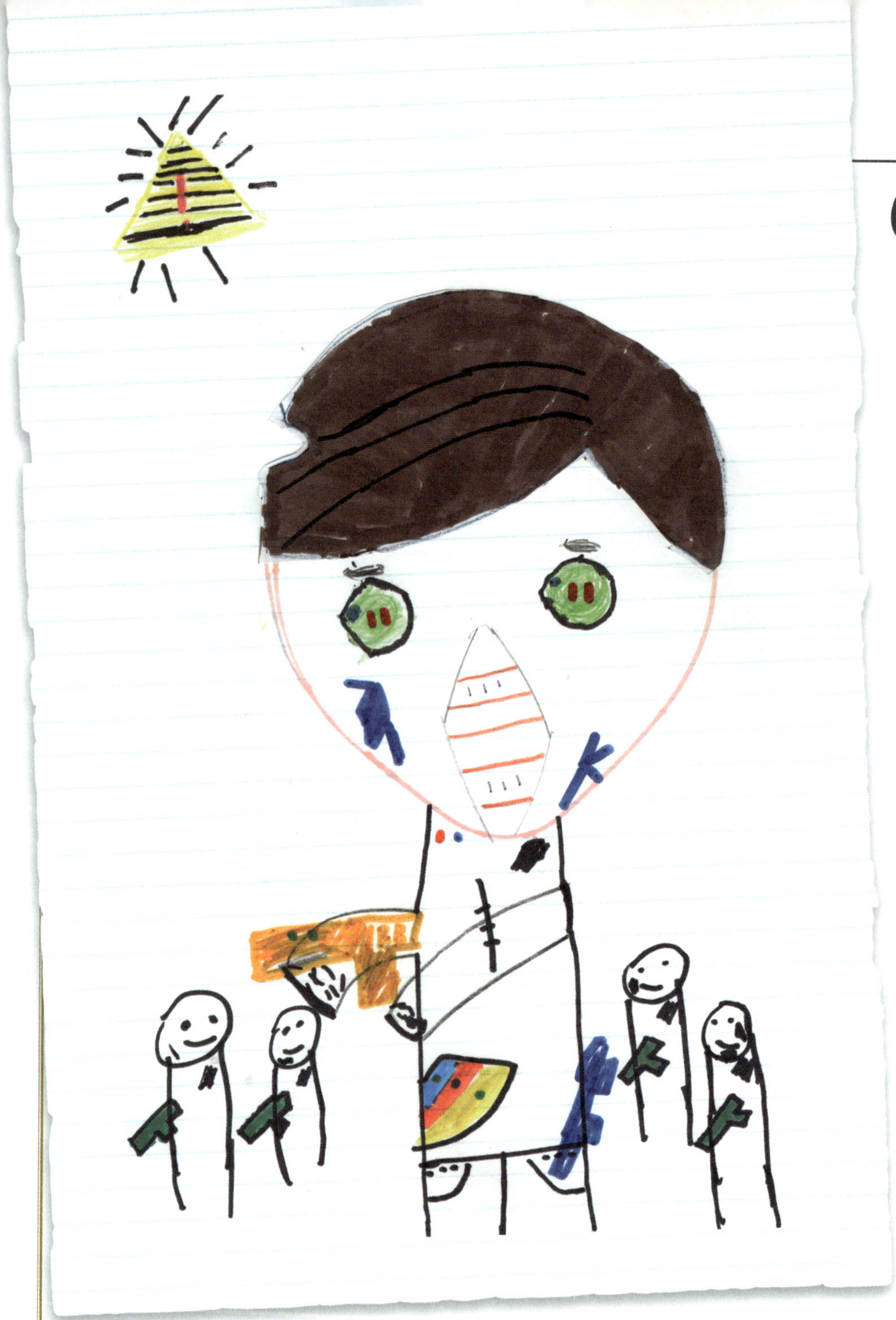

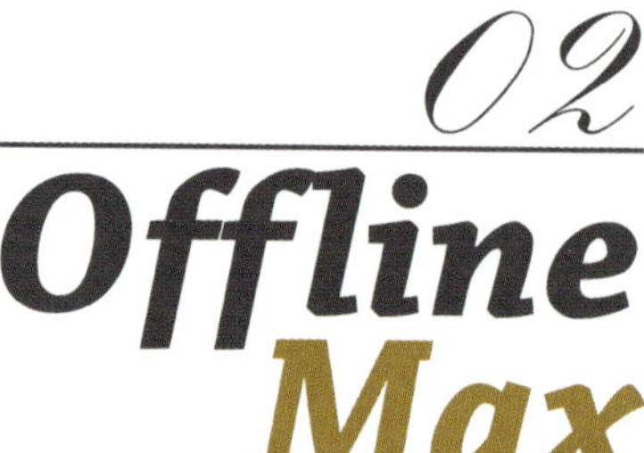

02 Offline Max

Thomas

Itsuki made this drawing at the same *Tokyo Sky Tree* workshop. This one was a bigger challenge for me to reinterpret. The hair, the green eyes, and especially the rainbow pockets are unexpected details difficult to combine. My final version is very 80s cyberpunk, which is a style I certainly wouldn't have come up with on my own.

Itsuki

At the beginning I wanted to draw a picture of Dad. I started with his hair, but after seeing that my brother was making a cool-looking monster I changed my mind and decided to make some sort of robot. Dad's drawing really looks like mine, since we can find the same details. But his is better. It looks like a character from a manga!

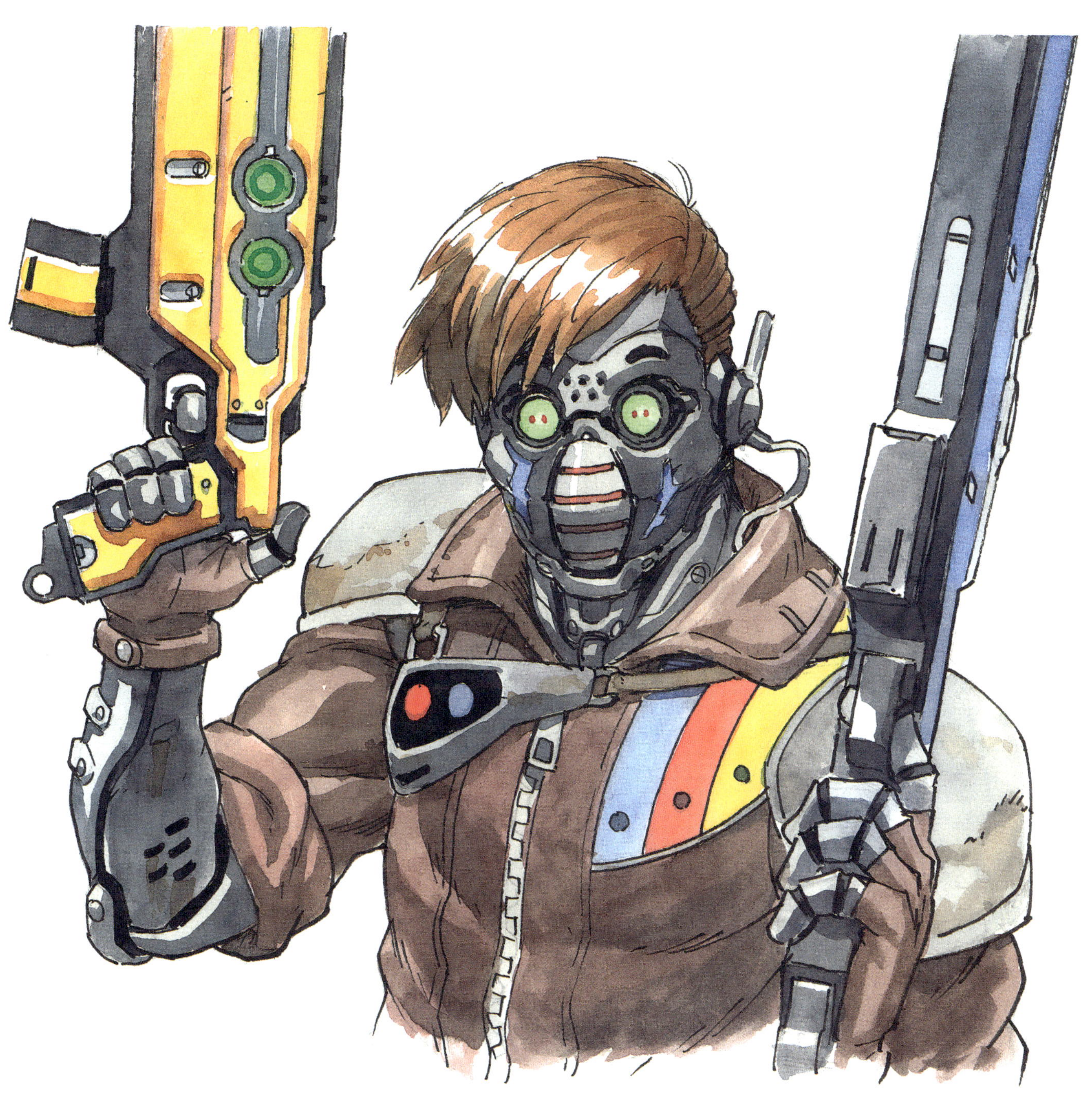

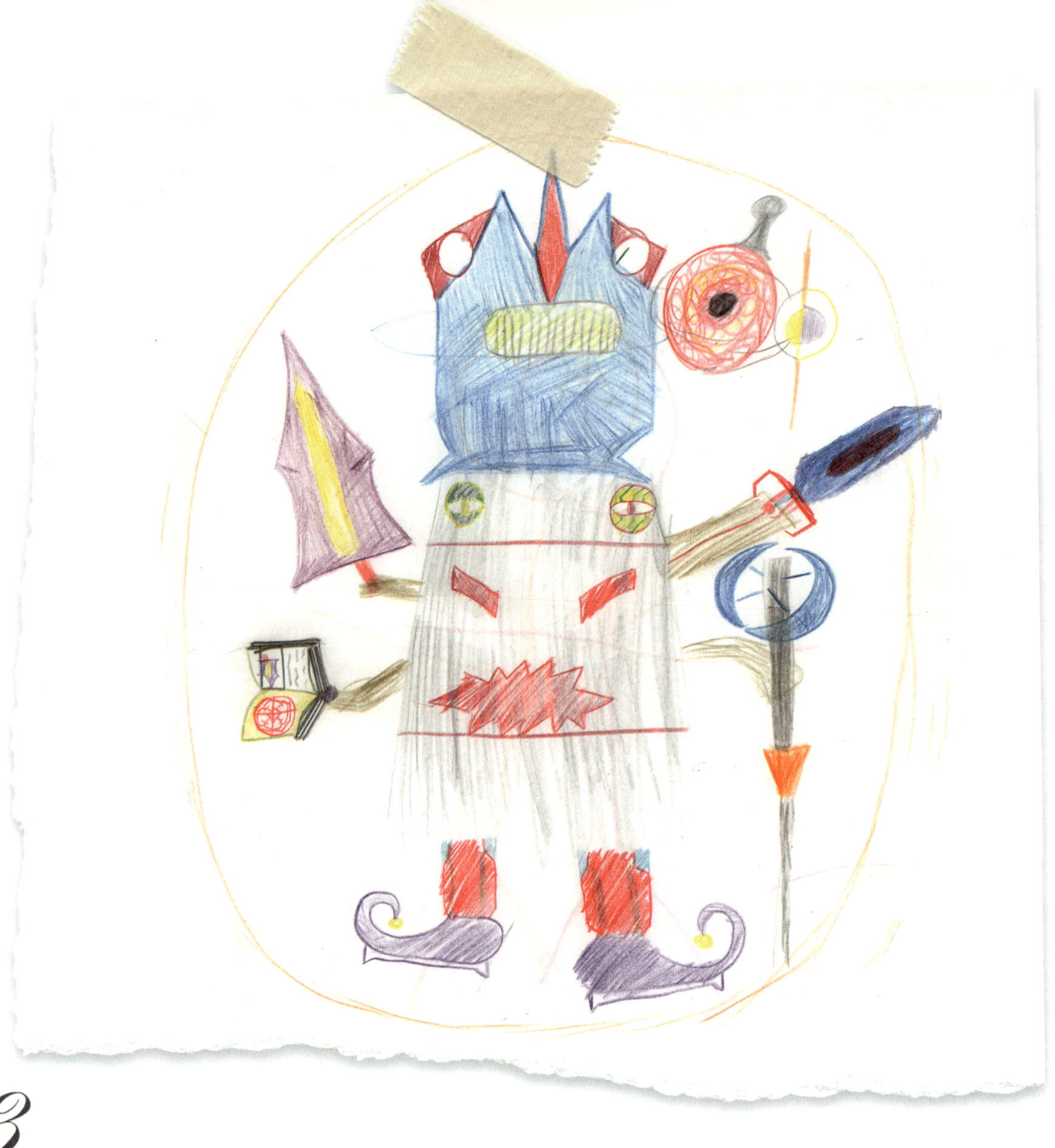

03

The Mage Knight of the Astronomical Order

Thomas

It is from this drawing that this project became a series. To find a new subject for inspiration, I plunged into Ryunosuke's sketchbooks. While all his preceding drawings were little more than stickmen, this one was far more detailed and had the elements necessary to become an excellent character. The orbs that revolve around his head reinforce the magical aspect. His primary colors and cartoonish proportions make him feel like he'd be right at home in the cult video game, *Dragon Quest*. Like many artists of my generation, I find Akira Toriyama to be a big source of inspiration.

Ryunosuke

The two left arms do normal attacks, and the two right arms specialize in magical attacks. In spite of his cute appearance he is a formidable fighter. Other than that, now that I look at this drawing again, I can see how much better I got since then. It's very encouraging! What I really like in Dad's version are the precious jewels.

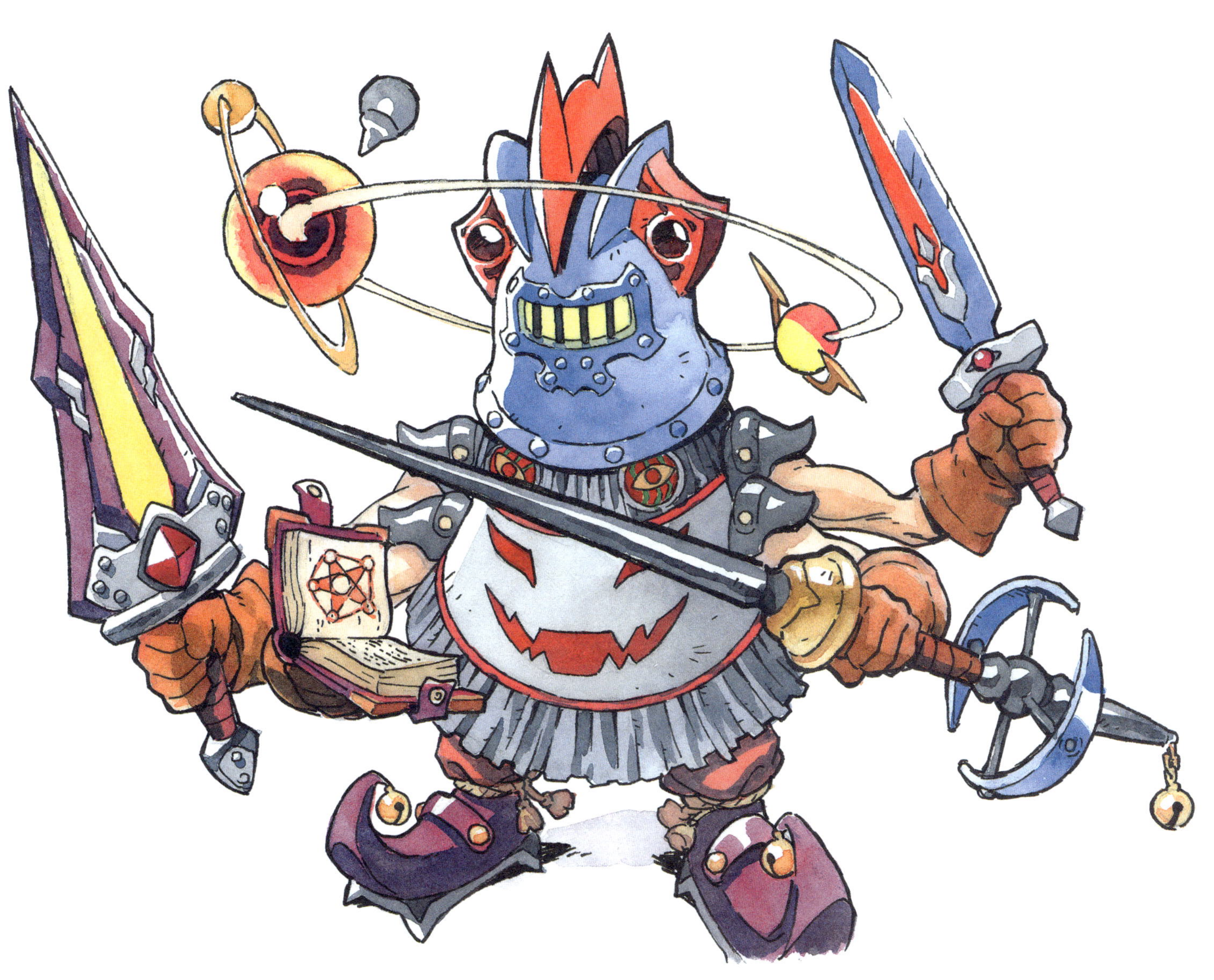

04

The Scarlet Doctor

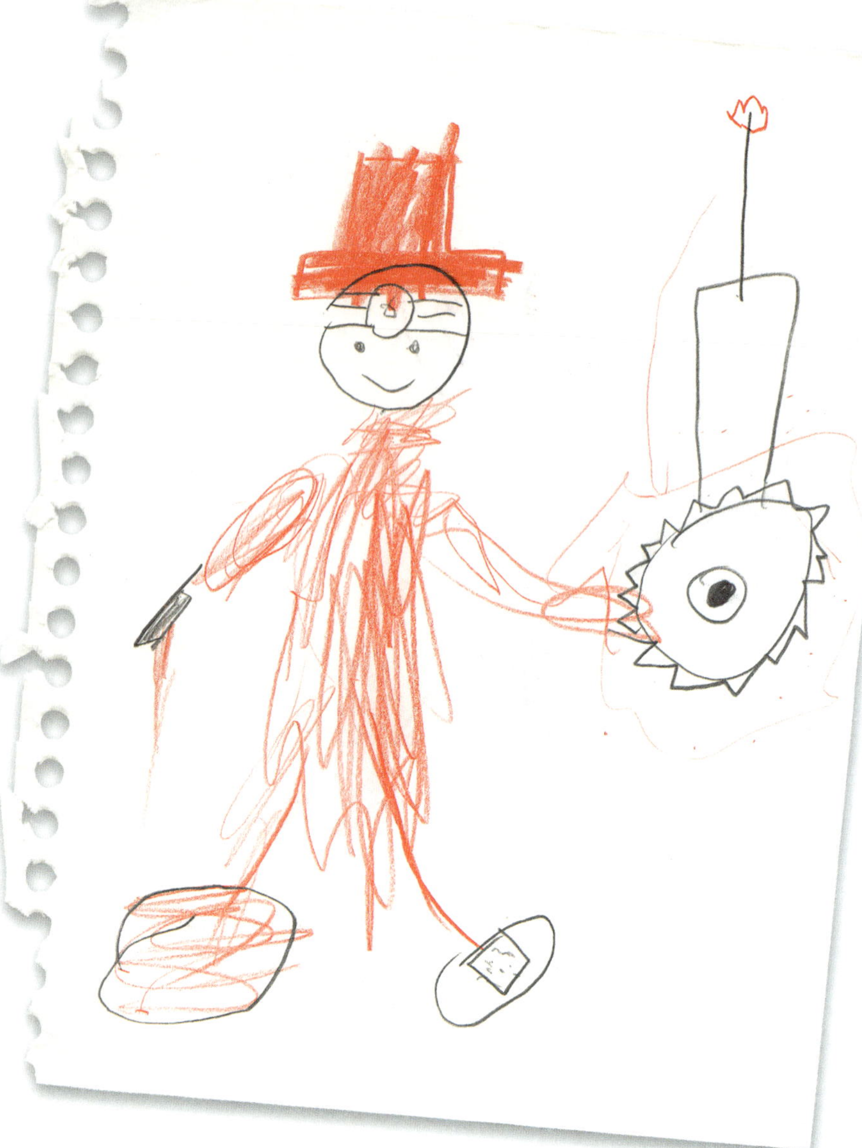

Thomas

Itsuki made this drawing back when he was in the 1st grade - he was only six years old at the time. It's certainly the most stick figure-y of all, but I find it has a particular force in its simplicity and design. The scalpel and the head mirror immediately identify him as a doctor. The top hat gave me the urge to give him a steampunk-coded look. This character went viral on the net and helped popularize our collaborative project. We even got some fanart of him!

Itsuki

This was one of my favorite drawings, and what Dad made was even better. This doctor is really cool! The thing he's holding is a candle, but Dad took its general form and made it a syringe. That was a good idea because it goes with the look of bloodiness I wanted to give him by using lots of red. I even named him Chi Ningen, which means 'Blood Man'.

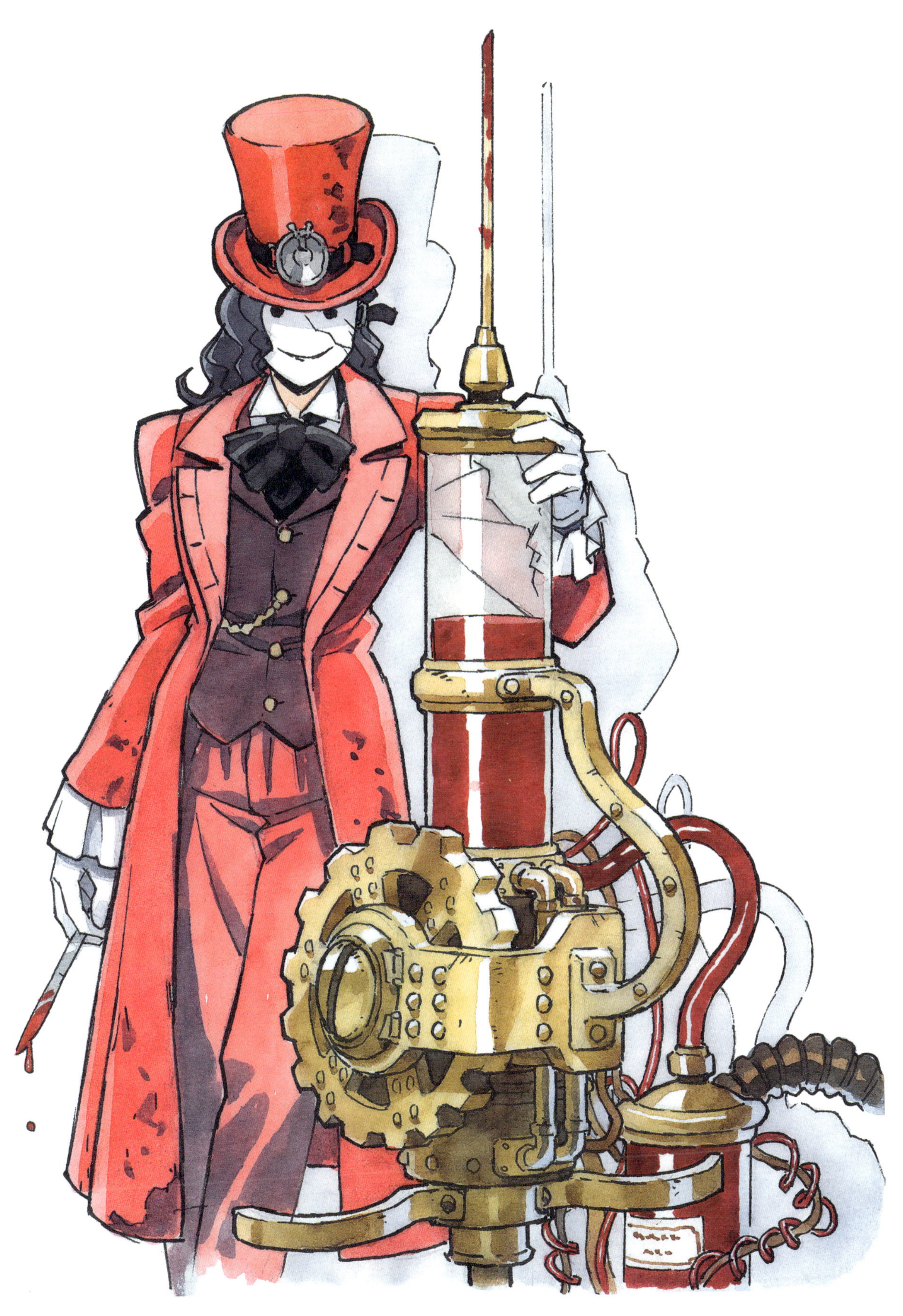

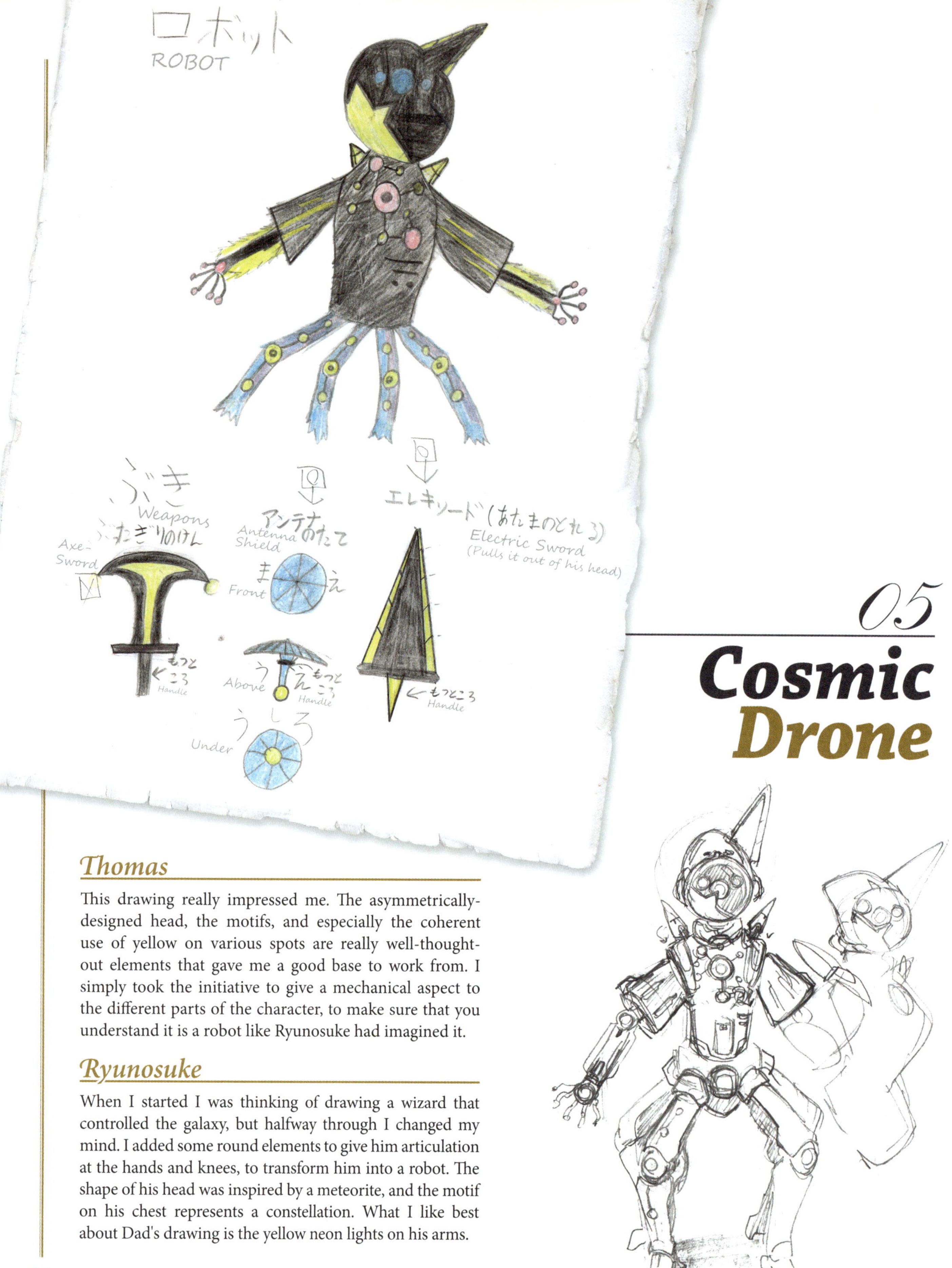

05

Cosmic Drone

Thomas

This drawing really impressed me. The asymmetrically-designed head, the motifs, and especially the coherent use of yellow on various spots are really well-thought-out elements that gave me a good base to work from. I simply took the initiative to give a mechanical aspect to the different parts of the character, to make sure that you understand it is a robot like Ryunosuke had imagined it.

Ryunosuke

When I started I was thinking of drawing a wizard that controlled the galaxy, but halfway through I changed my mind. I added some round elements to give him articulation at the hands and knees, to transform him into a robot. The shape of his head was inspired by a meteorite, and the motif on his chest represents a constellation. What I like best about Dad's drawing is the yellow neon lights on his arms.

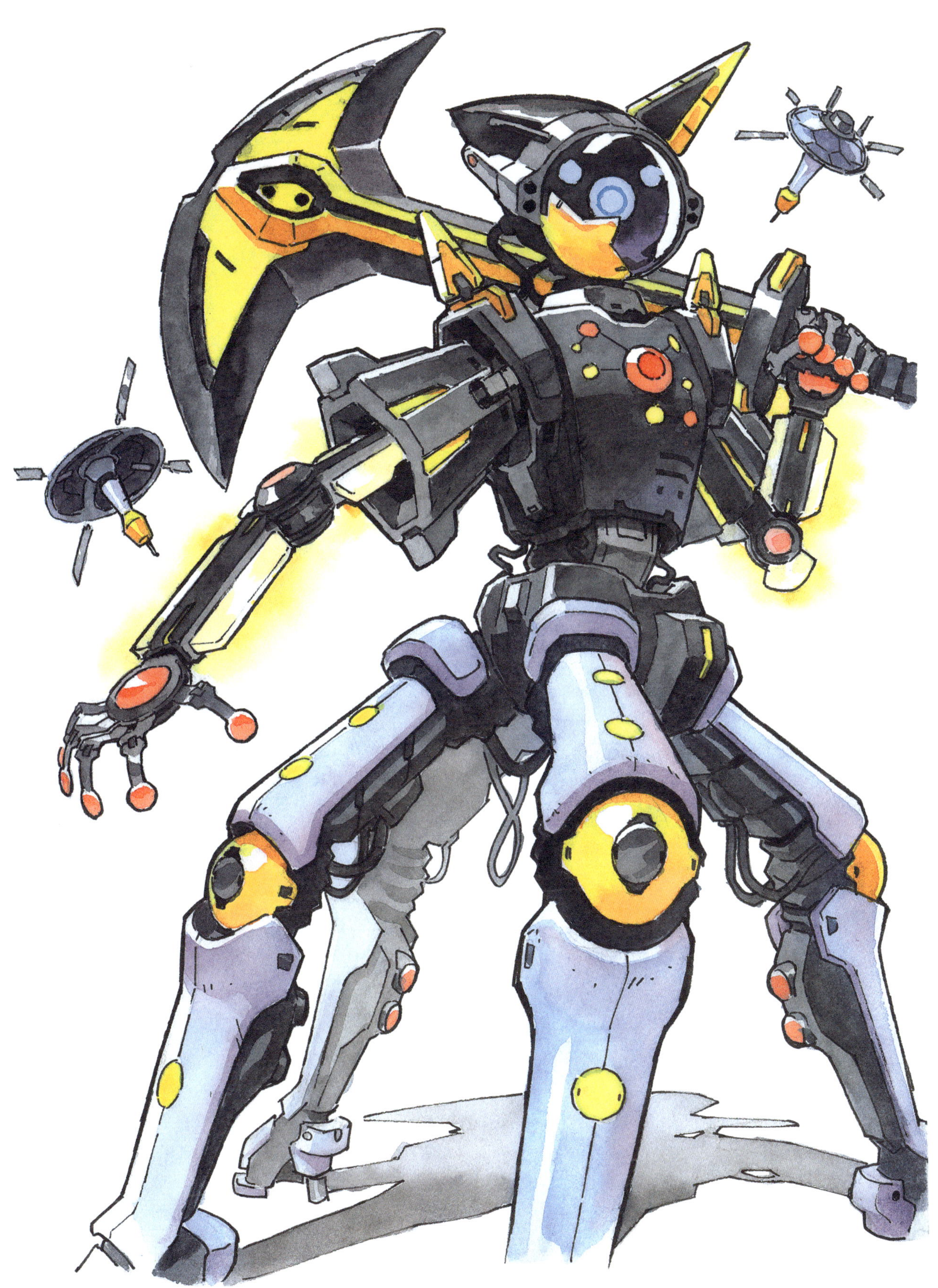

06

The Tulip Brothers

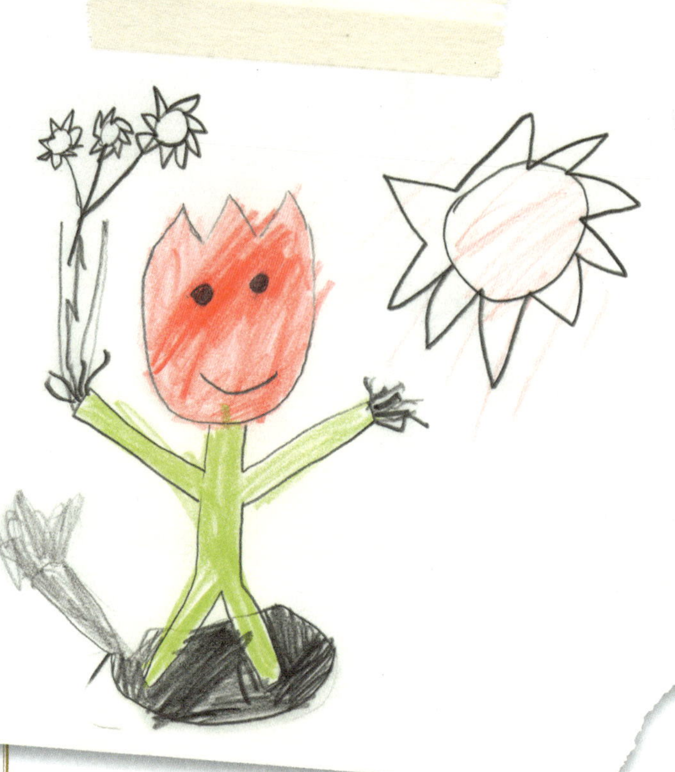

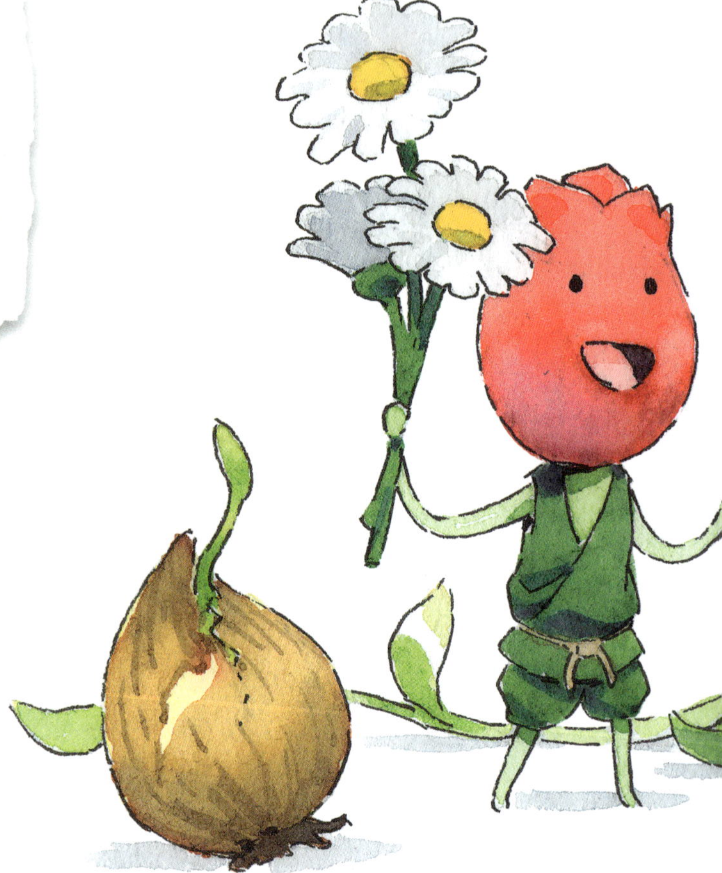

Thomas

The style of this illustration is different from the rest of the series. Itsuki's cute and minimalist drawing is self-sufficient, so I had no desire to stretch it out into a more elaborate design. I therefore decided to create a tiny diorama with several variations of the character. The inclusion of the flowerpot as a background element permitted me to pose the tulip brothers in an interesting manner while varying their attitudes.

Itsuki

Dad really respected my drawing - what's more, he made an entire group! My favorite is the little baby who is really too cute. This is Mom's favorite illustration. She wishes we'd do more cute drawings like this one, because we make too many robots and monsters.

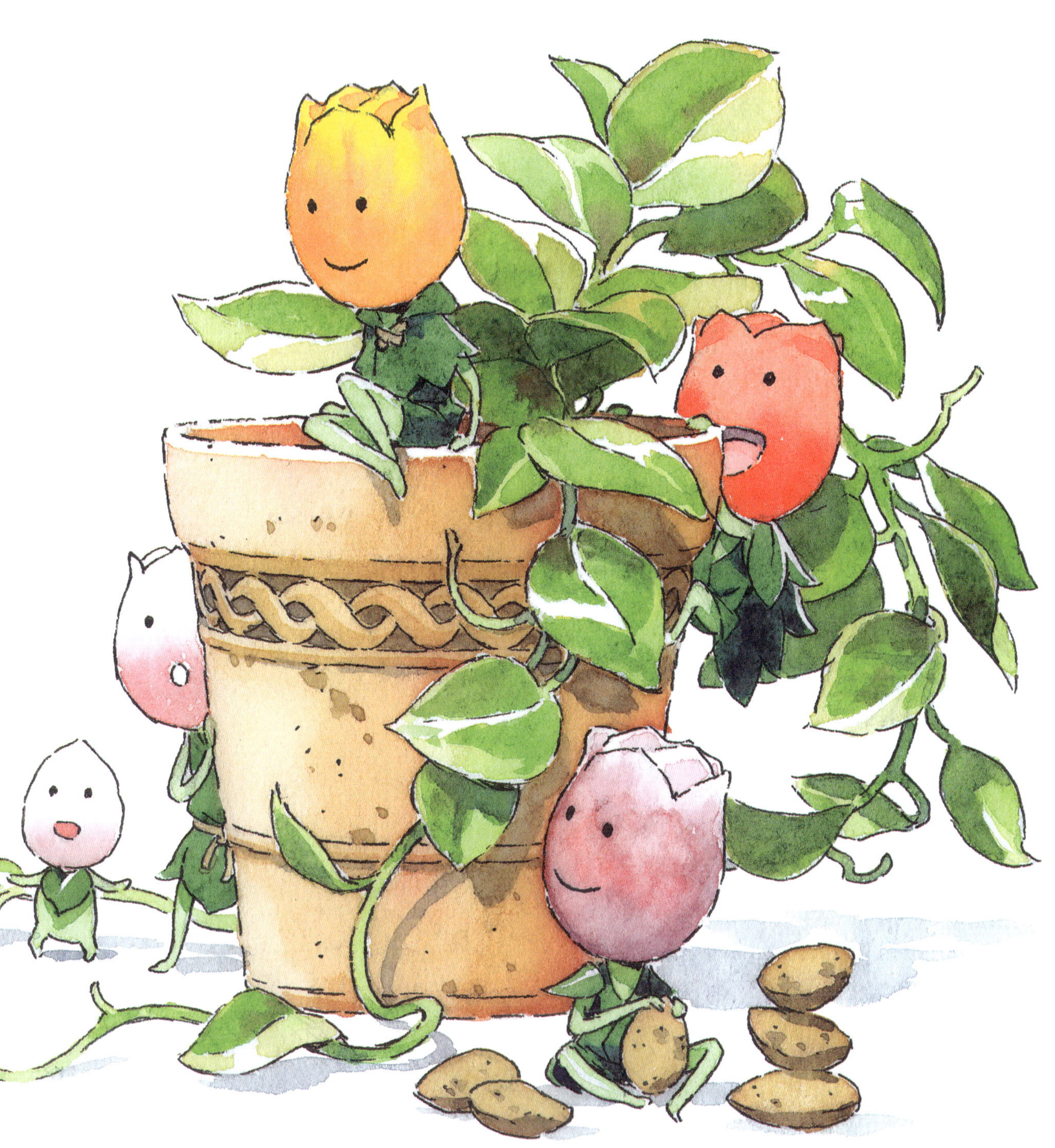

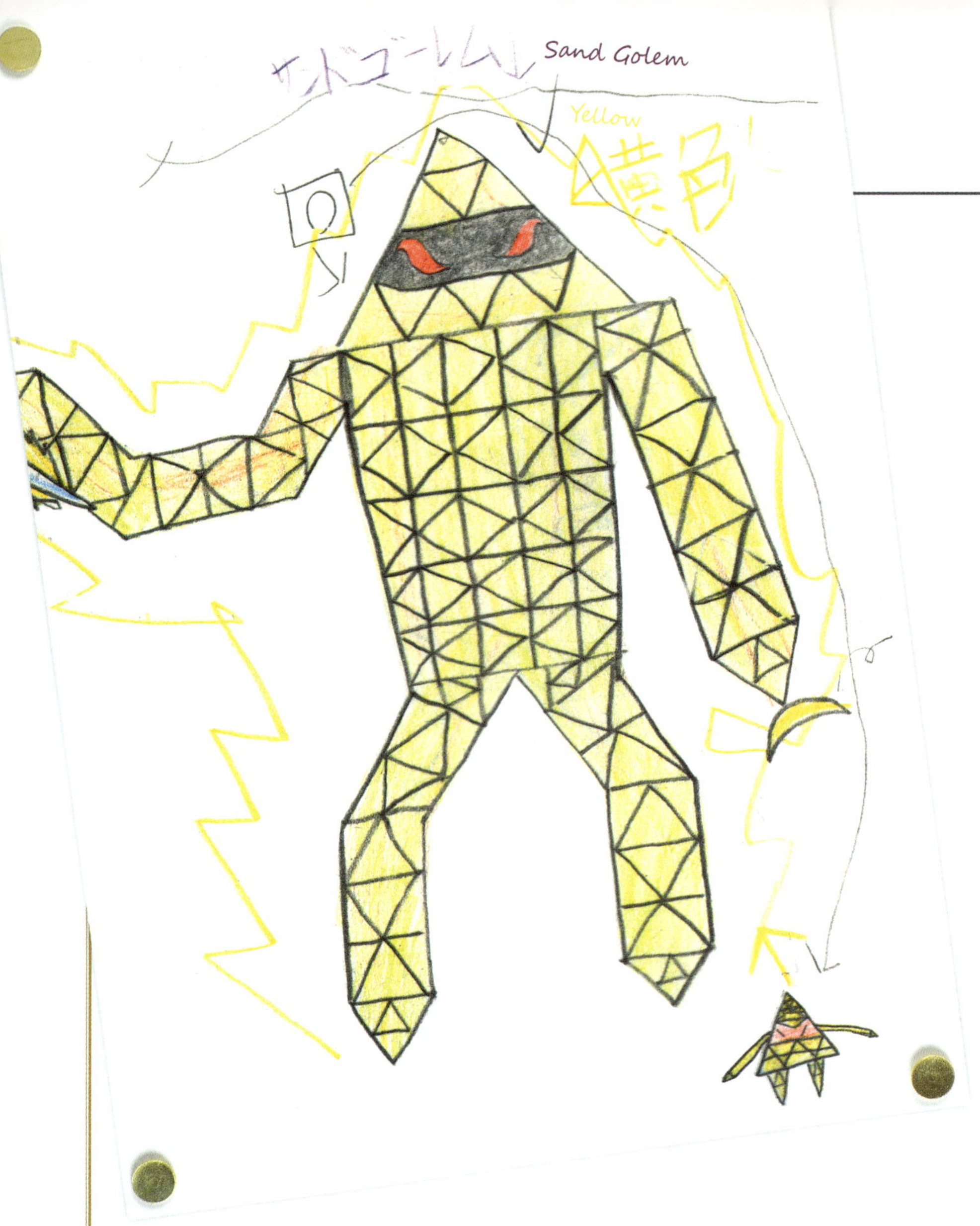

07 Trilith the Sand Golem

Thomas

Having become more at ease with my watercolor technique while proceeding with the series, I attempted a more ambitious illustration here by placing the character in the background. The effect pays off, as it permits me to show off the sheer scale of the golem in contrast to the tiny houses. Ryunosuke's triangular design, visibly inspired by the Egyptian pyramids, naturally called for a Middle Eastern-style environment.

Ryunosuke

I got the idea for this golem while I was at school. I like the shape of the eyes that I gave him, but I found the motifs on the body a little boring, so I didn't think Dad would pick this one. He wound up making the motifs not flat but in three dimensions. I think that was a great idea; I never even thought of that. Also, I never would have guessed that he'd draw him so big!

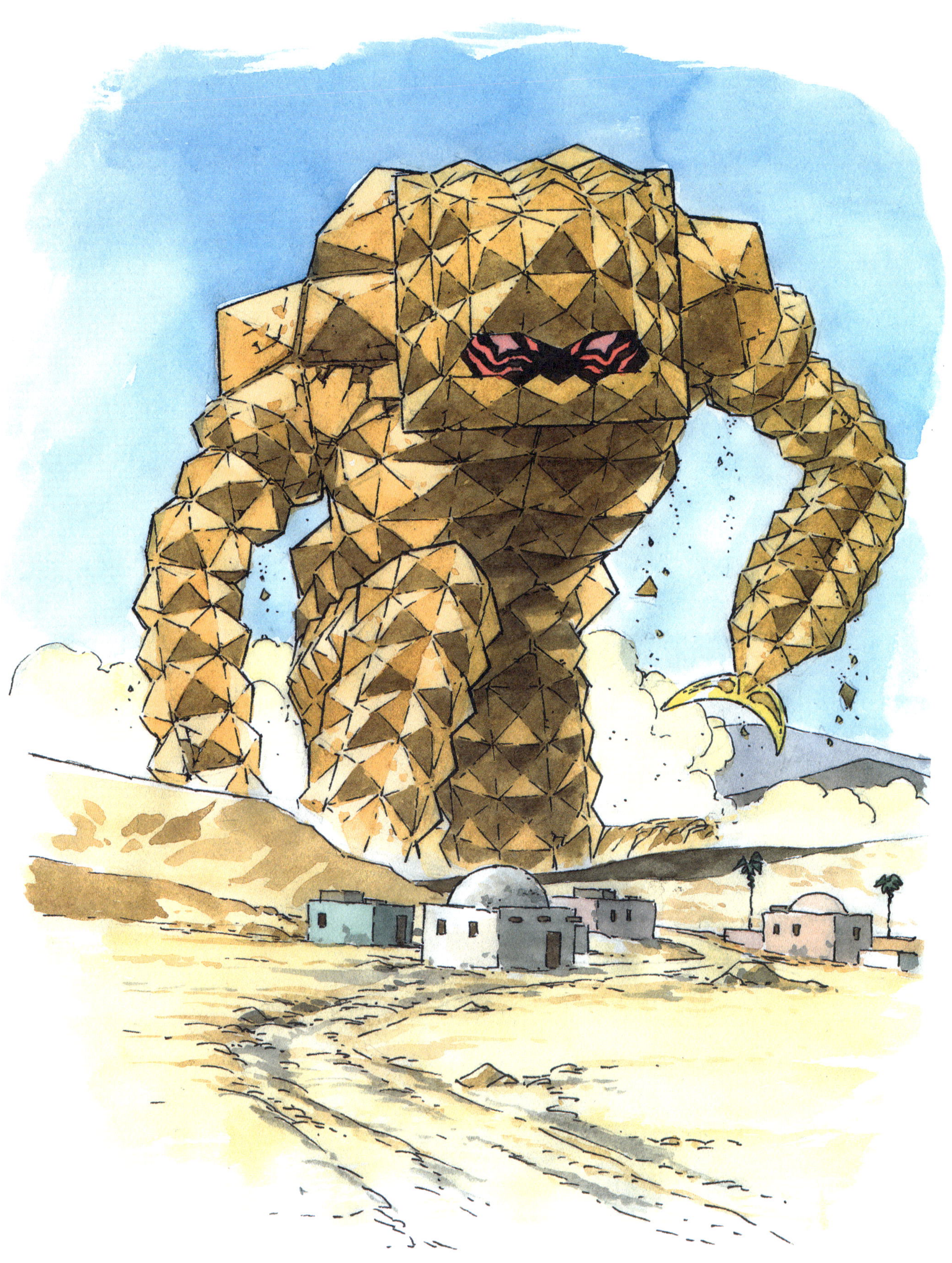

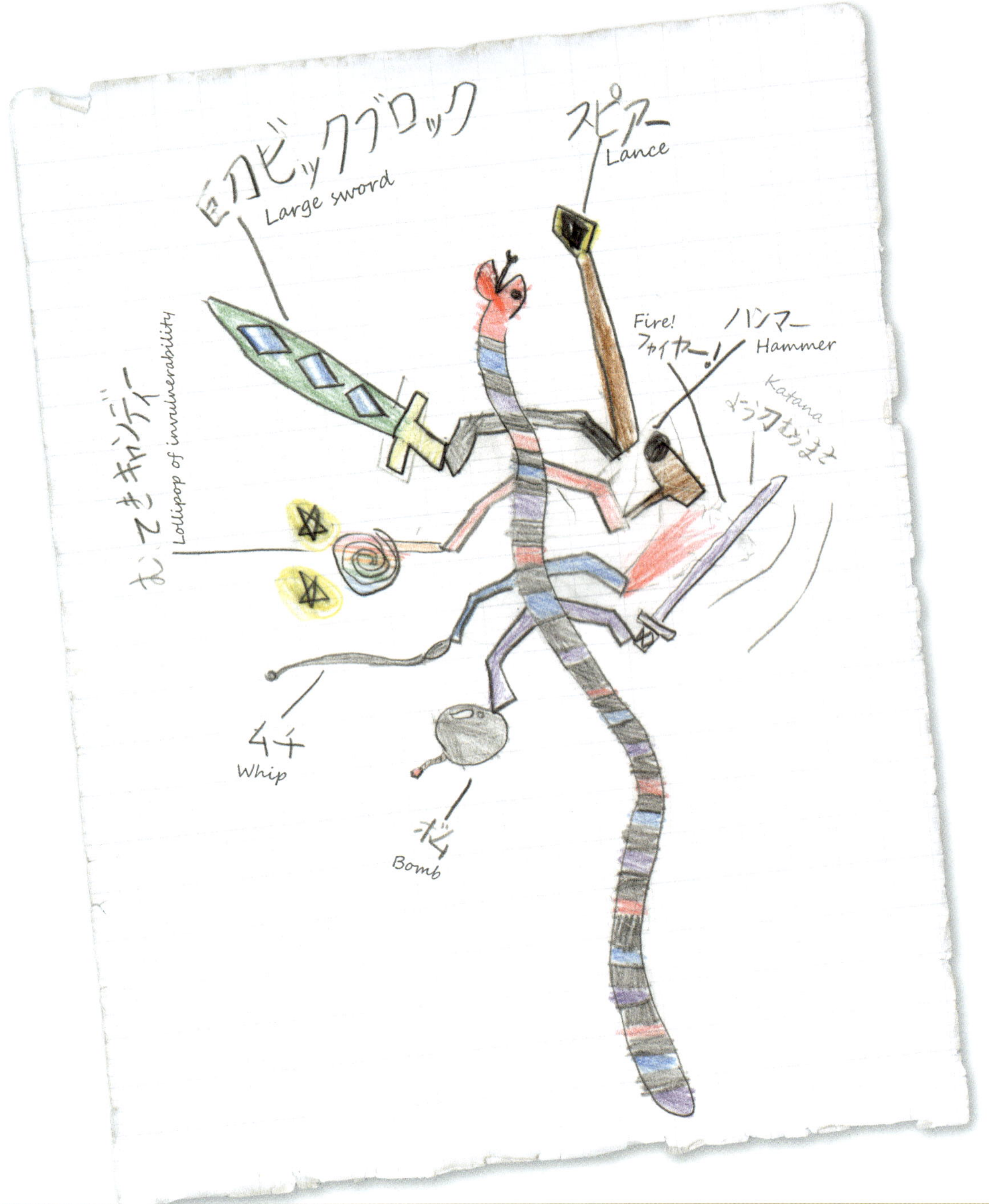

08

Warrior of the Vydra caste

Thomas

The biggest challenge here was sorting all the arms and weapons. I also changed his pose and tried giving the character a more three-dimensional aspect, as the drawing itself was quite flat. But all the ideas were already in play, so there was no need for me to add much. I love the multi-colored stripes that Itsuki dreamed up. This warrior would no doubt make for a fun enemy in a video game.

Itsuki

I felt like drawing a snake that day because we went to see the animals in a reptile and insect store. I know that snakes have no legs, but what's great about drawing is that you can do what you want! For the arms I found my inspiration in the *Kirby* video games, which I love.

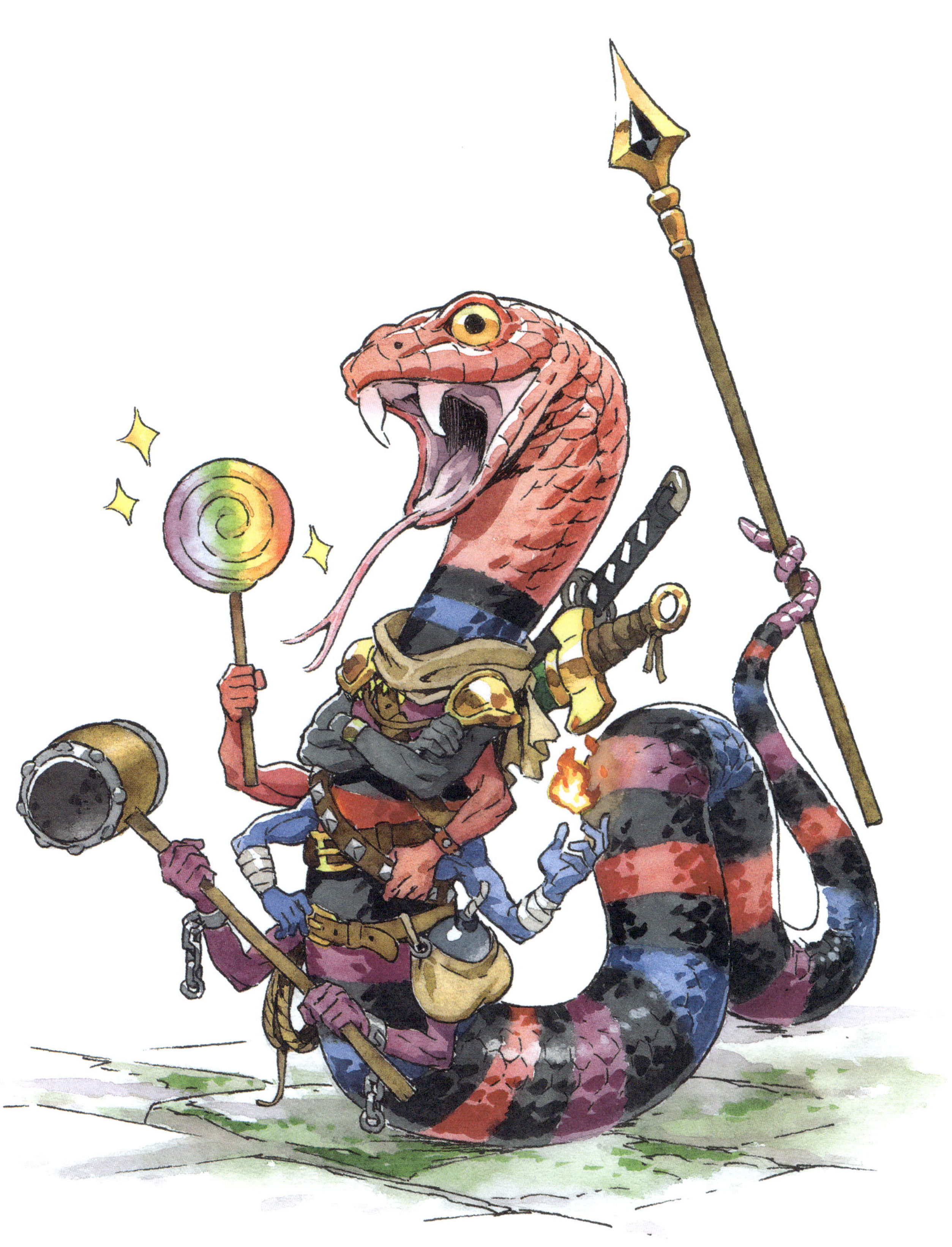

09

The Sentinel of the Purple Flames

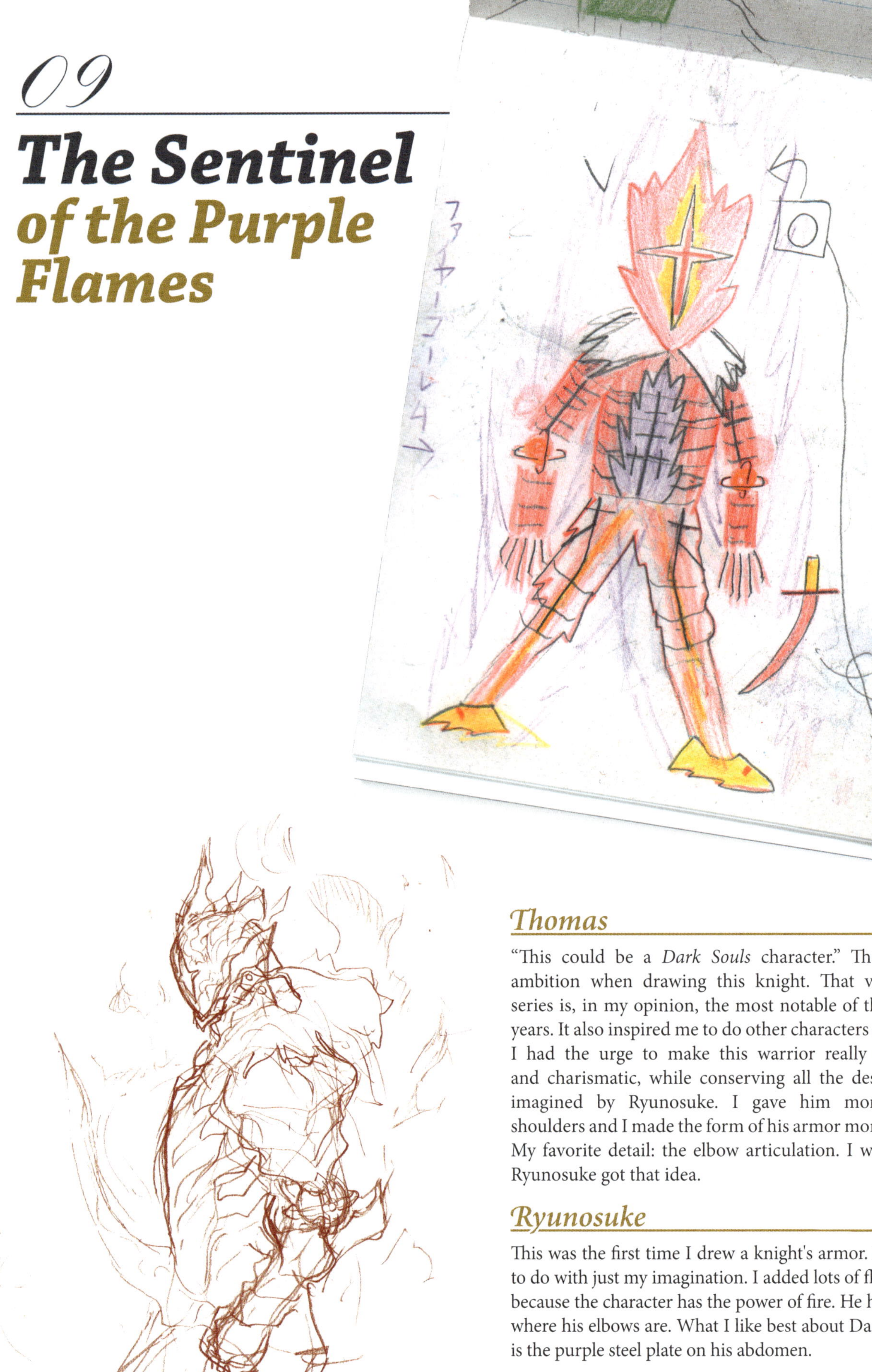

Thomas

"This could be a *Dark Souls* character." That was my ambition when drawing this knight. That video game series is, in my opinion, the most notable of the past few years. It also inspired me to do other characters afterwards. I had the urge to make this warrior really impressive and charismatic, while conserving all the design points imagined by Ryunosuke. I gave him more massive shoulders and I made the form of his armor more complex. My favorite detail: the elbow articulation. I wonder how Ryunosuke got that idea.

Ryunosuke

This was the first time I drew a knight's armor. It was hard to do with just my imagination. I added lots of flame details because the character has the power of fire. He has fire orbs where his elbows are. What I like best about Dad's drawing is the purple steel plate on his abdomen.

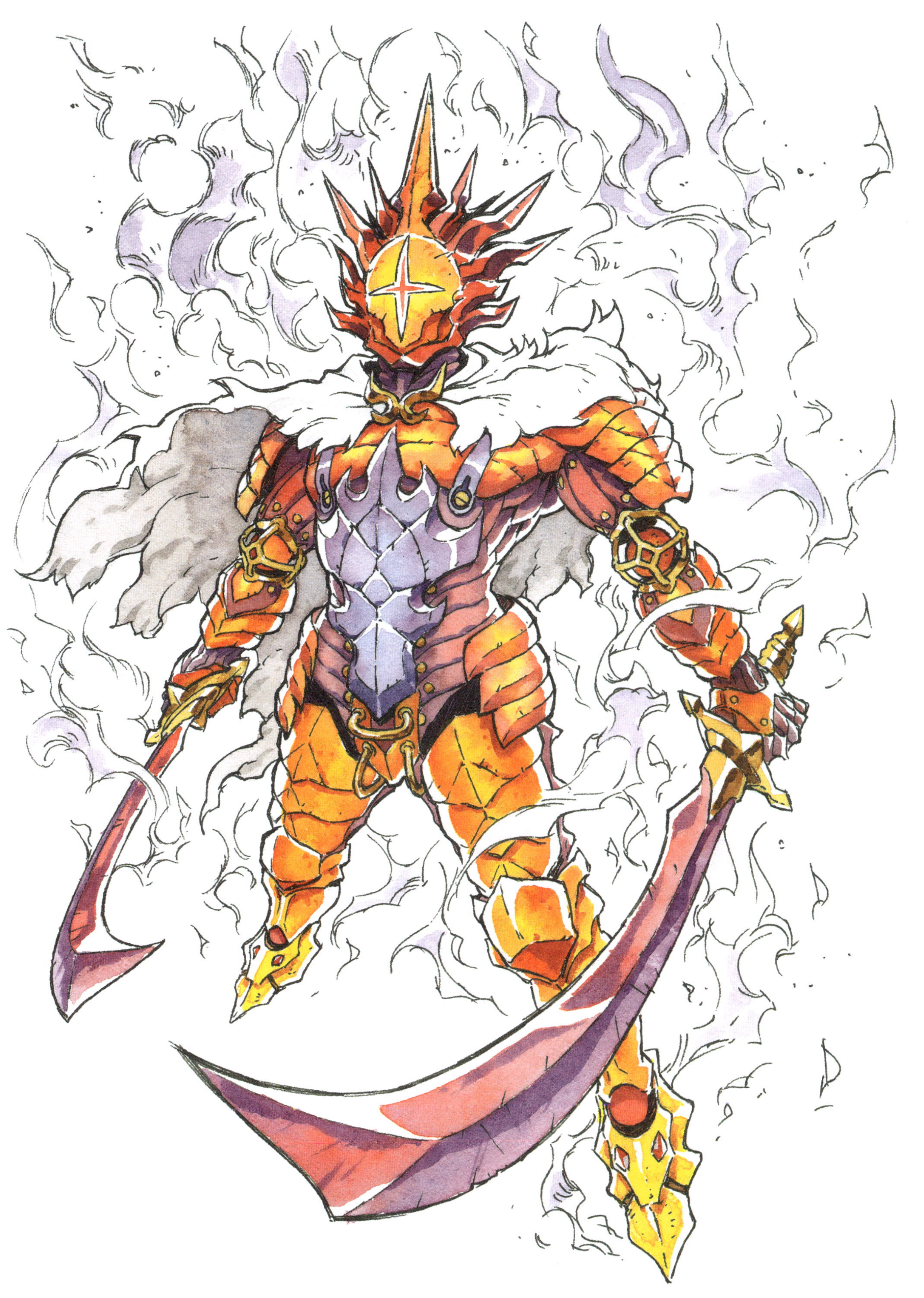

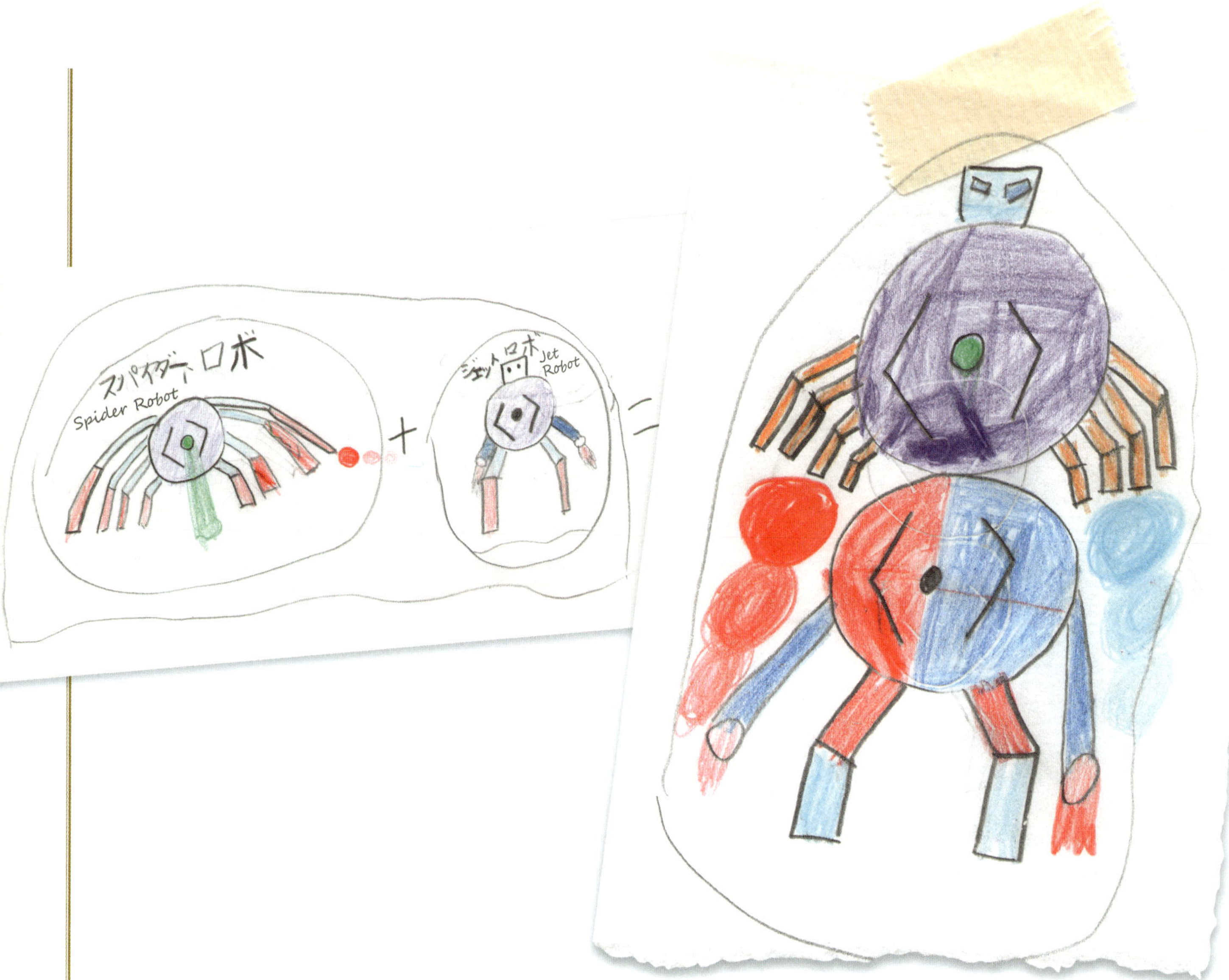

10

The Destructor

Thomas

This drawing by Itsuki reminds me of my own childhood. I remember how I would draw monsters and giant robots when I was little, influenced by *Goldorak*, one of the first anime series to be broadcast in France. To show the massive scale of this machine, I placed it against the backdrop of a meticulously-drawn town. Having worked for many years in Japan as an animation background artist, I had gotten used to drawing that type of environment. I also decided to add several metallic parts that reduce the abundance of colorful zones to make the robot look more menacing and less toylike.

Itsuki

The upper part of the robot is based on a spider. I don't know why, but that day I really wanted to draw a spider. However, I never thought that Dad would make such an impressive-looking robot. He has so many details and I love the light effect around its limbs.

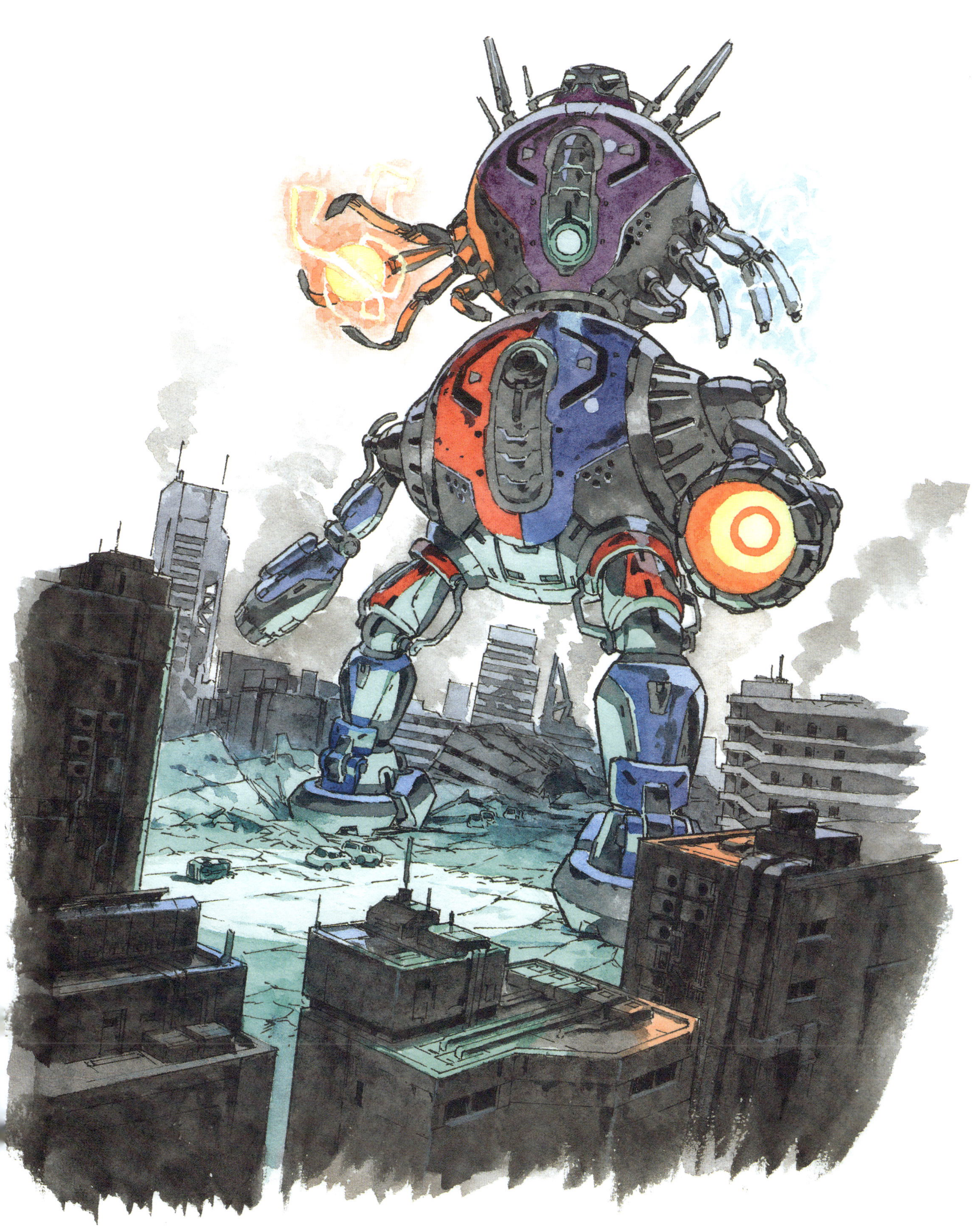

11
The Koomos
Inhabitants of Cloud Hill

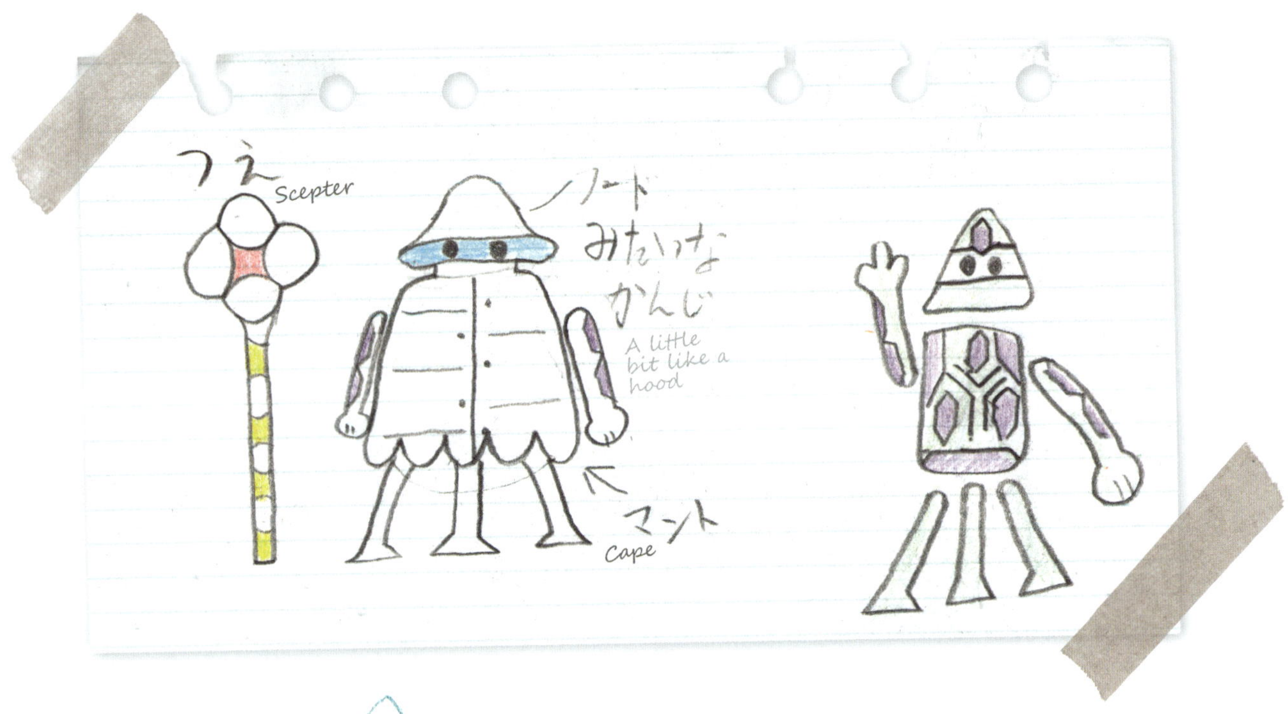

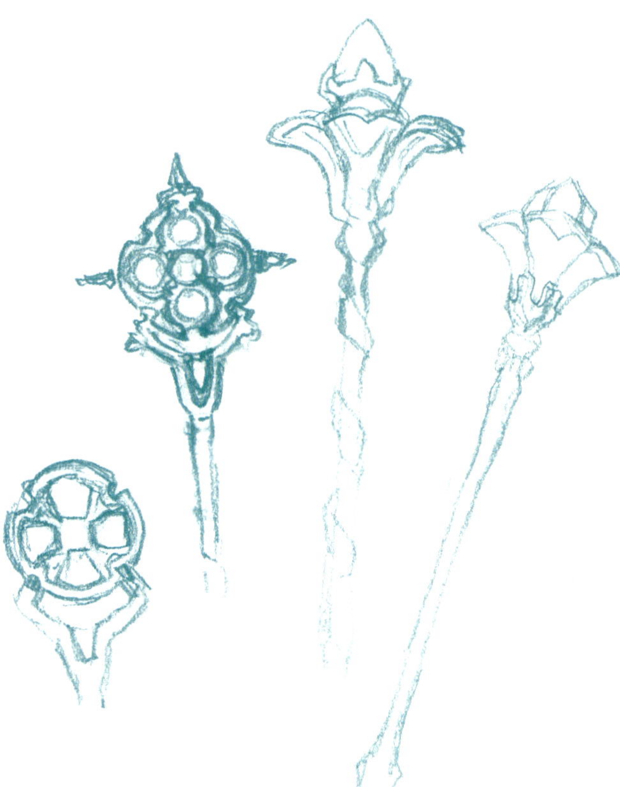

Thomas

Even though they look strange with their tri-legs, disembodied arms and violet-shaped gem motifs, I became very attached to these characters dreamed up by Ryunosuke. Seeing that their design was simple and well-executed, I chose to depict an entire tribe of them. The idea of their gathering around a lifeless body came from Ryunosuke drawing one without a cape. I wished to use both versions of the design and wanted it to make sense, while transmitting an emotion. I didn't know it at the time, but this image would become the first of a series allowing us to discover the adventures of the Koomo tribe.

Ryunosuke

When I started, I wanted to create a mushroom person, and the shape of the head made me want to give him a hood. This character is a being created by a mix of magic and technology. With his disembodied arms and three legs, we can see that it is not a tiny human. I really like the atmosphere in Dad's drawing, especially the flowers, whose cottony aspect harmonizes well with the cloud theme.

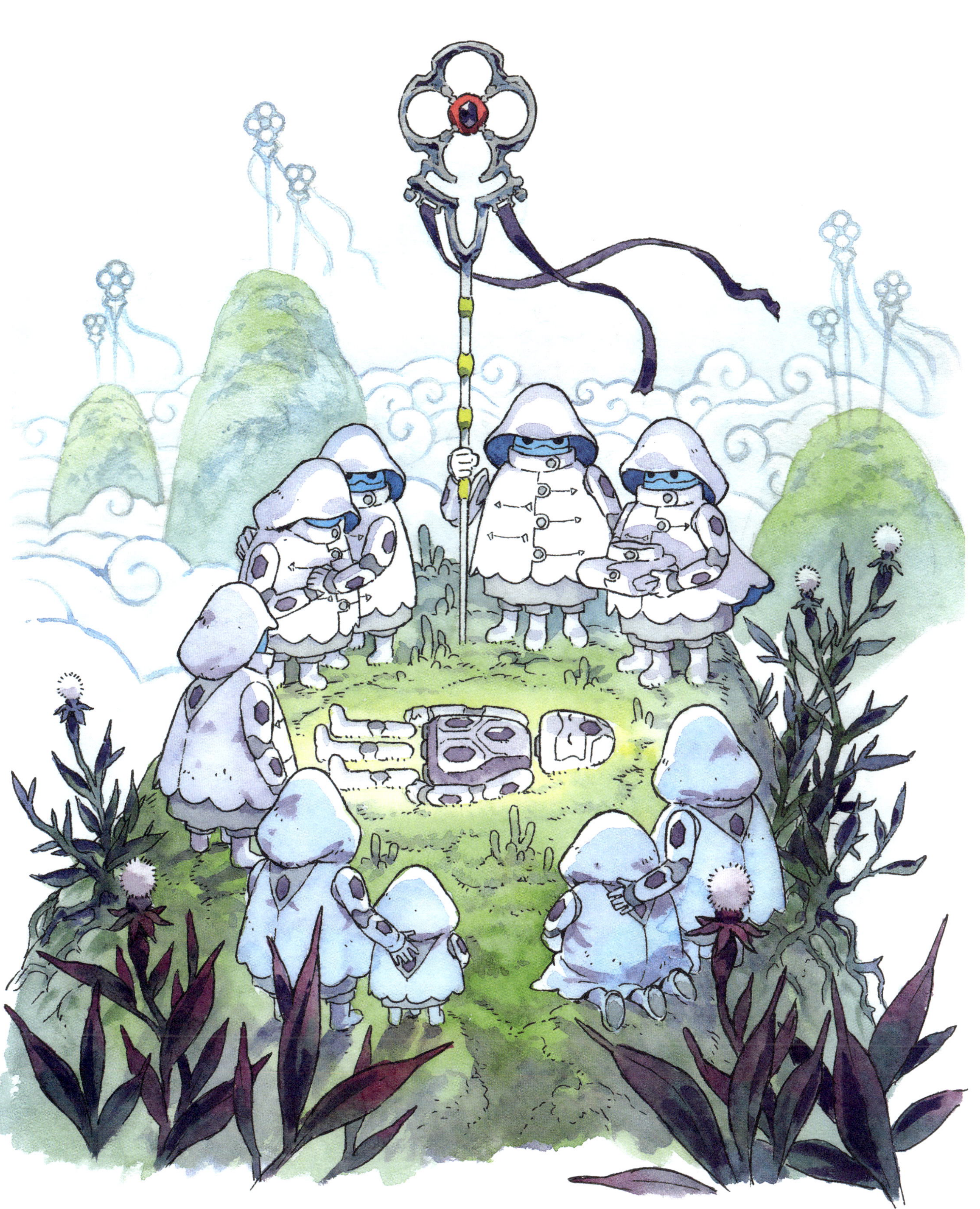

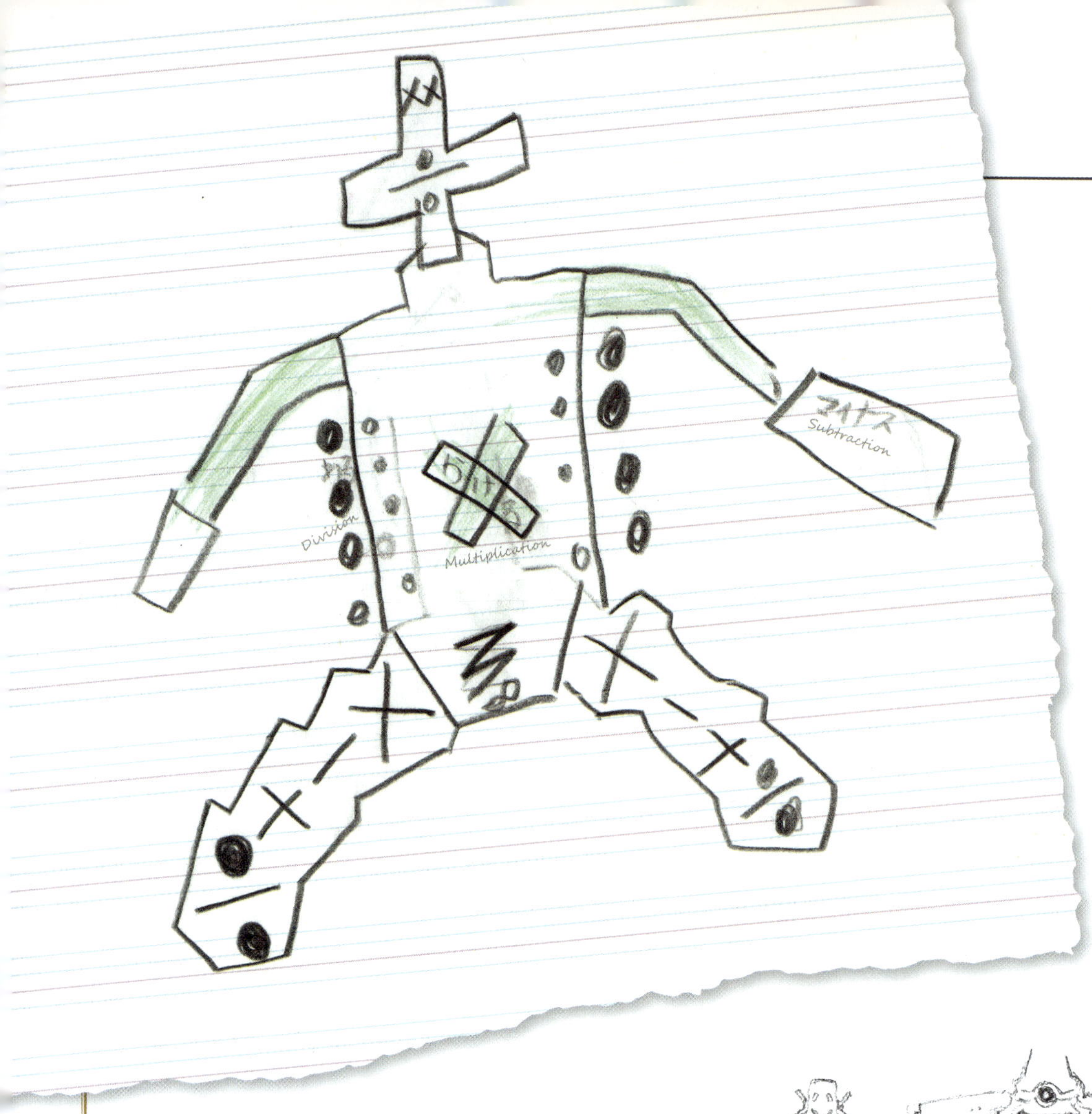

12

K-3

Thomas

Itsuki's drawings are very surprising. He makes them quickly, in minutes, but there is always has an original idea to take from them. This robot is composed of mathematical symbols: addition, subtraction, multiplication, and division. For my design I retained these graphic codes but made them more complex, to give the robot a more realistic and functional look. Since Itsuki used very few colors, I was able to give him a very sober aspect, close to something I could have done for a professional mecha design in Japan.

Itsuki

I got the idea for this character after learning how to do division in school. I also added the other math symbols and called him Keisan; that means 'calculation' in Japanese. Seeing as K is pronounced 'kei' and 3 is pronounced as 'san', Dad renamed him K-3, which suits a robot very well! He also gave him lots of details. I had no idea he would become so cool.

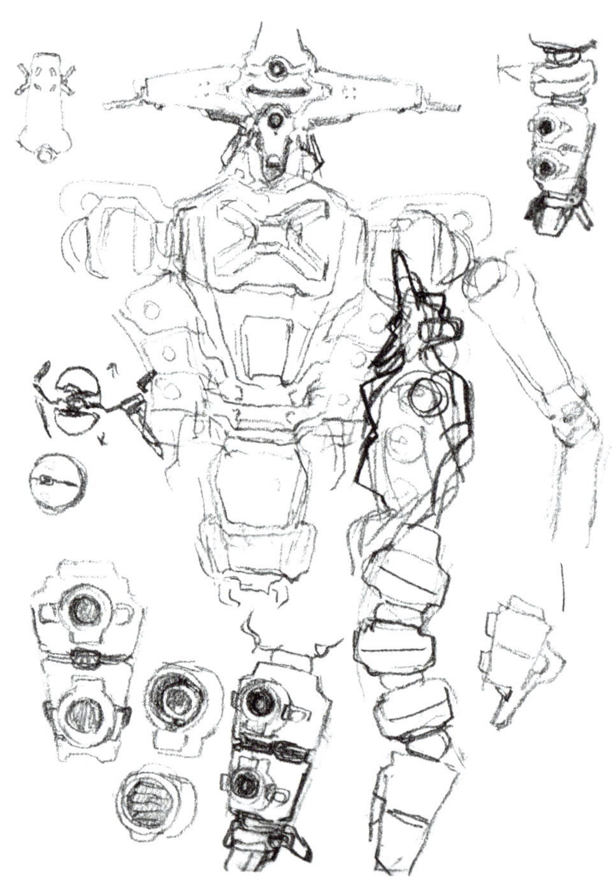

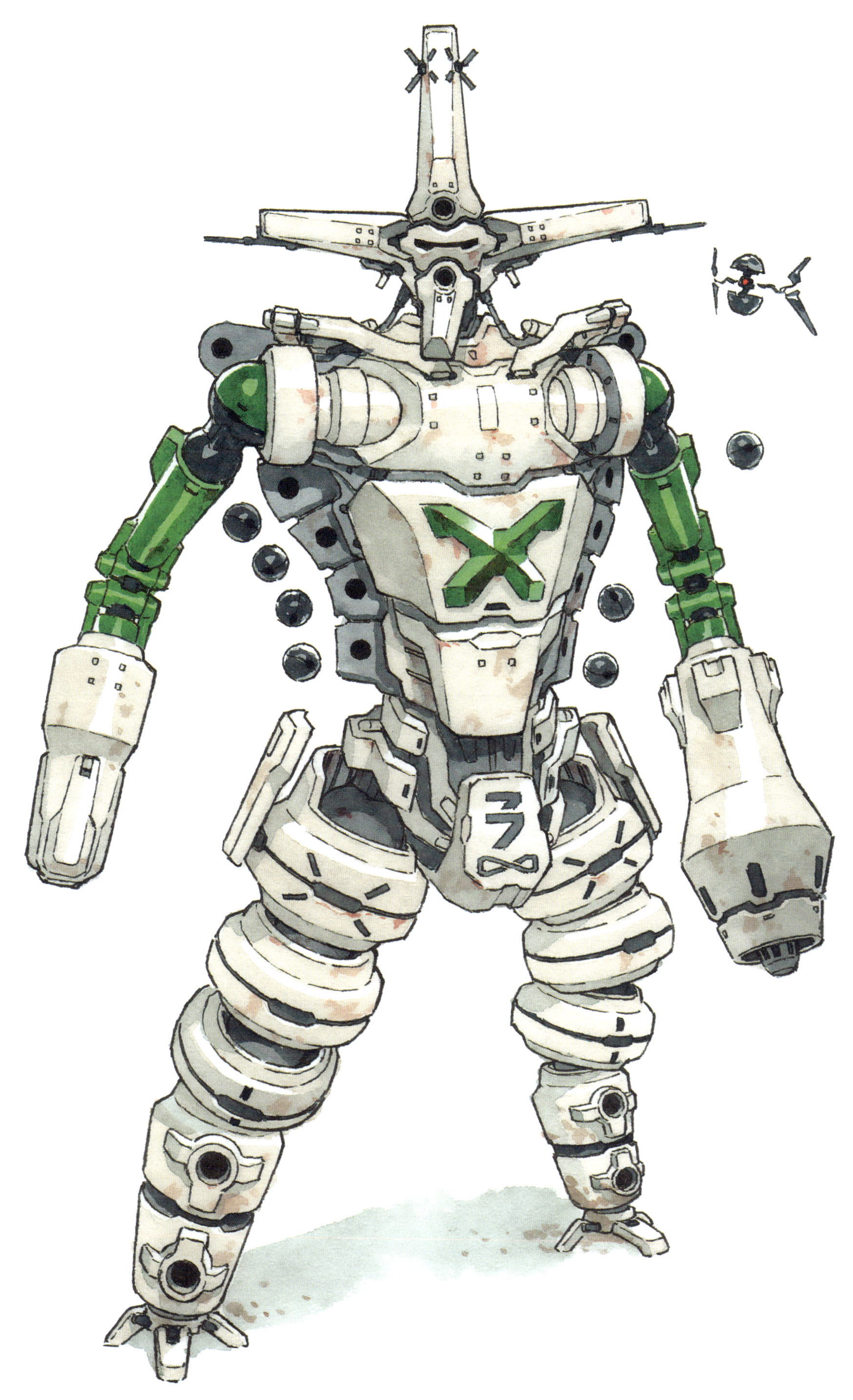

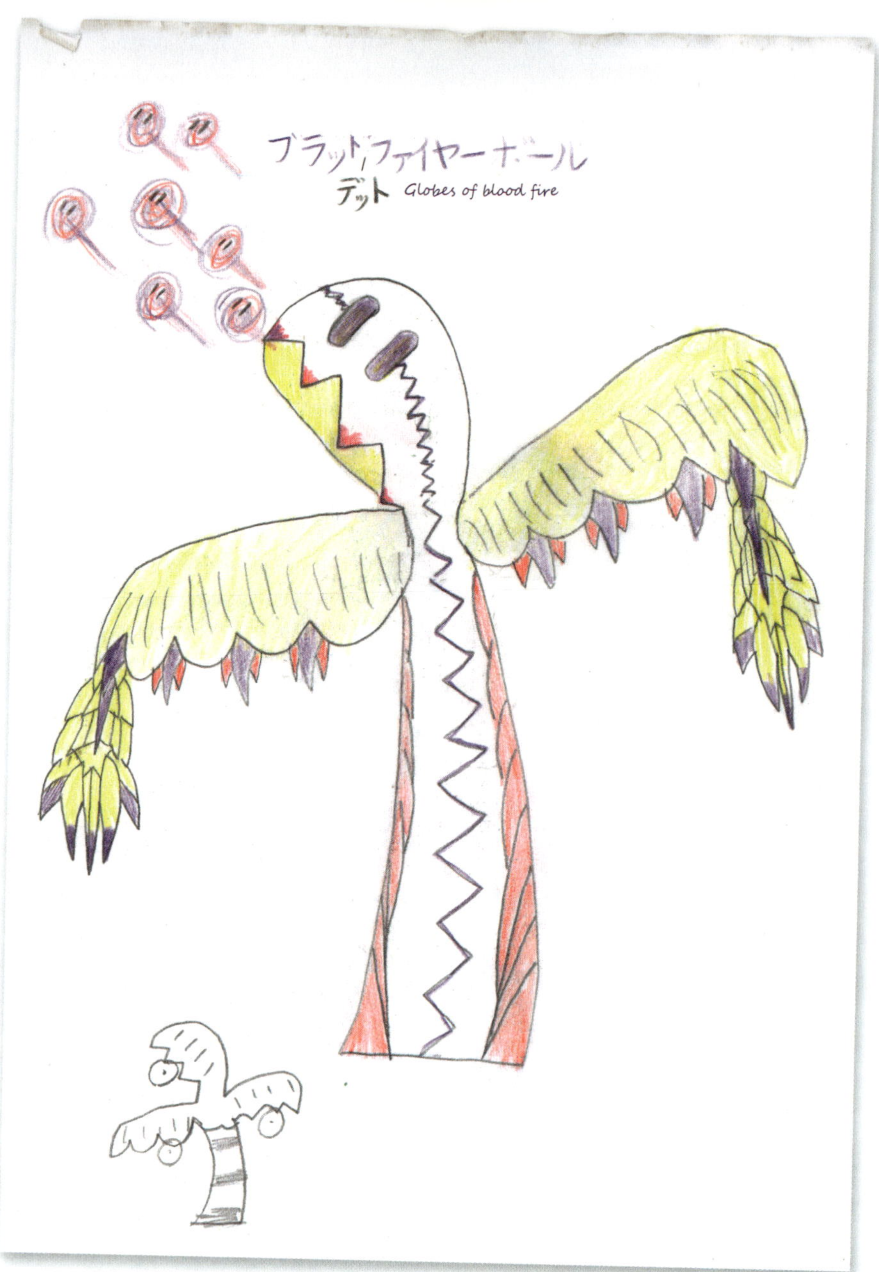

13 The Cursed Blood Prince

Thomas

I could have interpreted Ryunosuke's drawing in a much cuter manner, but I had the urge to orient myself towards *Dark Fantasy.* The red parts that Ryunosuke drew on either side made me think of muscle fibers. I then wished to give this creature a flayed-alive aspect, which contrasts with the refinement of the golden armor. This is a prince afflicted by a curse, which rendered him immortal and has altered his appearance little by little over the centuries.

Ryunosuke

For the outline of this character I found inspiration in the shape of a palm tree. I began by tracing the shape but then the idea of making it a winged creature came to me. Dad asked me if he could turn it into something scary, but I had no idea he would become so monstrous! All things considered, I think I like him anyways.

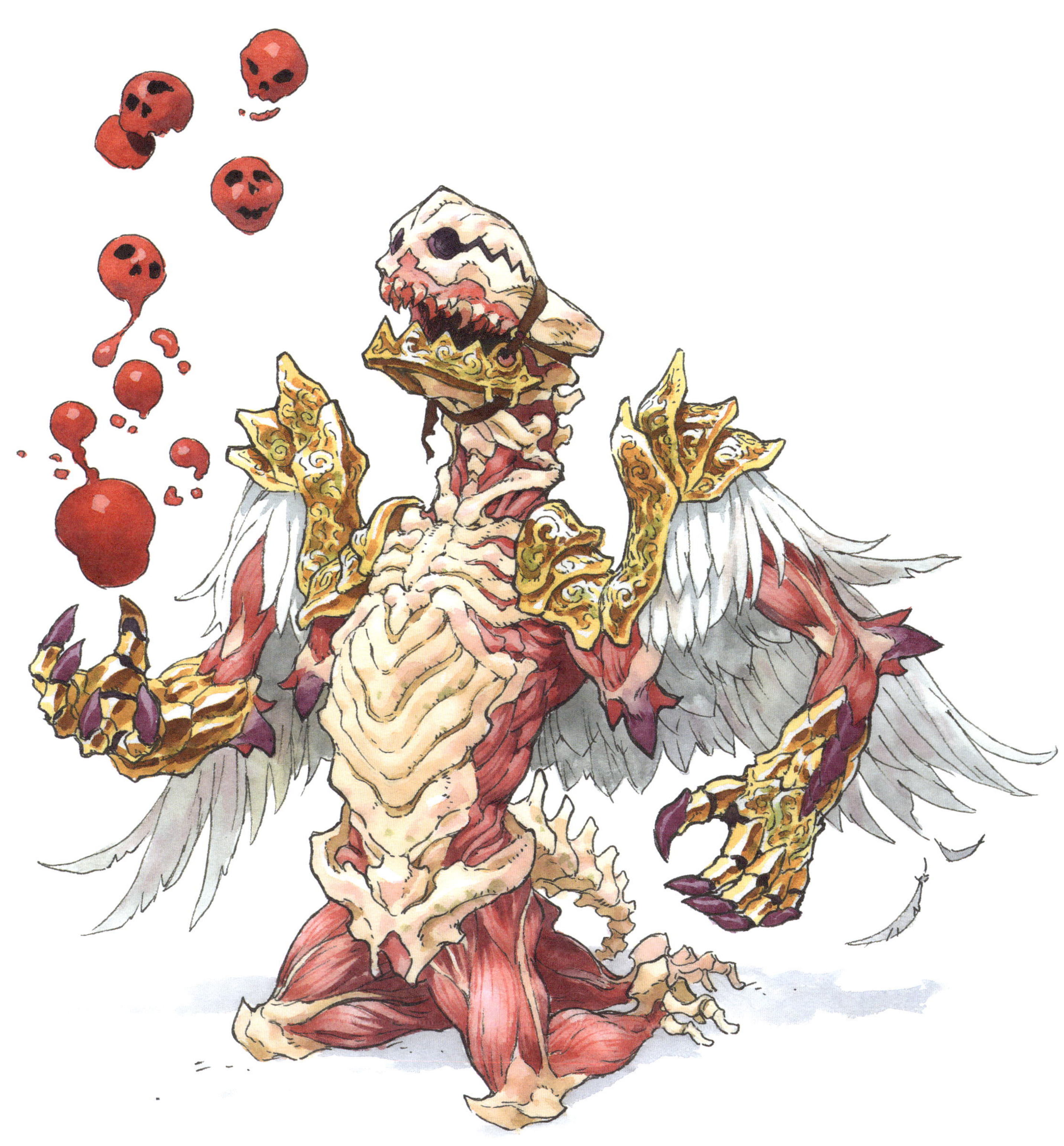

14

The Royal Tentaduse

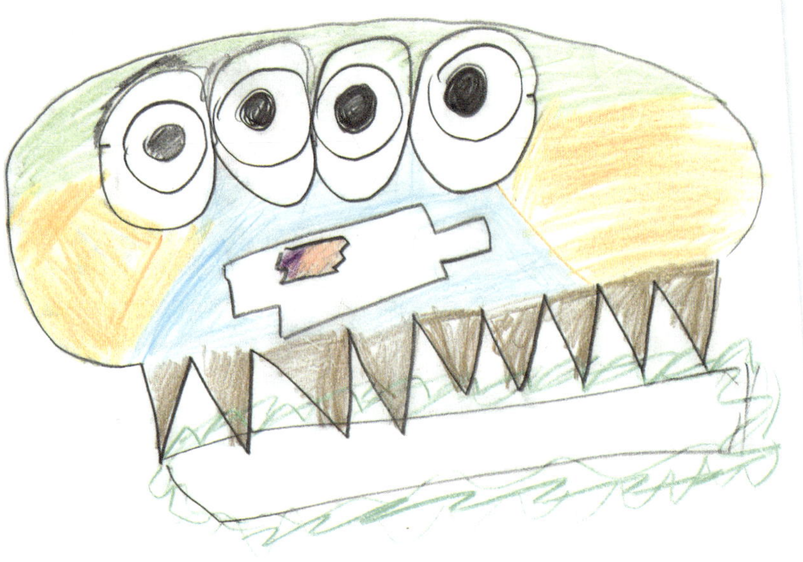

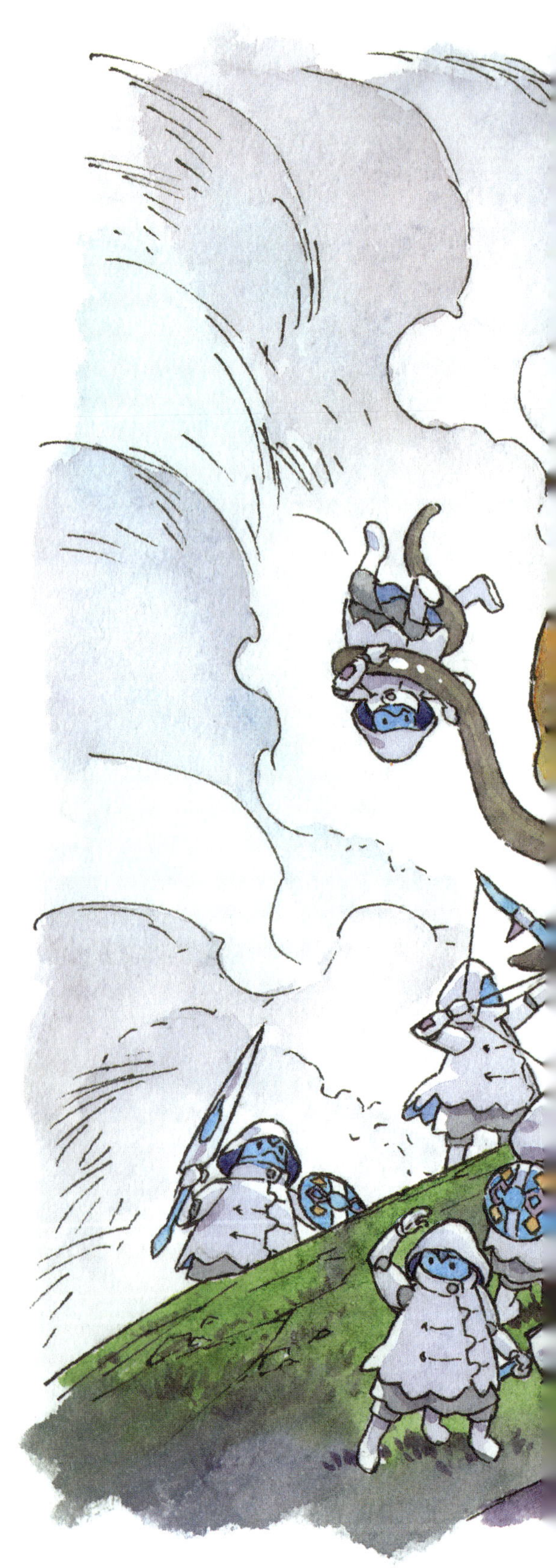

Thomas

To show off this simple yet amusing design by Itsuki, I had the urge to bring back the Koomos, and thus started to develop their world. Their village has been imperiled by a mysterious fog that brought with it a flood of menacing monsters. They decide to form a combat troop to defend themselves. They aren't very skilled in weapons handling, but their courage and solidarity are without equal. They will succeed in chasing off the Tentaduse, but their worries are far from over...

Itsuki

At home we have a book about deep-sea creatures that have all kinds of weird shapes. It also has some jellyfish. That's what inspired me to do this giant, flying, carnivorous jellyfish! Dad's drawing is way scarier than mine because of all the tiny eyes he added. I find that having Ryunosuke's Koomos fight him was a really good idea, because it gives a lot of life to the drawing.

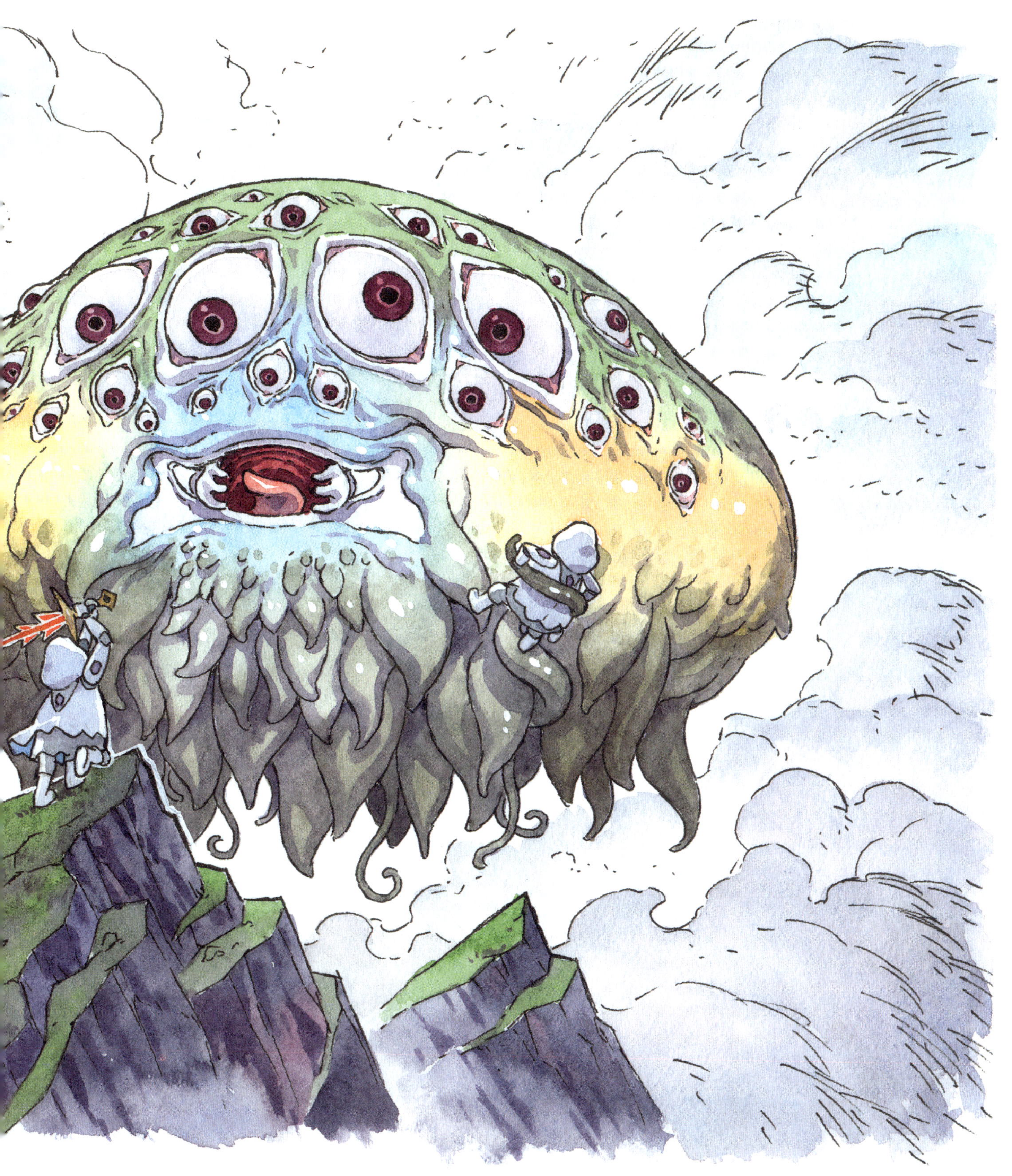

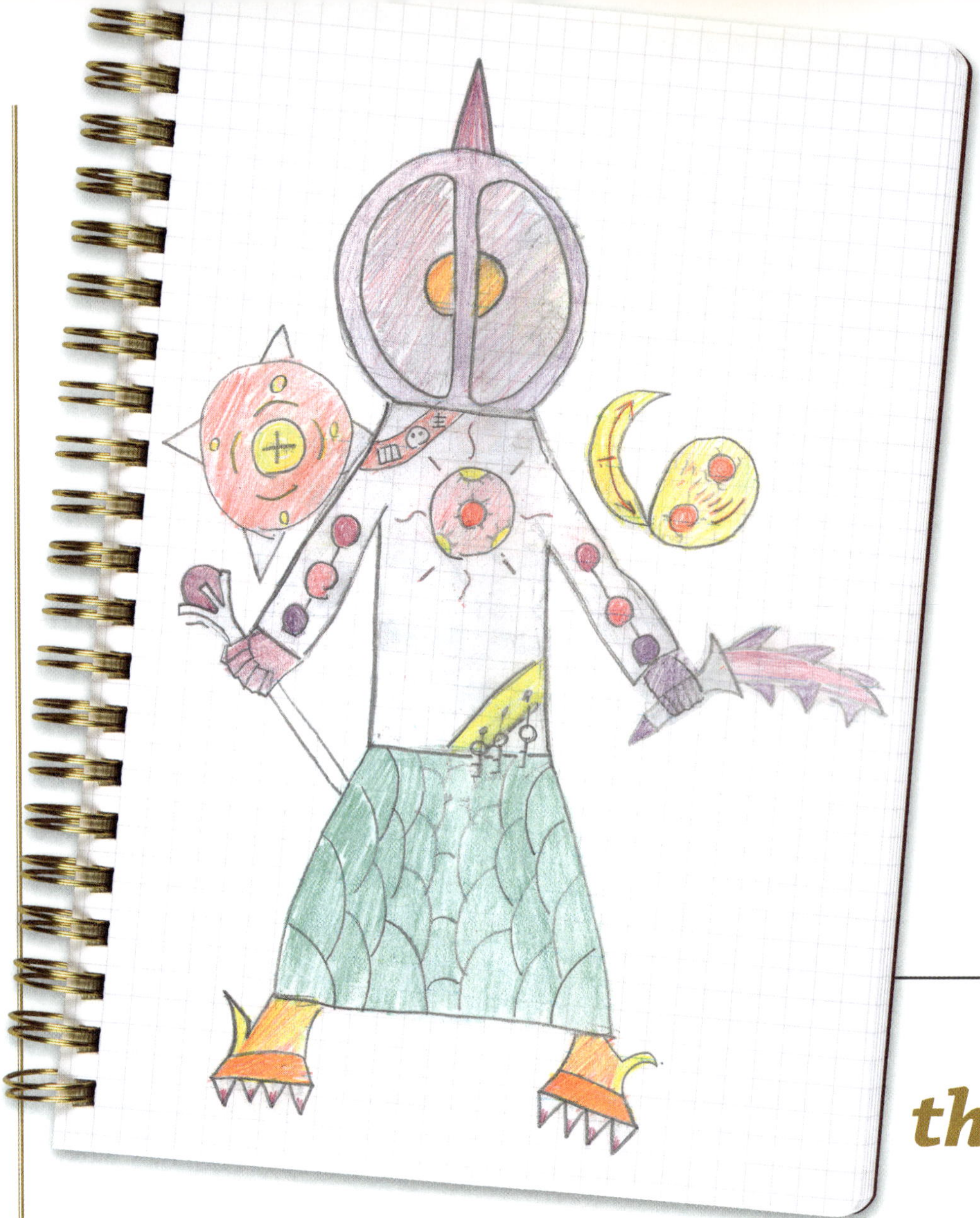

15

Scal the Dragon Trainer

Thomas

I took great pleasure in drawing this strange magician, who possesses the power to control the flying creatures known as the Narwhagon. His skirt made of dragon scales and his face (or rather the absence of one) really gives him personality. I imagine him as a kind of solitary and mysterious fighter, riding a fantastic mount, who would come to the aid of the hero or heroine, or even become a rival.

Ryunosuke

This is one of my favorite characters. I love the purple color, magic, and space, so I combined my favorite elements into one drawing. The two relics that float on both sides represent the sun and the moon. Dad got the idea to make the face empty with a ball of energy, like a tiny sun. This is even better than I had imagined it.

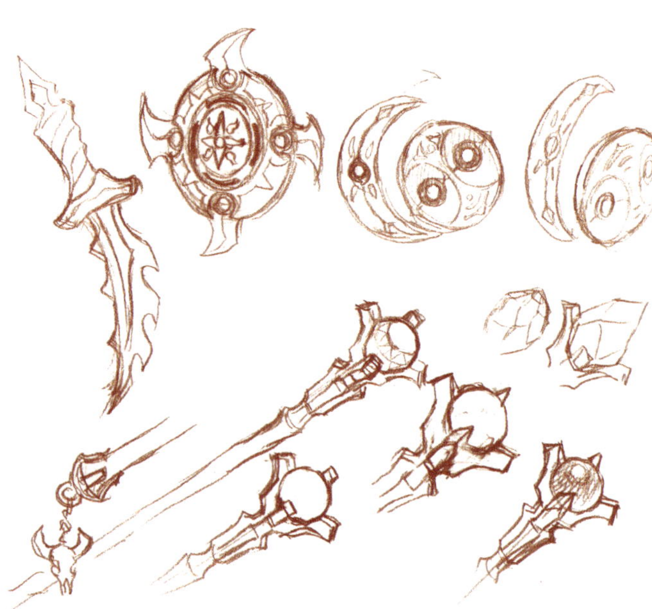

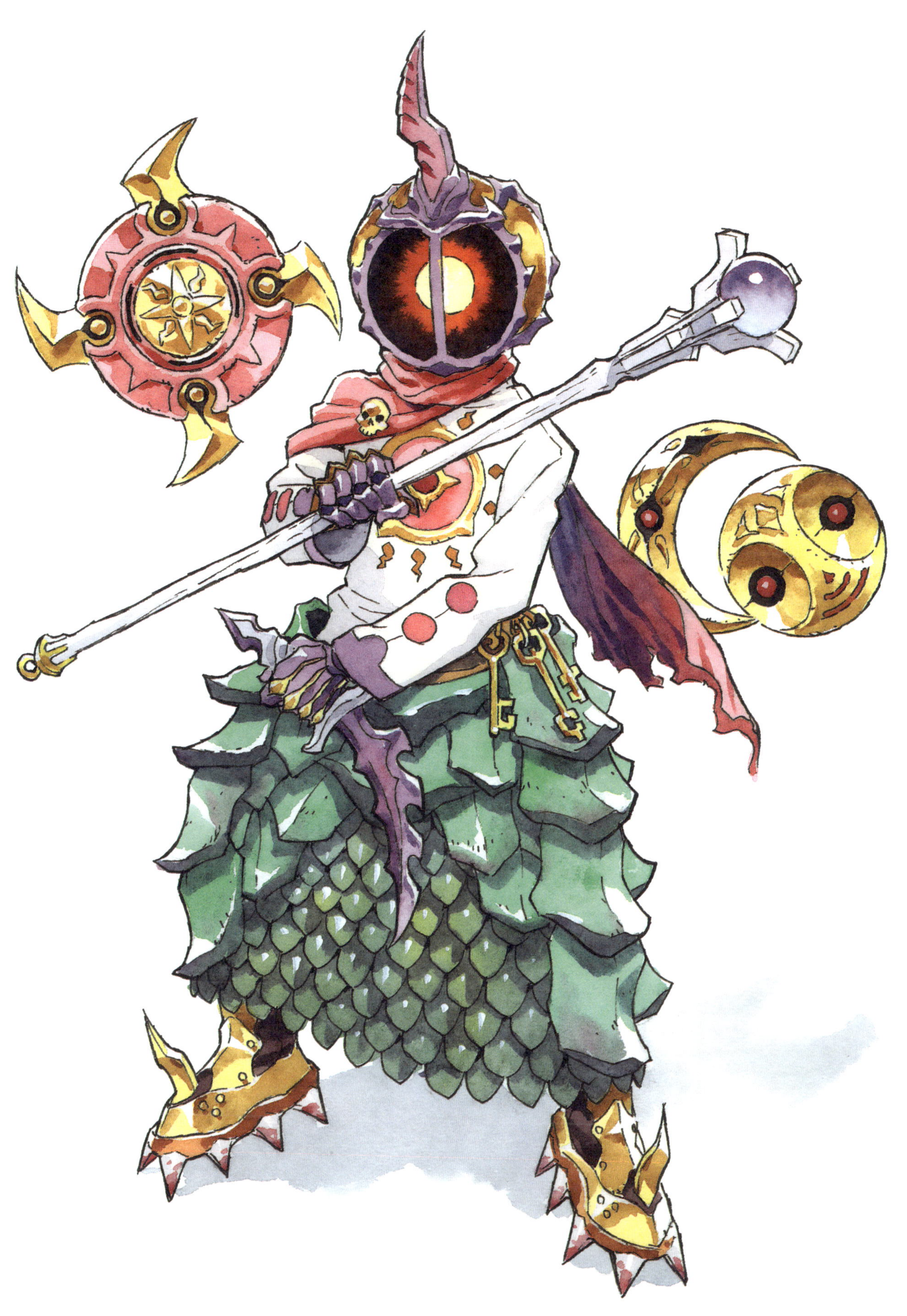

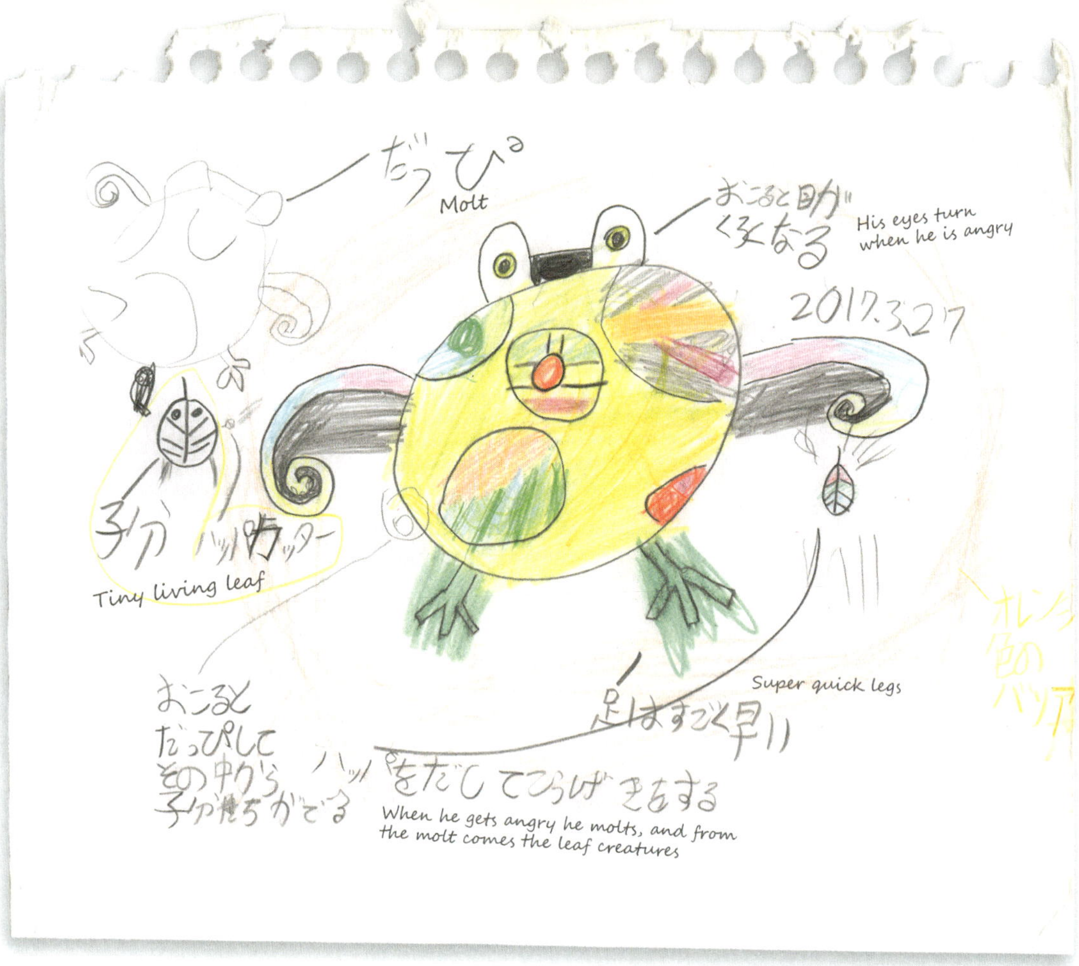

16

The Leafrogs

Thomas

Itsuki really likes to draw colorful abstract motifs on his characters. That's his style. He put lots of them on this tiny creature. I simplified them somewhat to give a more coherent design. I also tried to render the tiny creatures more expressive by giving them a mouth and manga-ish eyes. The leafrogs are generally cowardly creatures and prefer to stay in the shadows of plants, except for one, who won't hesitate to have fun in broad daylight in the middle of the forest without worrying about predators.

Itsuki

I drew a lot of robots before this, so, to change things up a bit, I thought up this forest creature. It can use leaf-based attacks, but Dad didn't show them in his drawing. On the other hand, he made the leafrogs way cuter than I ever did. Also the background is pretty. The idea for the shape came from a foam balloon that my brother and I play with outside. It's hollow with holes on all the sides. I really liked that shape, but instead of the holes I drew the colorful motifs.

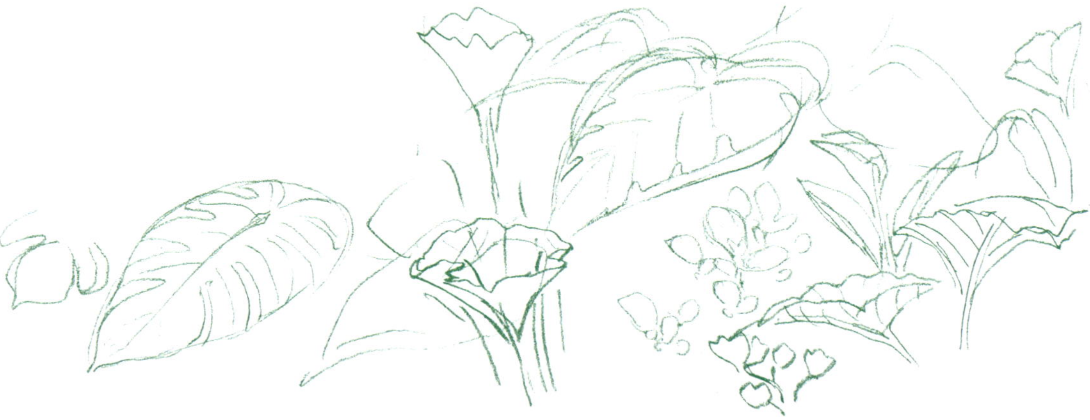

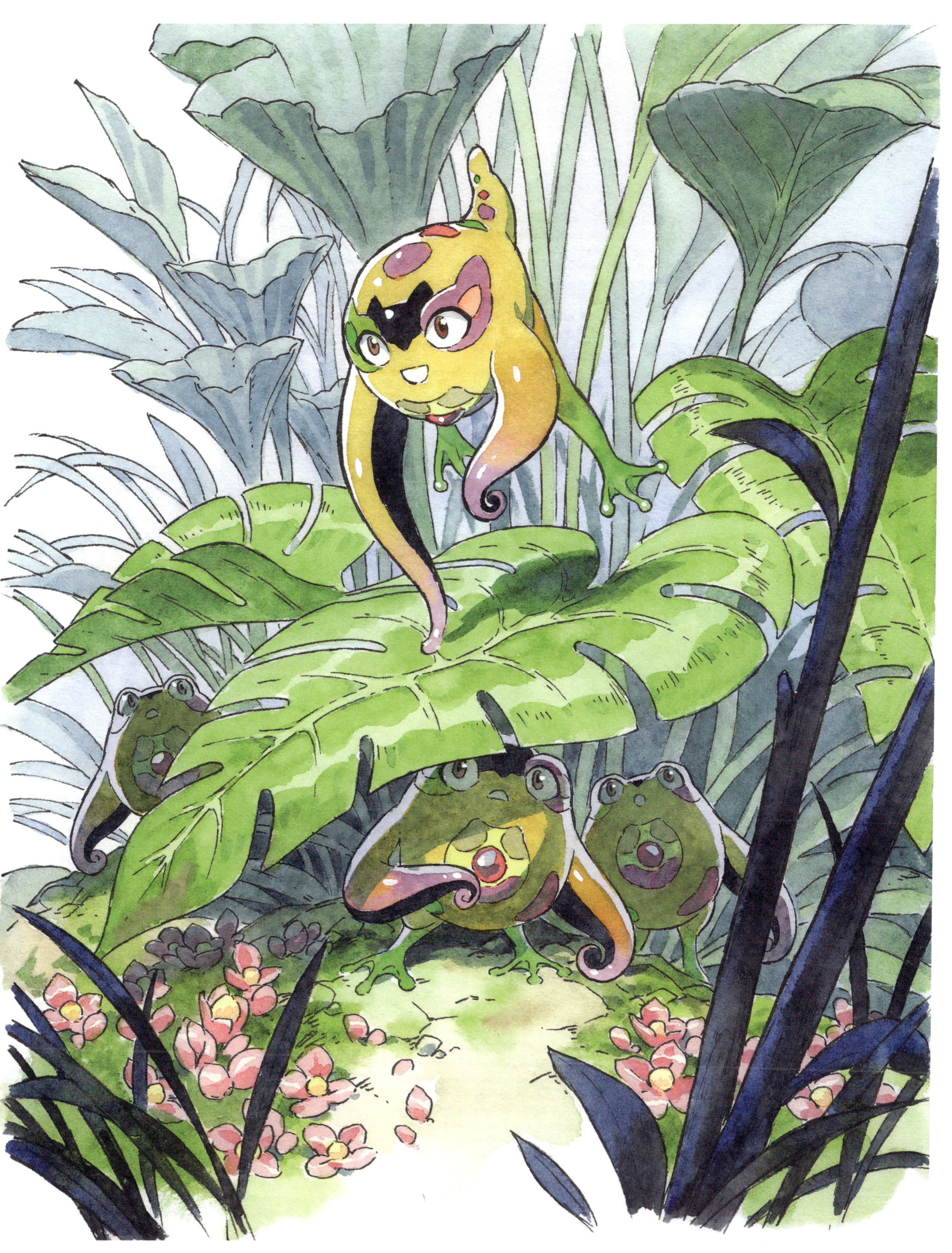

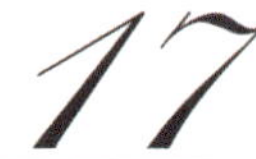

The Wings *from Bone Mountain*

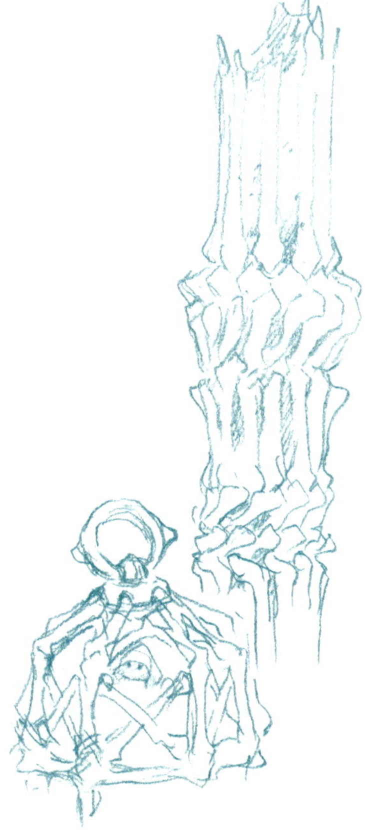

Thomas

The sketch of the cage gave me the idea to bring back the Koomos and transform them into prisoners. Rather than using steel bars I preferred to use bones. This gives a primitive touch to the design and renders it more plausible that the winged creature could have built the cage itself. The theme of bones comes back in other background elements, as well as in the creature's own skull.

Ryunosuke

I remember making this drawing during an animation conference that dad gave at Ikebukuro, a neighborhood in Tokyo. I was in the back of the room. Since what he was saying was really boring, I went ahead and started drawing a bit. The character I made is a kind of ghost that captures people with large hands that come out from under his robe, to make of them its offerings. Dad made him into a strange bird, which I wasn't expecting. I don't think it's bad, and looking back at my own drawing, it's actually quite faithful. I like the twisted legs and the cage of bones, which goes well with my idea of mystical sacrifices.

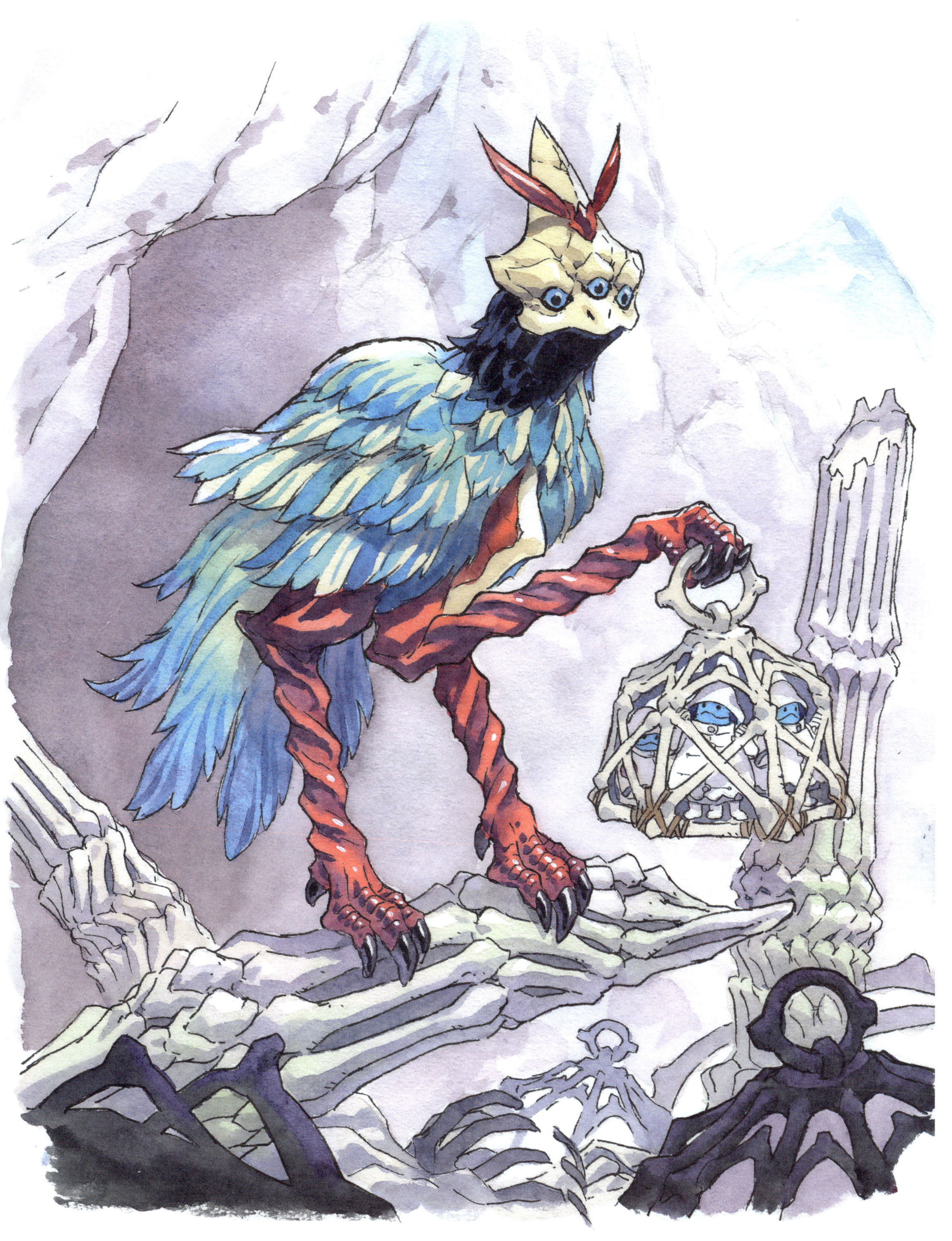

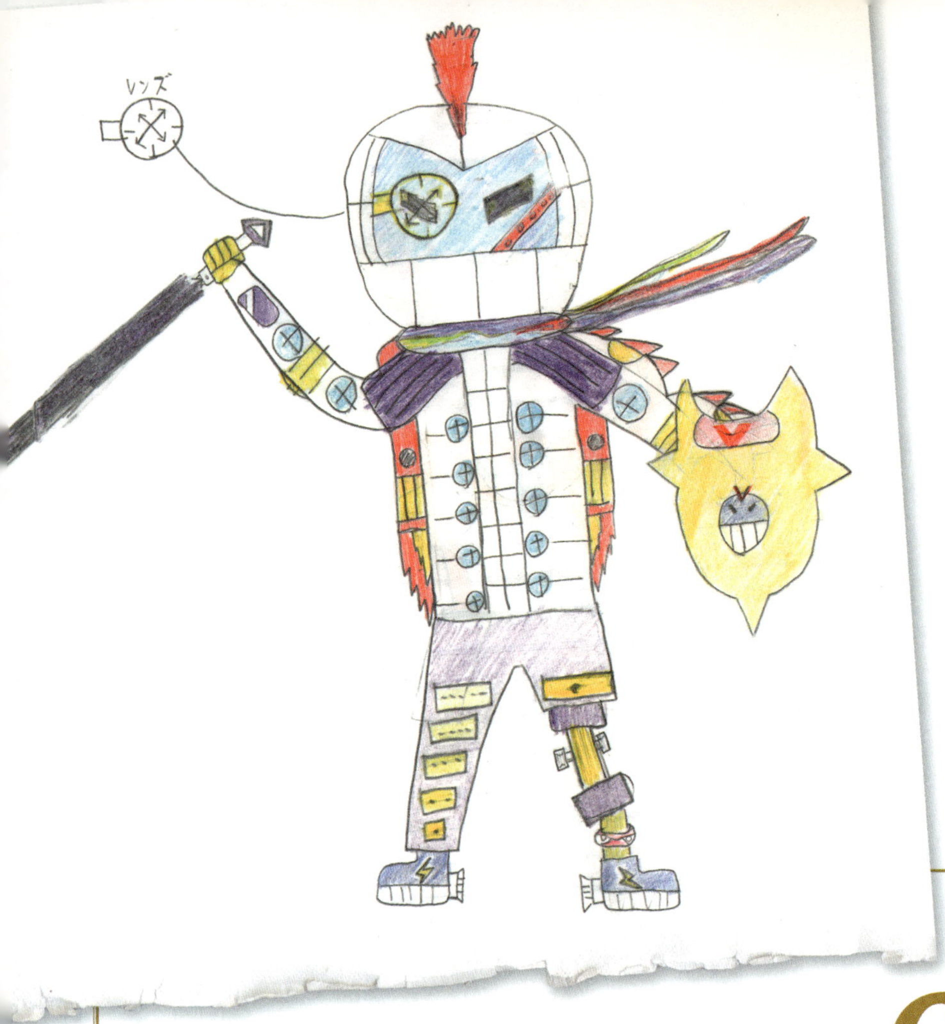

Bonus 01

Cyber-Gladiator

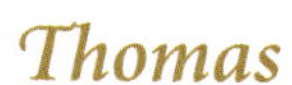

Thomas

This drawing was made at the request of a Japanese TV show. During their report about our father/sons collaborative art project, they wanted to film me creating a brand-new illustration. It was quite stressful, so I chose a more humanoid-looking character as they are the easiest to draw. The drawing by Ryunosuke was excellent, as it has a little *Mad Max*/post-apocalyptic side to it that I adored. I made several attempts at finding a dynamic pose before finally deciding on this more relaxed one. Since I couldn't show the tag on the shield from that angle, I went and drew it on the wall.

Ryunosuke

The helmet is based on a Roman helmet, only a more high-tech version. I integrated a lot of futuristic elements with little touches here and there, like the cybernetic leg. There is a lot of violet because I love that color. What I like the most about the final illustration is the touch of contemporary clothing, like the jeans and the vest. That gives a realistic presence to the character.

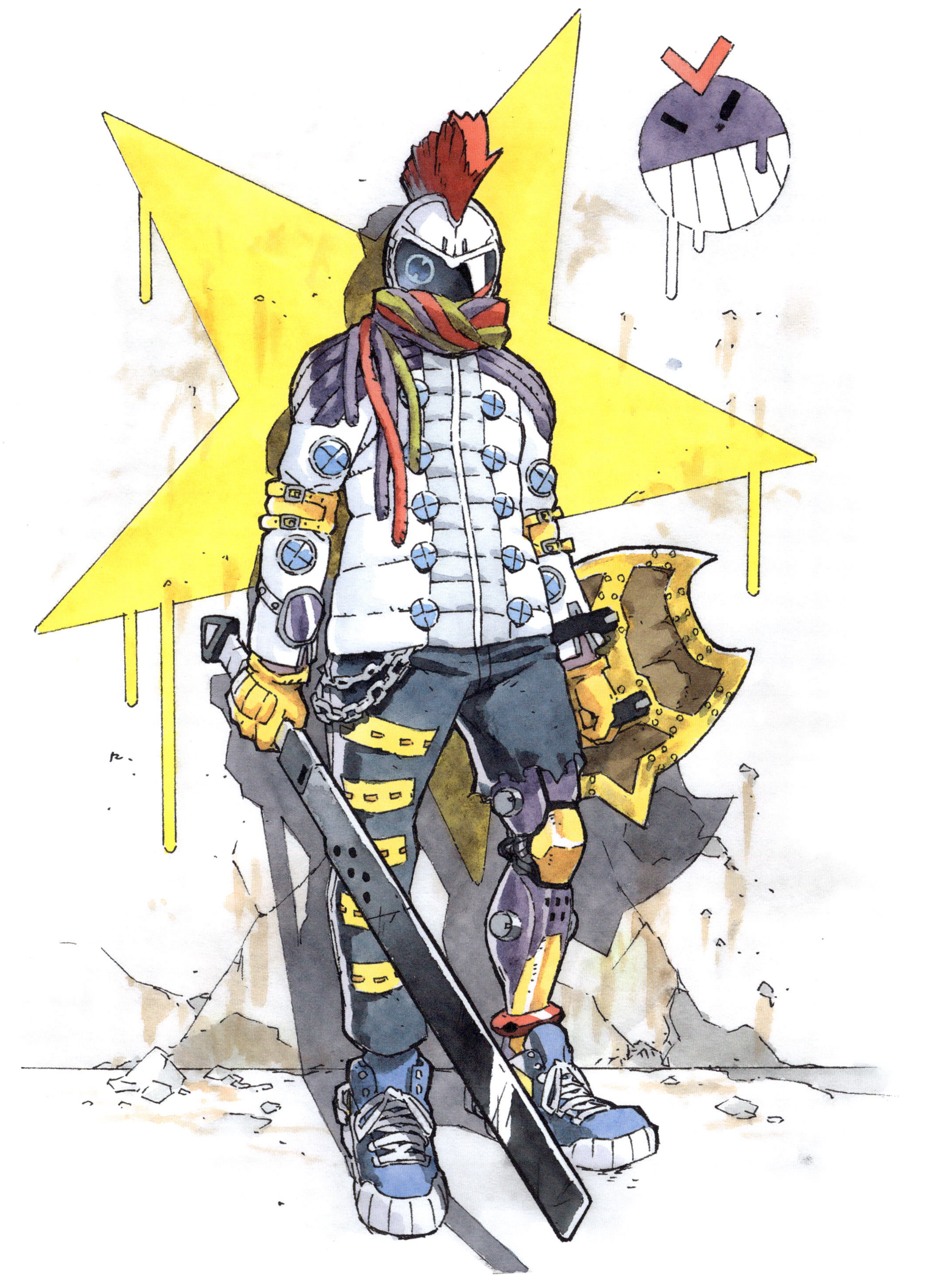

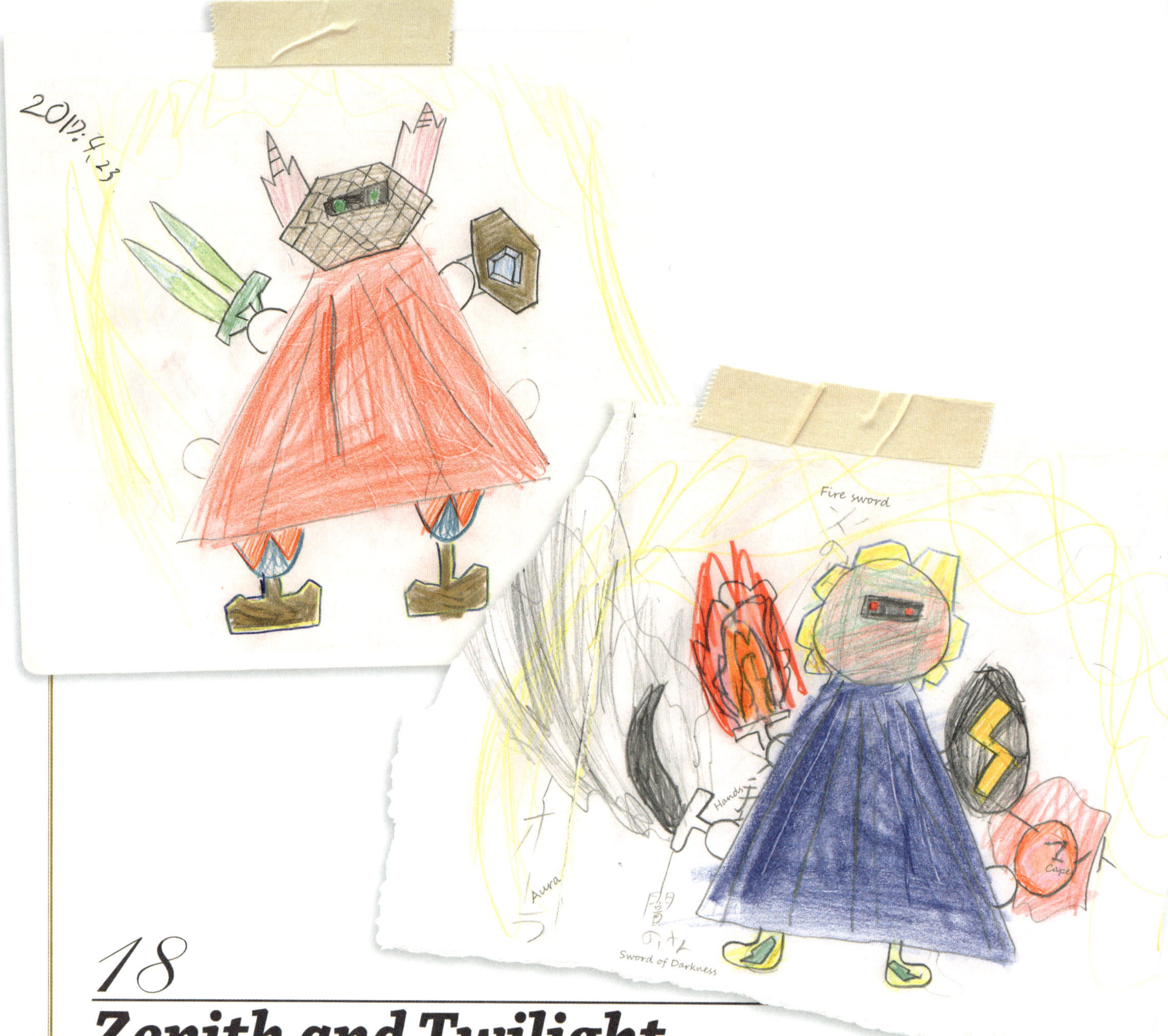

18

Zenith and Twilight the Brothers in Arms

Thomas

Itsuki drew the blue character first. I thought he had potential, but was a little too simple to make the subject of a single illustration. I then asked him to make a second one in the same style. I was really surprised by his good ideas. All the little design elements he imagined are just perfect. The horns, the double sword, the ornate shield with a blue gem, the hammer-like feet... a real pleasure to draw. We can almost imagine their quests in a world of legends. My favorite is Zenith, the warrior in the red cape. And you? Who's your favorite?

Itsuki

This one is a little hard to explain. Dad had brought home a small plexiglass stand made to illuminate anime figurines. This object has two small red diodes in a rectangular hole, which is what inspired me to create the face of Twilight, the blue knight. I imagined him with four arms, but I realized after talking with Dad that we didn't always have to give lots of arms and legs to every character. Sometimes it's better to be simple.

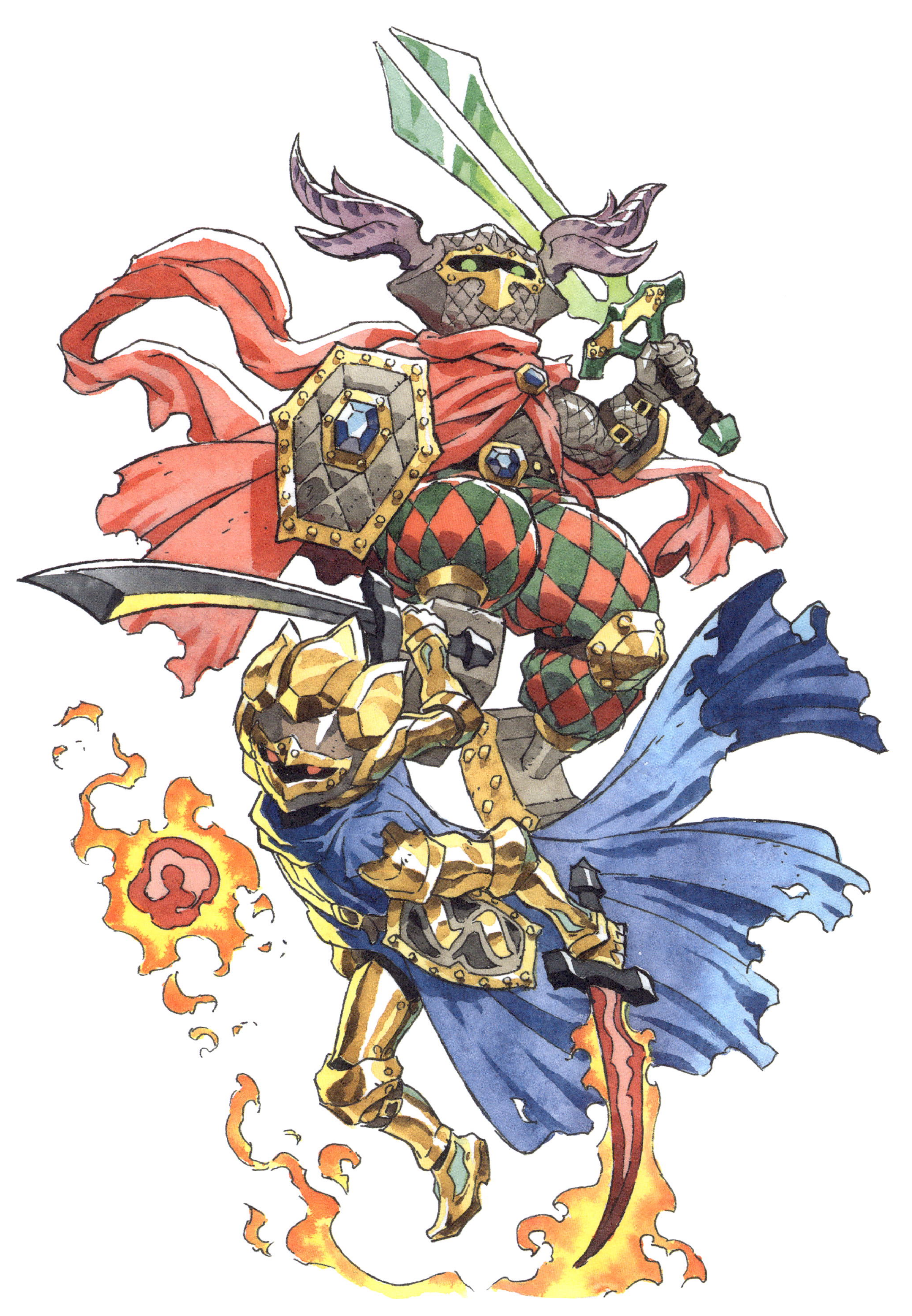

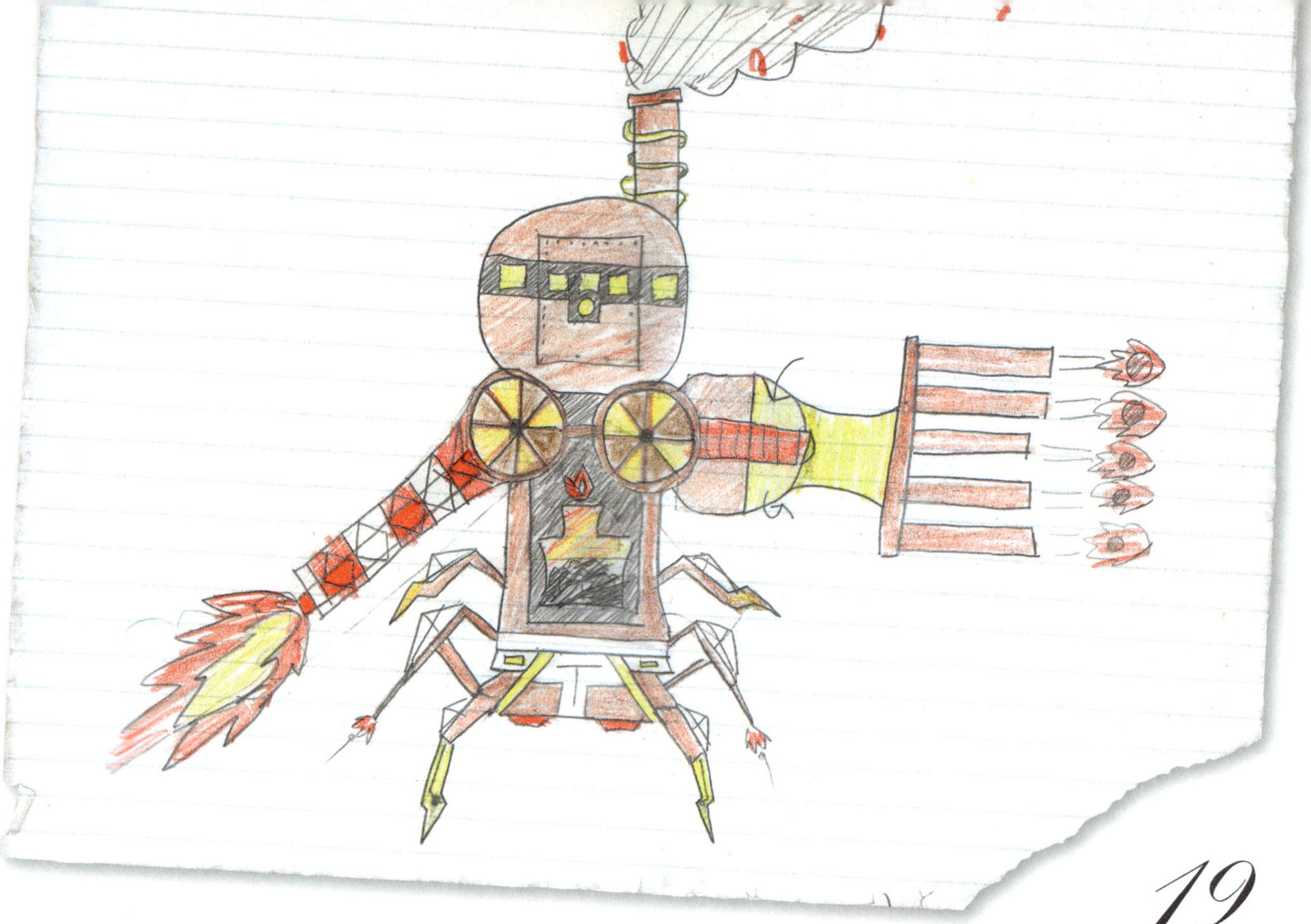

19

The War Machine

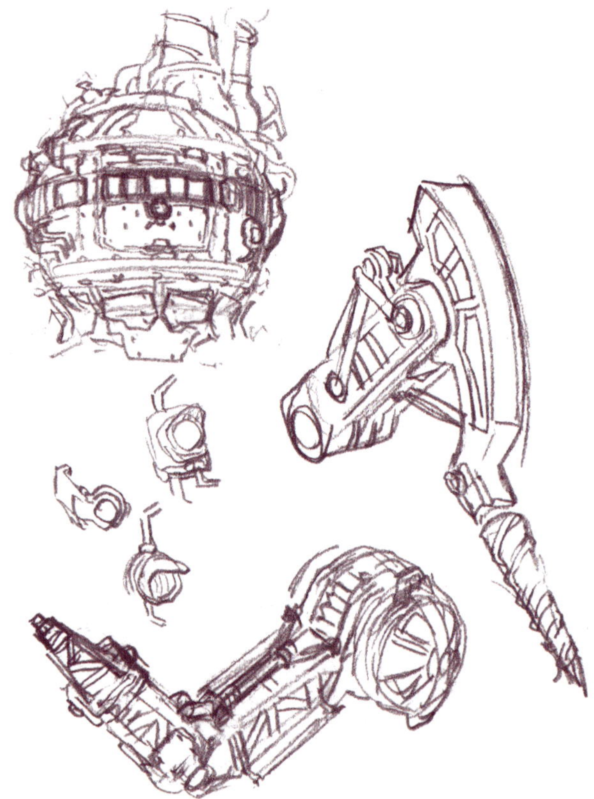

Thomas

The rivets and smoke and even the metallic armatures drawn by Ryunosuke gave this impressive machine a retro aspect, which put me back on the steampunk path. After drawing several prep sketches and seeking out reference images (notably ancient pumps and oil rigs) to help me design the legs, I was ready for this ambitious illustration. This one took me more time to make, as the machine is quite detailed. This drawing also gave me the opportunity to train myself to draw smoke effects. The icing on the cake: I placed the Scarlet Doctor at the top of the destroyed building.

Ryunosuke

My idea for this drawing was to mix elements of factories and thermal power plants to make a robot. I'm pretty happy with the dual-colored arm, as it makes it look a little like Tokyo Tower. I had no idea Dad would make such a complicated drawing out of that. It really has a lot of tubes and little details to look at. I really like the effects of the rust and the incandescent embers as they flutter off in the wind.

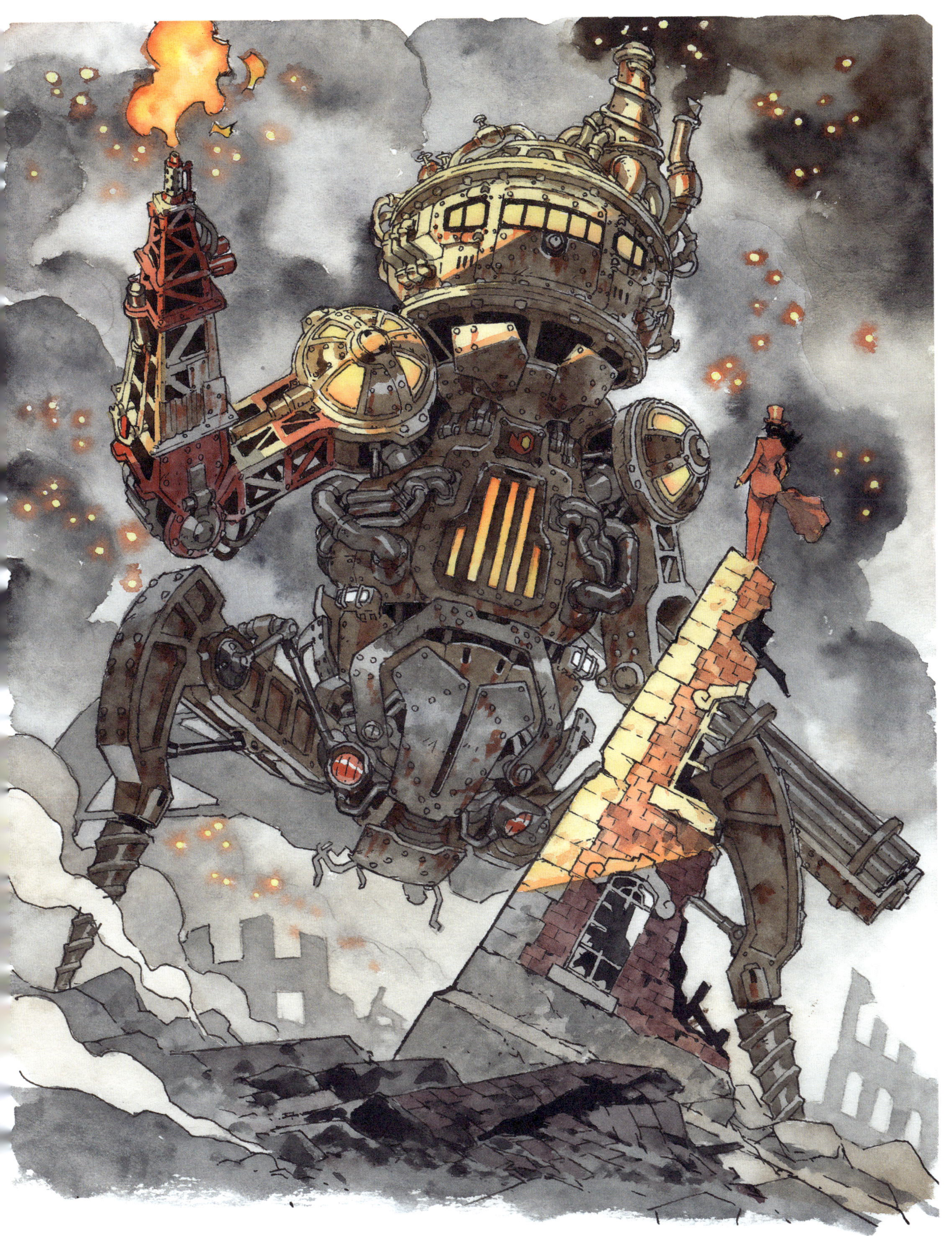

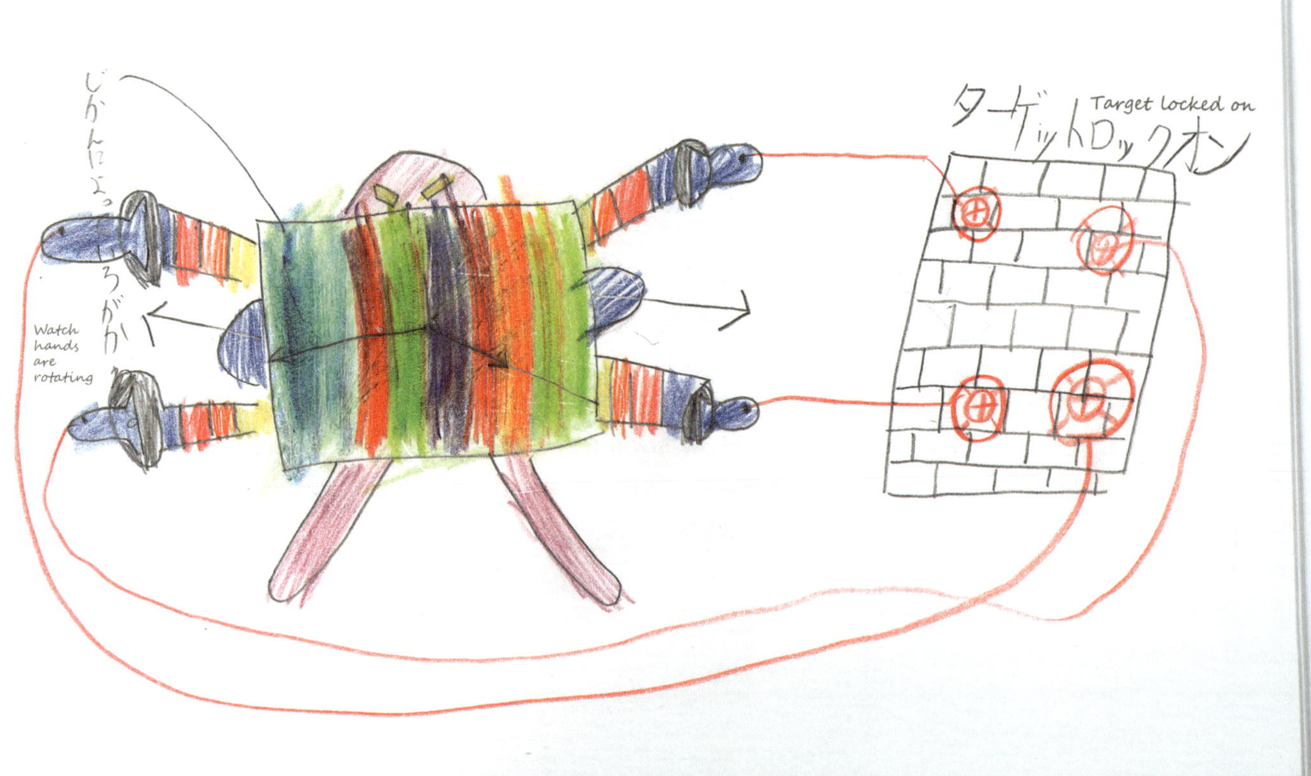

20 The Time Octopus

Thomas

I think this was the drawing by Itsuki that gave me the most trouble. I had to make a few little adjustments to make it something coherent in my eyes. The fish missiles put me on the path towards an aquatic theme and the multiple arms gave me the idea to make it a kind of futuristic octopus. I clearly reduced the size of the giant watch so it wouldn't take up too much space on the character. In the end, the design of this squid is one of the most fun and colorful. Is he obsessed with the passage of time, or does he possess the power to travel the ages in order to track down his enemies? It has yet to be imagined.

Itsuki

I didn't have many ideas that day. So I inspired myself with what was around me: the small clock on my desk, and the fish we had for dinner that night. I gave him multicolored stripes because I love that. What I like the best in Dad's drawing is the fish missile that's heading right for us.

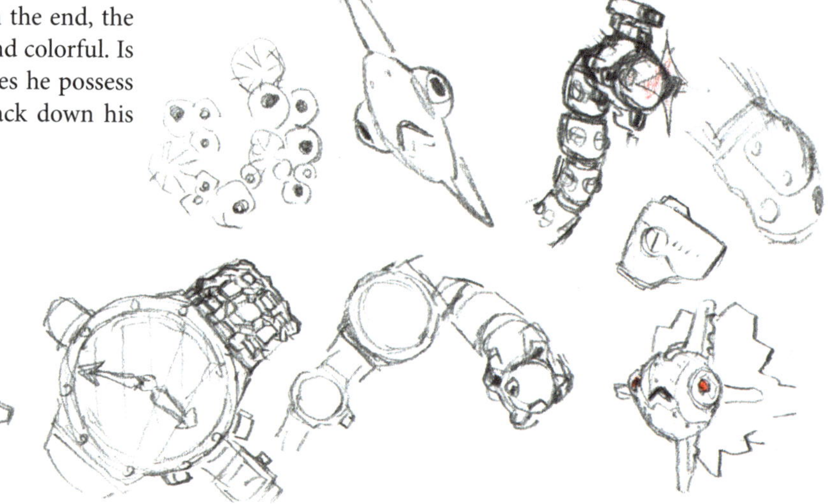

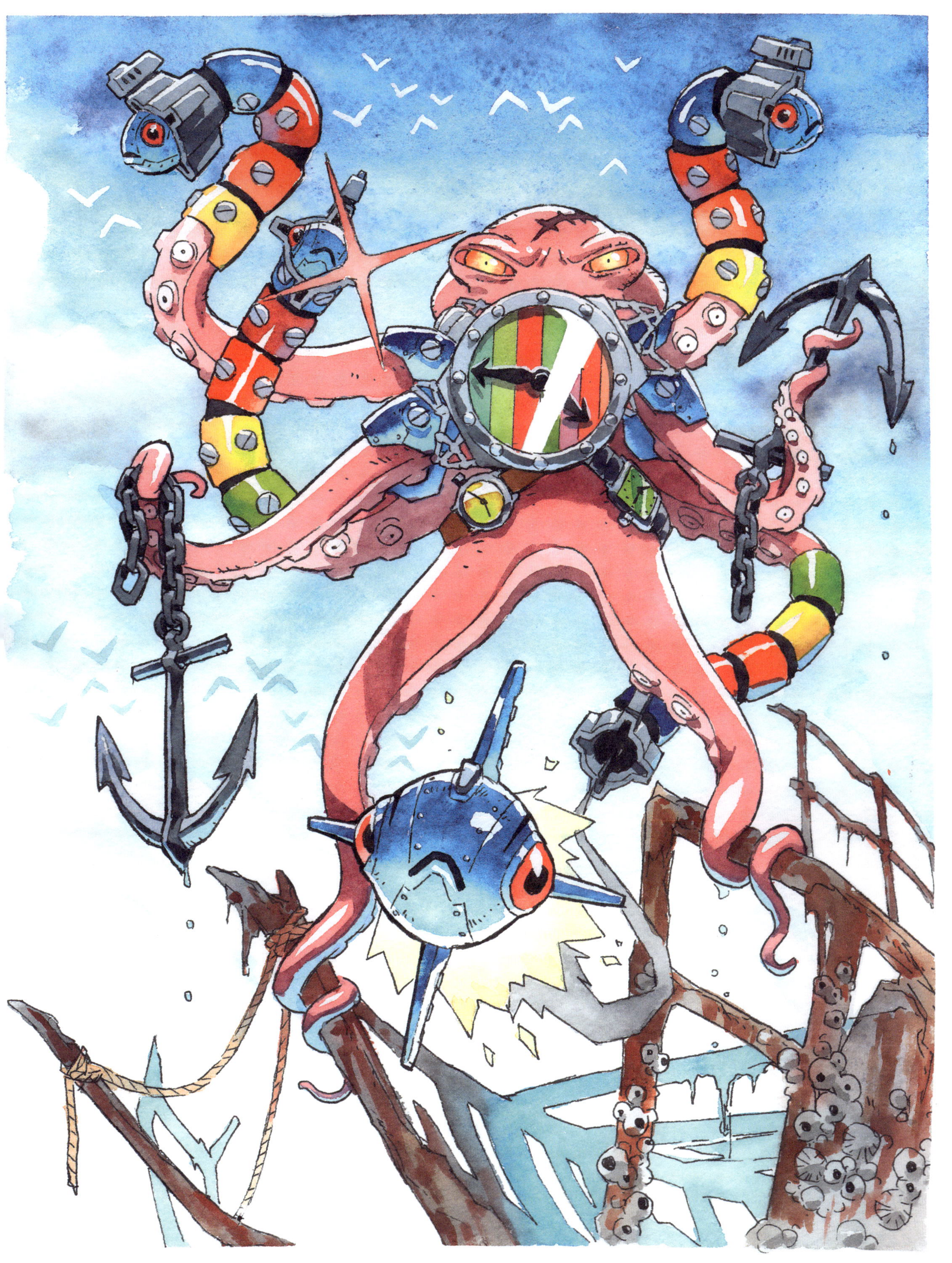

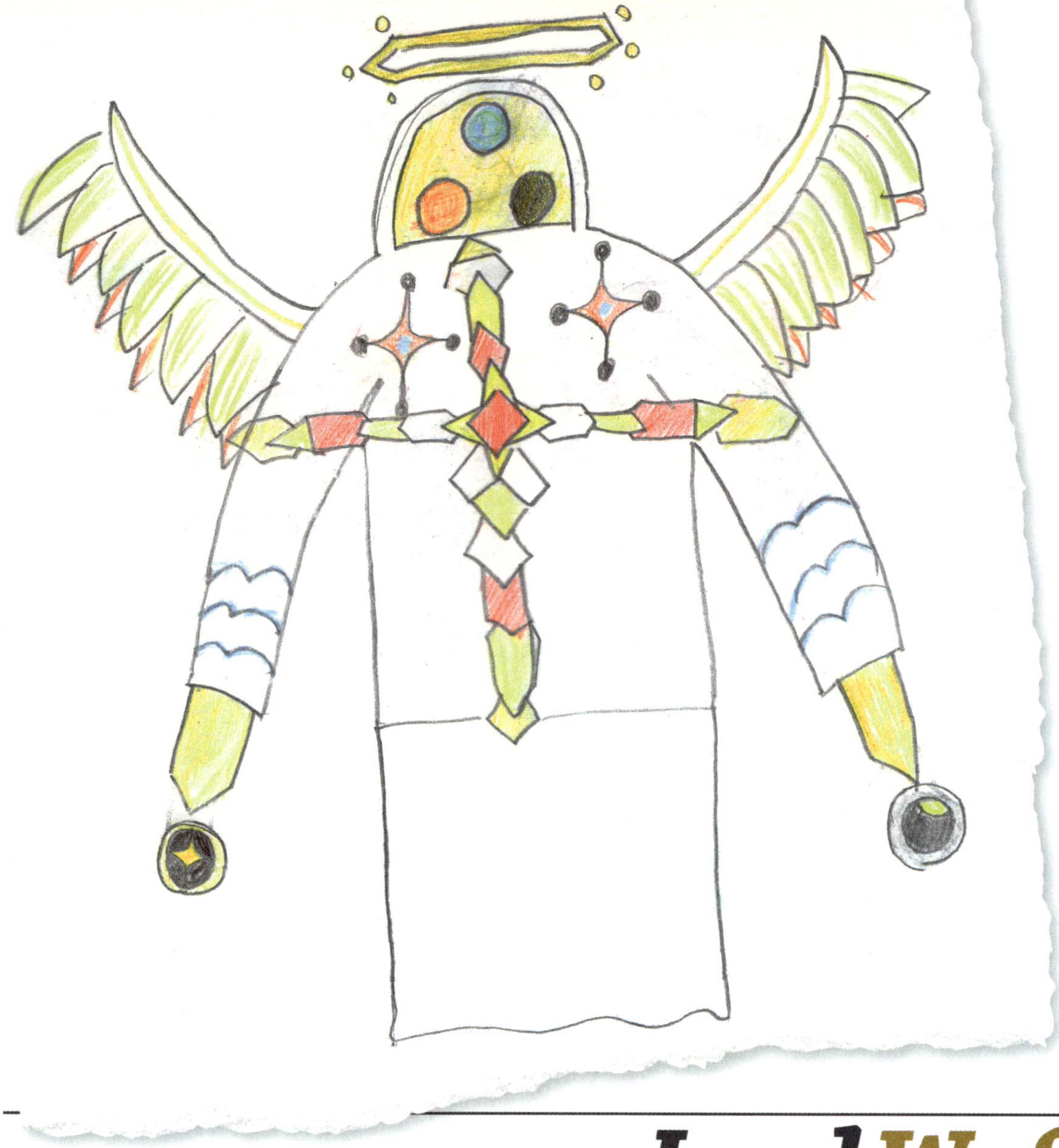

21

Lord Wafida

Thomas

A well-balanced design by Ryunosuke. I love the stylization of the face devoid of expression, which gives the character a mysterious and impressive allure. The many motifs and graphic details on the body are indicative of the richness of the costume. Lastly, the white and gold colors evoke both purity and power, the perfect combination for this imaginary divinity. For my half, I added the light effects in the background and the cloth drapes, to accentuate the idea of a religious image representing a glowing icon. The name Wafida comes from the combination of the first syllables from the words water, fire, and darkness - elemental powers associated with blue, orange and black, the colors that make up the face.

Ryunosuke

What I wanted to draw was an all-powerful god. The white, the wings, and the halo over the head are all borrowed from the look of angels. The colors of the eyes represent the colors of the sky. Blue for day, orange for dusk, and black for night. I didn't tell Dad that when he made his drawing. I love the motifs he drew. They are really neat. It makes me want to do more detailed drawings.

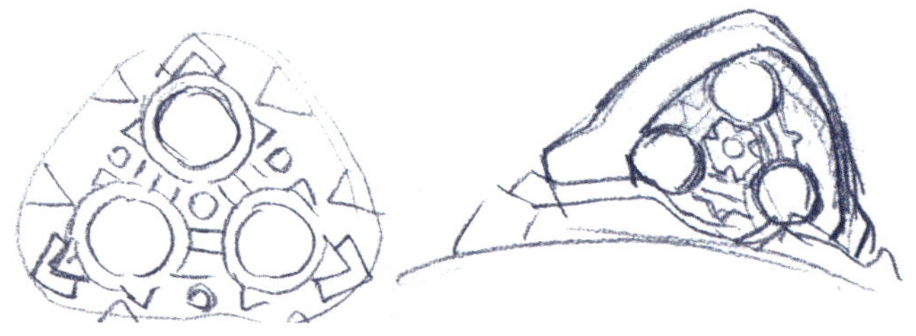

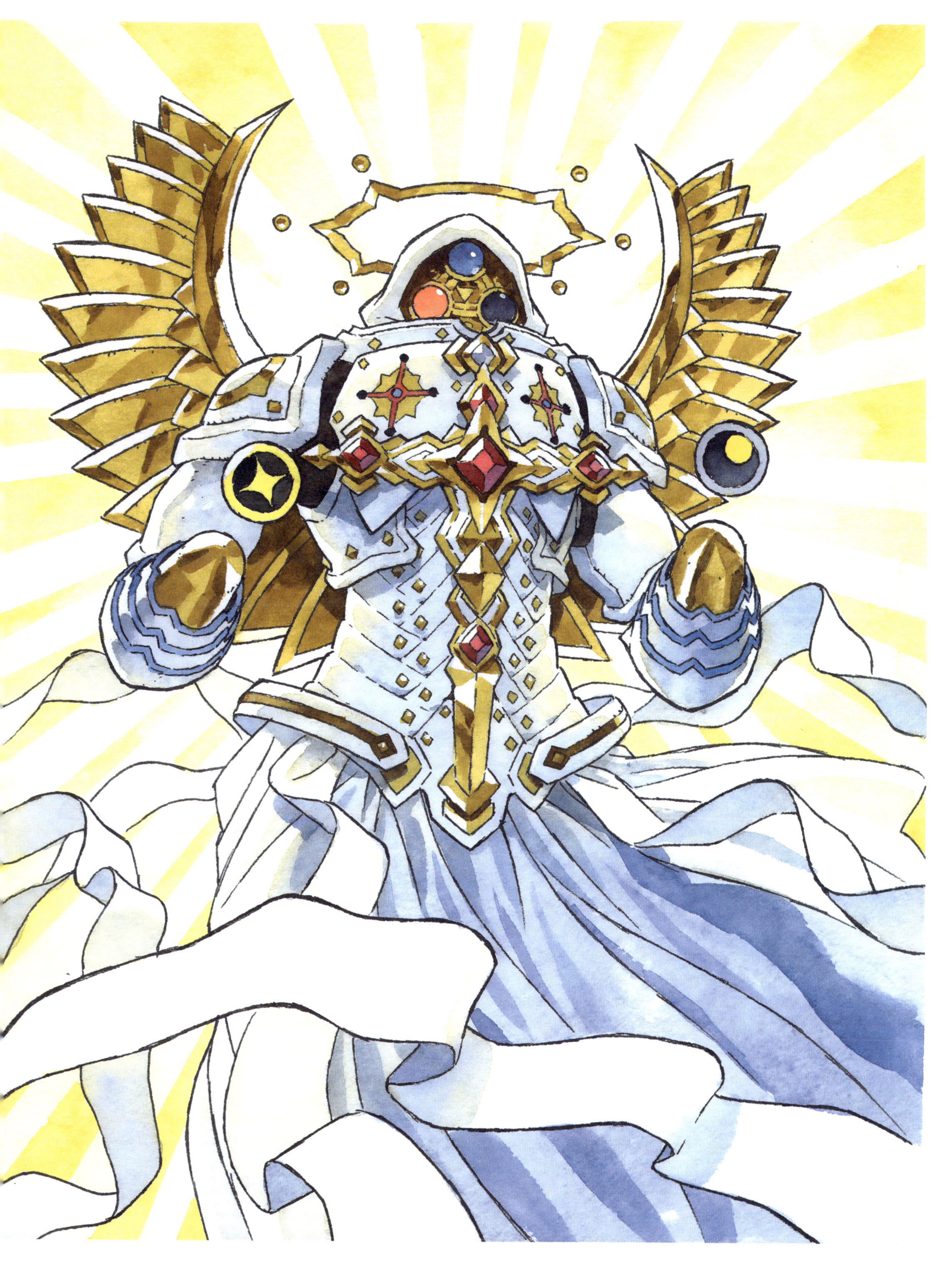

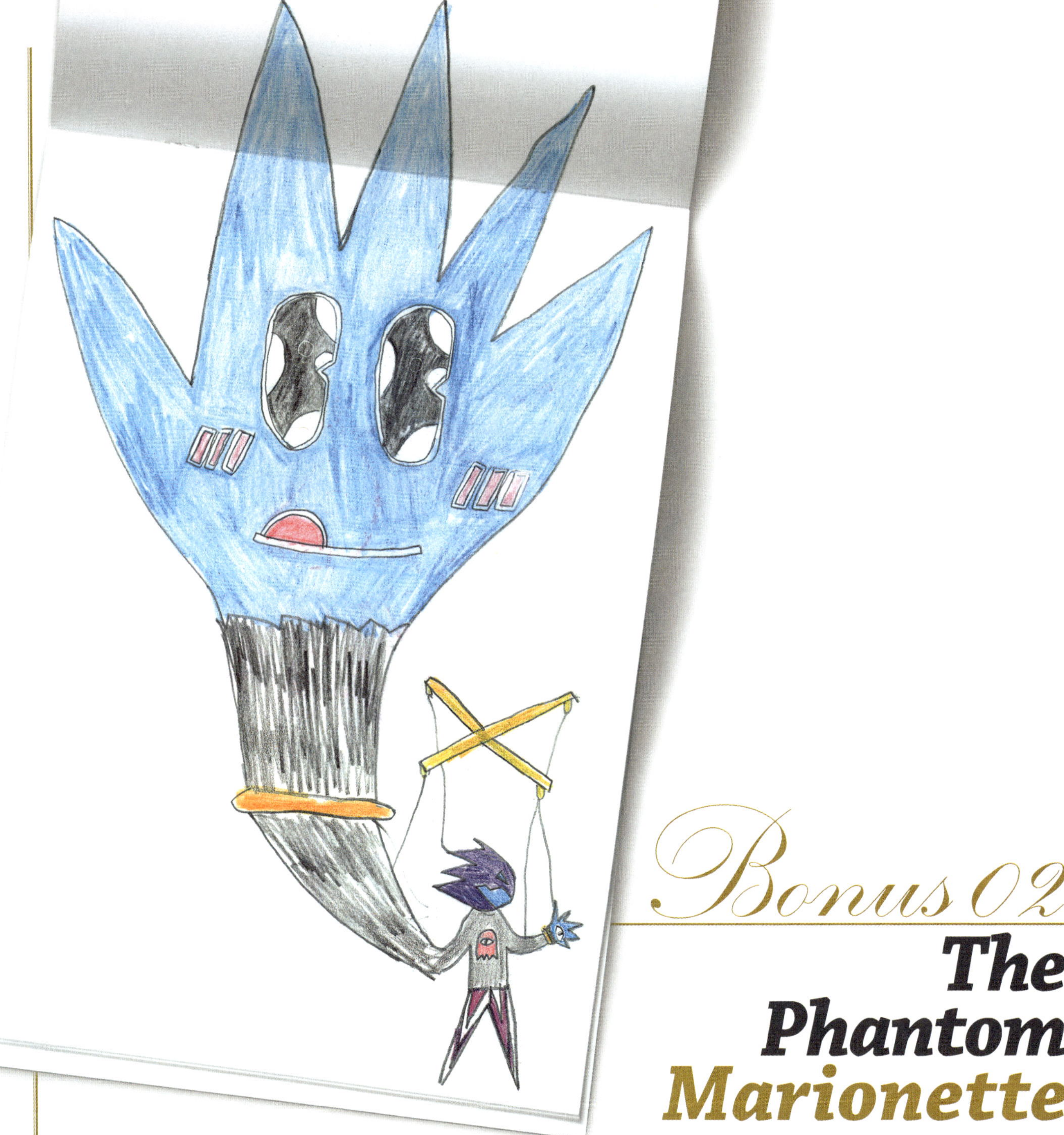

Bonus 02

The Phantom Marionette

Thomas

I modified a lot of the proportions from Ryunosuke's drawing: the hand was really too big, and the body far too small. This permitted me to add a third face in the image, that of a marionette with a worrisome expression. The design, being quite simple, caused me to work particularly on the pose of the character and the composition of the image. The goal was to give a very disjointed attitude to this marionette.

Ryunosuke

At first, I only drew a cute face. It stayed like that for several weeks in my sketchbook while I was working on other drawings. Then I had the idea to place it inside a hand, and then to stretch it out towards a marionette's body. After seeing Dad's drawing, I told myself that I should have tied the strings to the legs as well. That would have been way more logical. What I like the best about his version is the palm of the hand. With its long hanging tongue and its dark eyes, his expression is both cute and malicious.

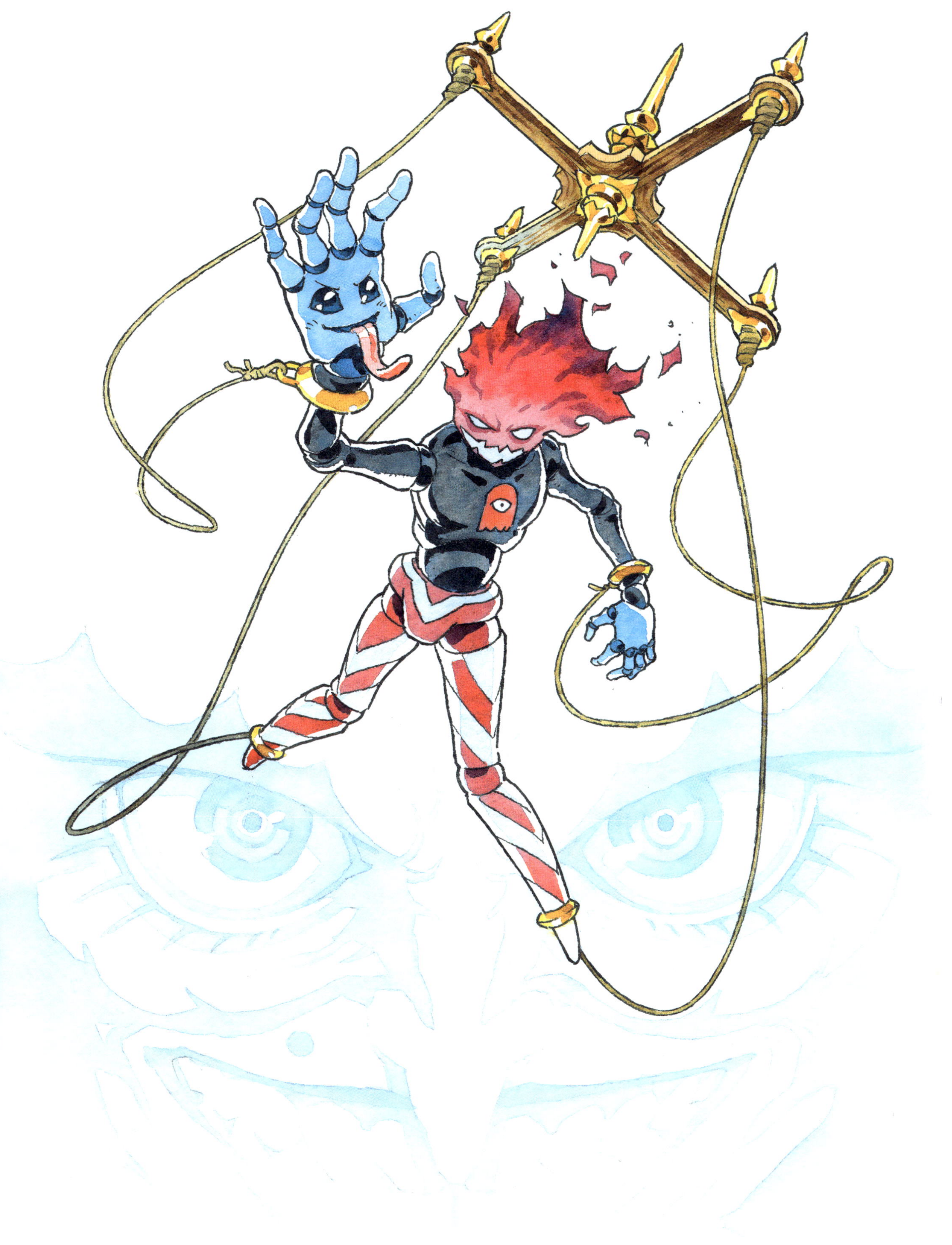

22

The Boomerang-bot

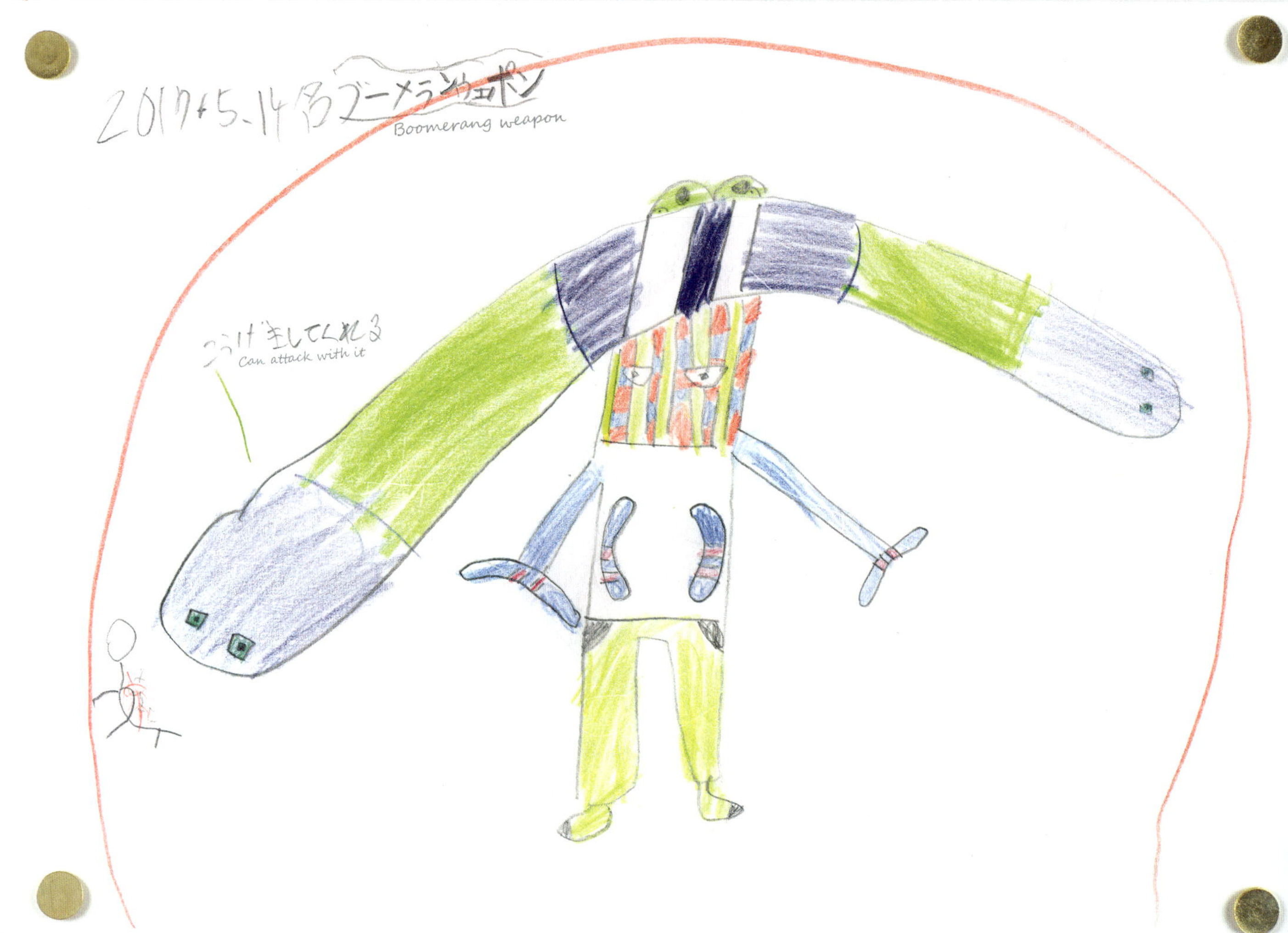

Thomas

The shape of Itsuki's drawing is really hilarious. I first tried to make it a creature but I wasn't convinced by the first test. I then chose to roboticize it. Placing it in a natural background helps create a good contrast on a material level. The green moss on the stones and the blueish atmospheric attenuation in the background call back the colors of the robot and produce a harmony within the image. This robot is really fast - I can imagine him bounding from mountain to mountain, using his large ears for gliding. His hands are a cross between claws and boomerangs.

Itsuki

My French grandmother gave me a small multicolored boomerang. That's what led me to draw this character. I used the shape of the boomerang for the head, the hands, and the pockets. I didn't think about making it into a robot, but I find the final result quite good. It reminds me of the robots we see in Japan in videogames or on TV. I also like the shape of the stones. Dad says they are called basalt columns and that they really exist.

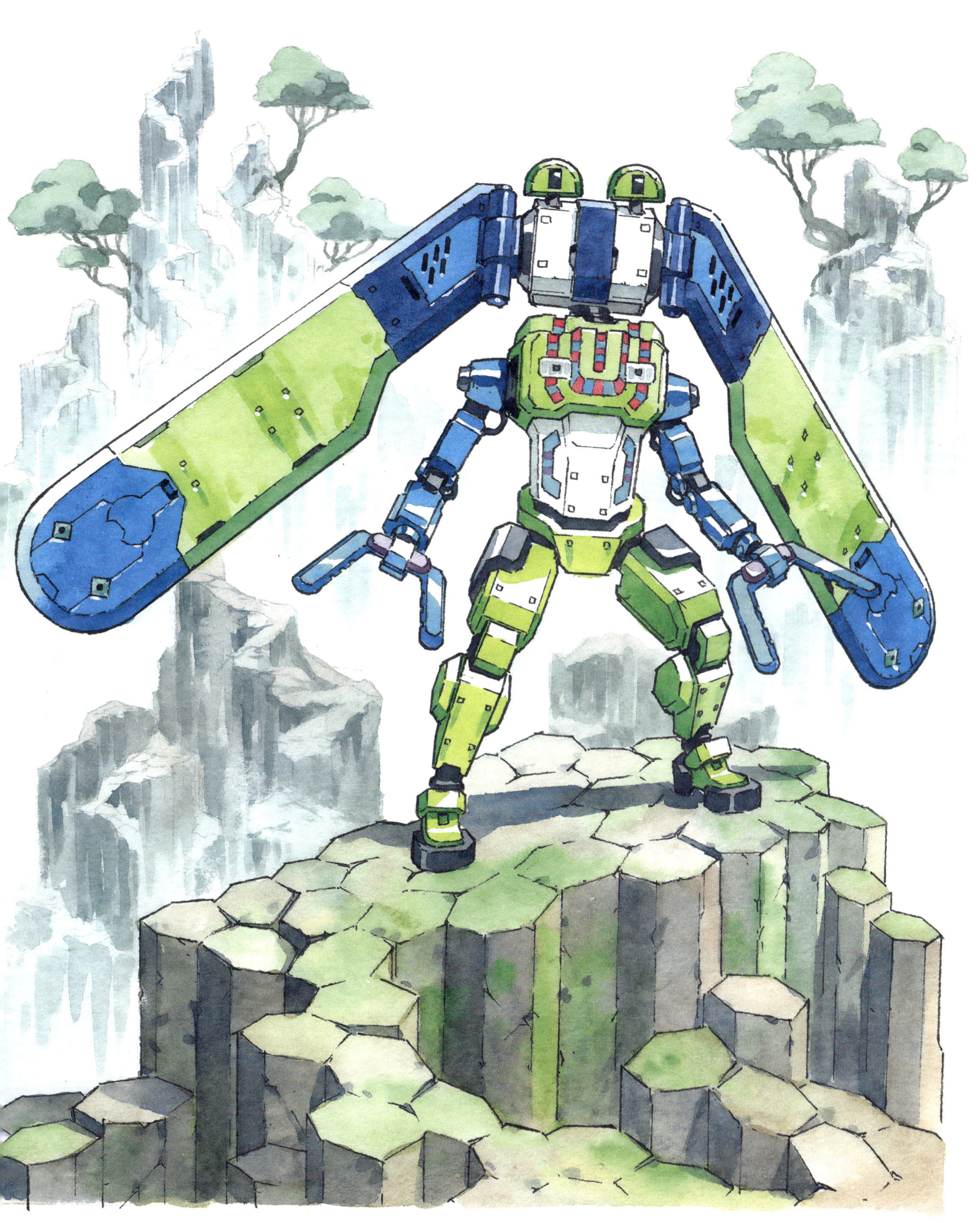

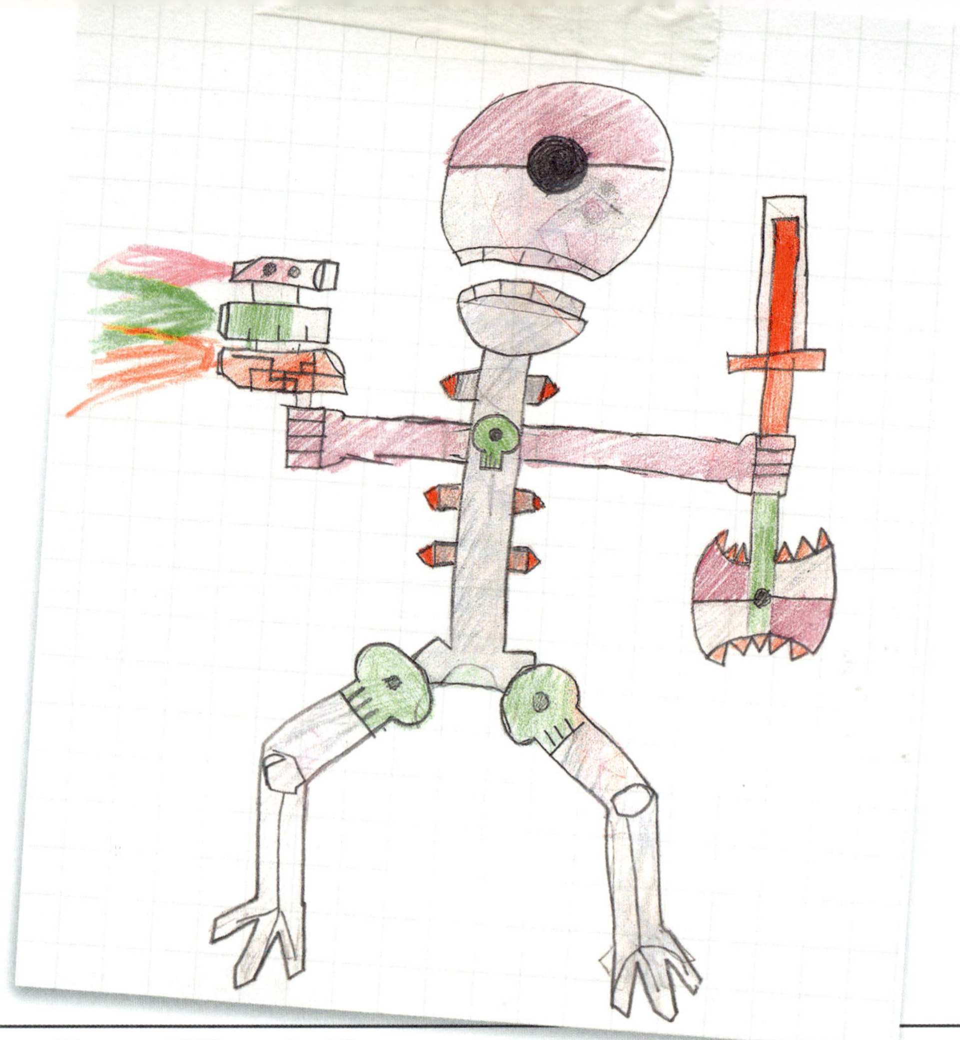

23
The Skulloid

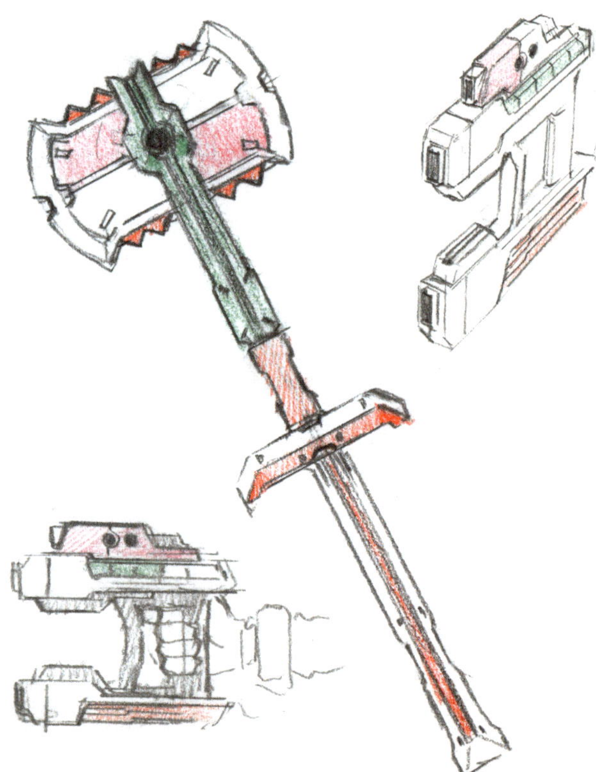

Thomas

The Skulloid is a cyborg who, despite his robotic appearance, is composed in part of organic tissue. The technology from which he was conceived is quite mysterious, but one thing is certain: he is a most tenacious adversary. Entire legions march up and down the devastated avenues of the cities in a dystopic future, searching for human survivors to enslave. Such is the context we could imagine upon seeing Ryunosuke's drawing. Personally, I love the combination of the pink and the green, very pop colors that contrast with the not-so-friendly look of the character.

Ryunosuke

"I made the head way too big." That's what I told myself when I saw Dad's version. With more realistic proportions, a bigger body that's more in proportion to his face makes him much scarier. The green skulls on the costume have a really great design on the final, very futuristic. On the other hand, why do we see severed heads on the ground? Did the Skulloid turn on his brothers because of a glitch? Or was he hacked by rebels?

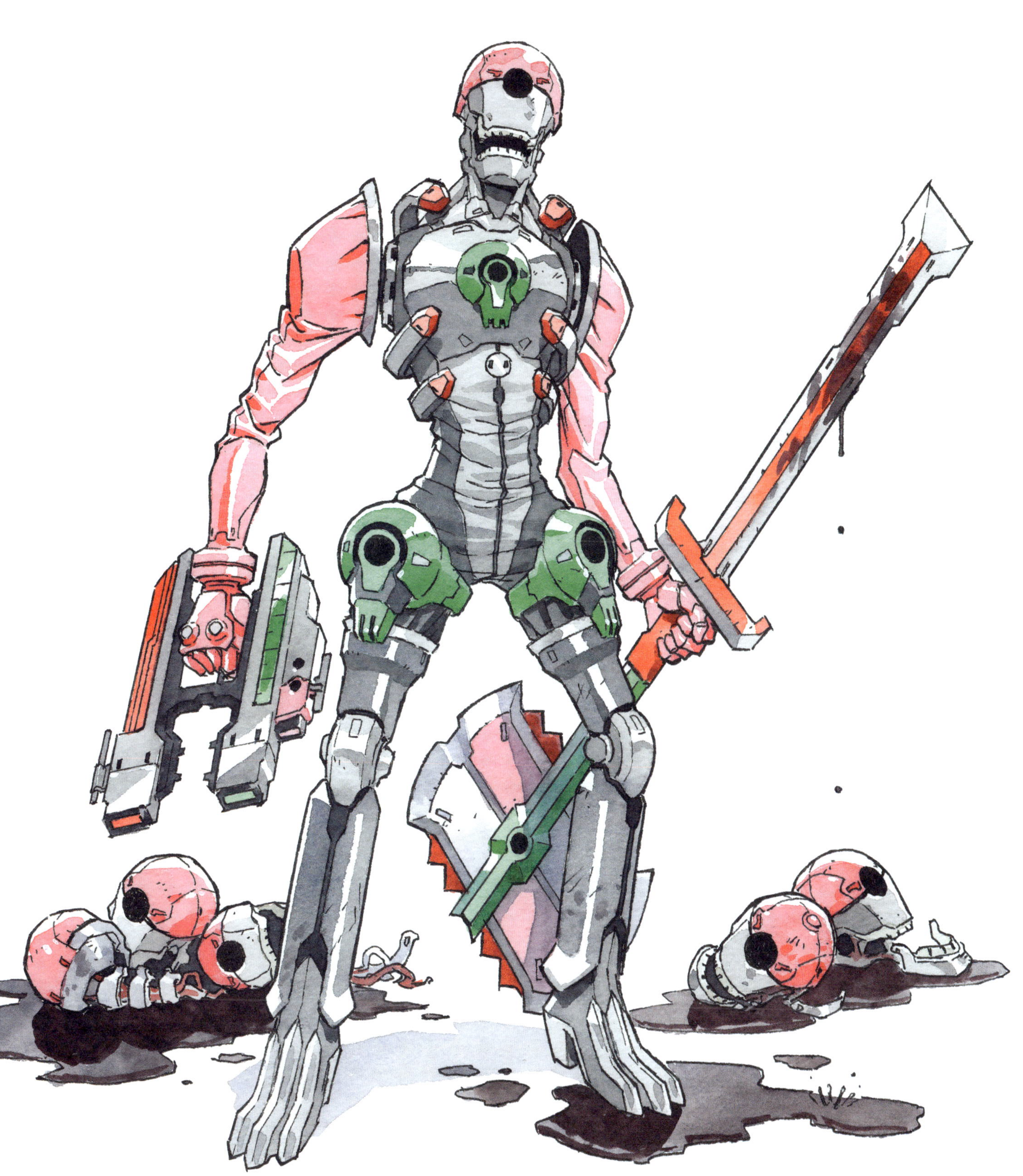

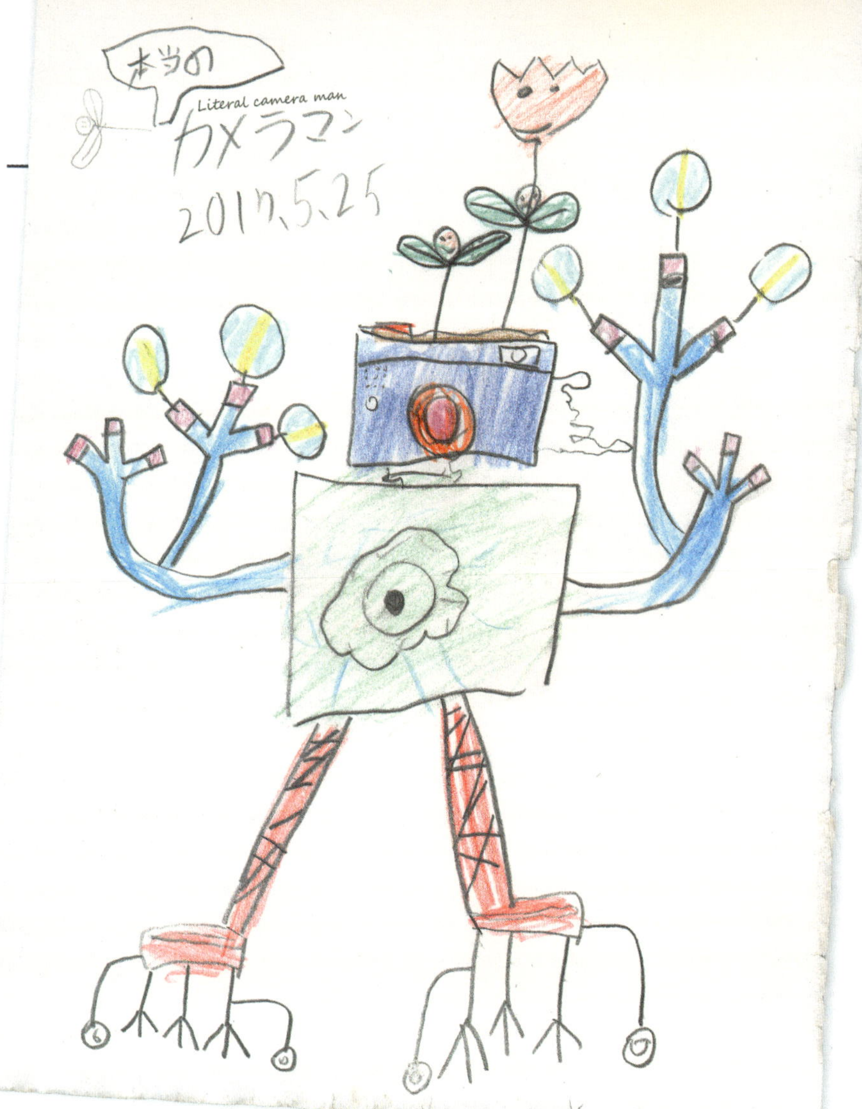

24 The Forgotten Giant

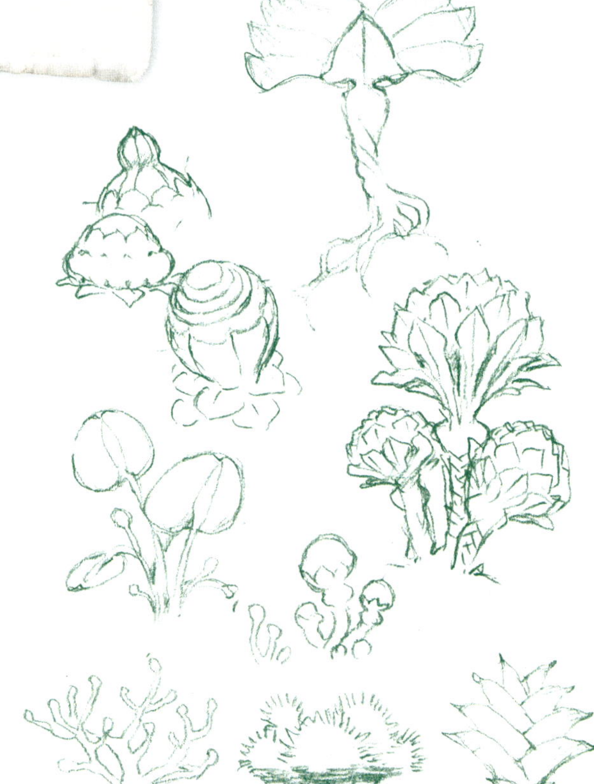

Thomas

Relic of an ancient civilization, all traces of its technology vanishing several centuries ago, this giant is little more than an abandoned carcass covered by moss. At its summit grows a rare flower, the sap of which possesses a great power, and, as such, is of great value. The tiny Koomos are on a mission to obtain it. The atmosphere of this drawing evokes that of certain Hayao Miyazaki films, such as *Nausicaä Of The Valley Of The Wind*. These movies, that have now become classics, are some of the works that gave me the urge to settle in Japan to work in the animation industry.

Itsuki

I started on the head by making a kind of camera. Then I went on to the robot's body by mixing in nature-inspired shapes. I like the ambiance of the final drawing a lot. The colors blend one into another - it's quite nice. And seeing the Koomos that are venturing into the forest, it's like we're travelling with them; we feel like we are discovering this location with them.

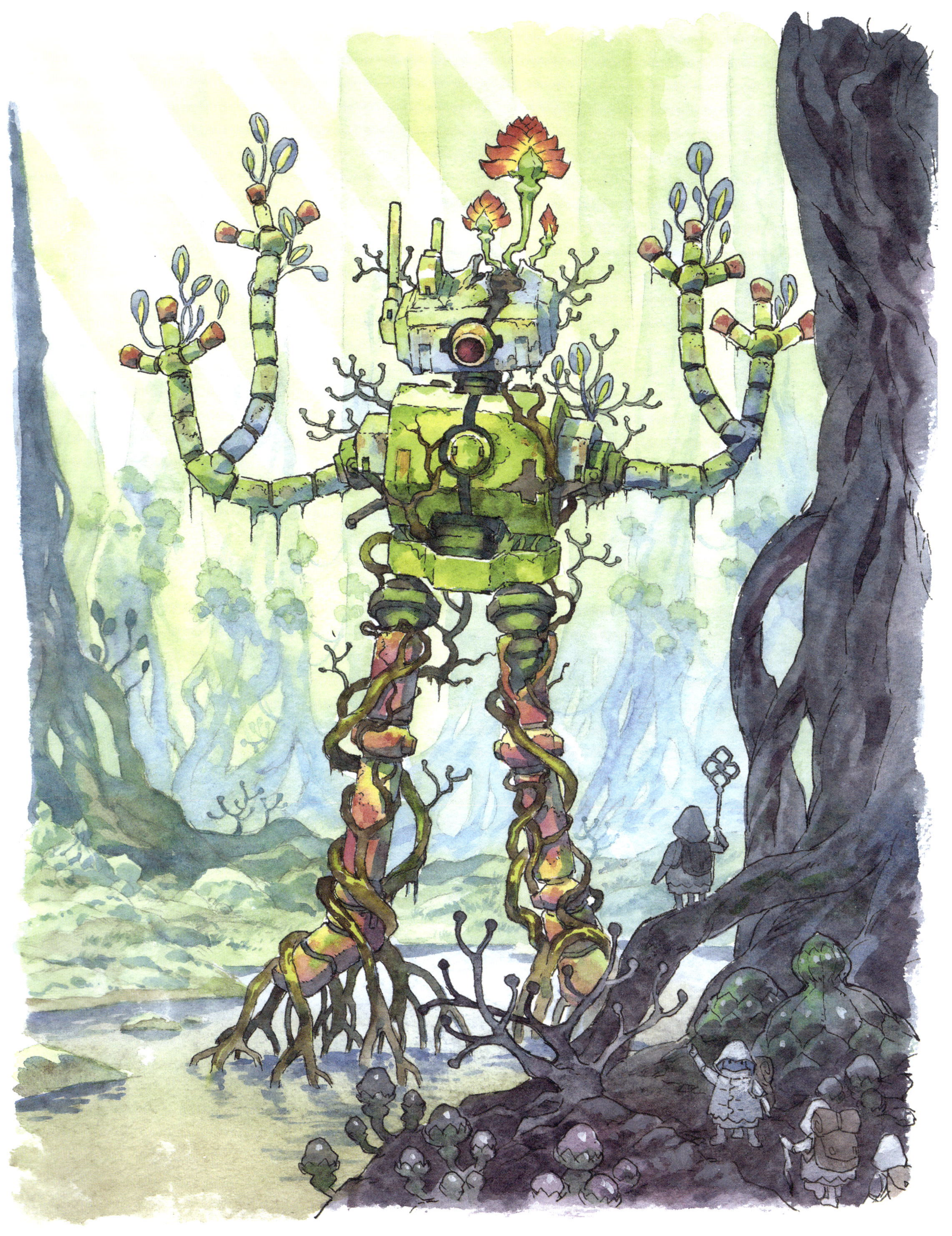

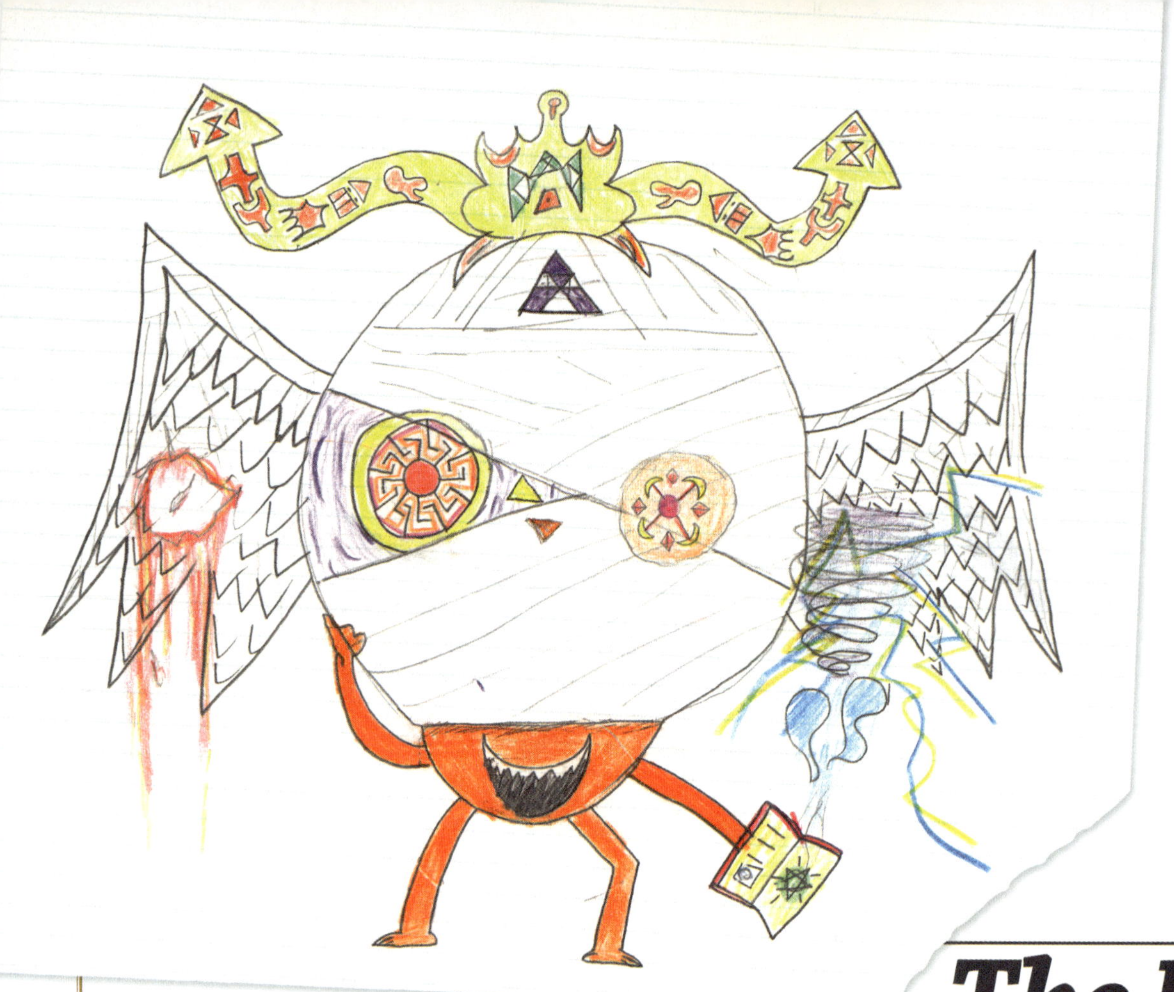

25

The Baby Mummydemon

Thomas

I was immediately won over by the general balance of Ryunosuke's drawing as well as by its silhouette, which was very different from those he had made up until now. I didn't have much to add other than a few bandages and some of the finer details on the golden parts. For the background, I used the tiny violet tornado coming out of the book. I transformed it into a spectacular electric cyclone, at the heart of which I placed the demonic baby. Around him spin magical tomes.

Ryunosuke

The entire upper part of the character is a cursed relic that is thousands of years old. When someone wears this headdress, it takes control of their body. This is what happened to the orange character. The bandages are supposed to contain magical power - under no circumstances are you to remove them! I find that the tornado makes the drawing quite dynamic in the final image. I also like the details of the magic eye.

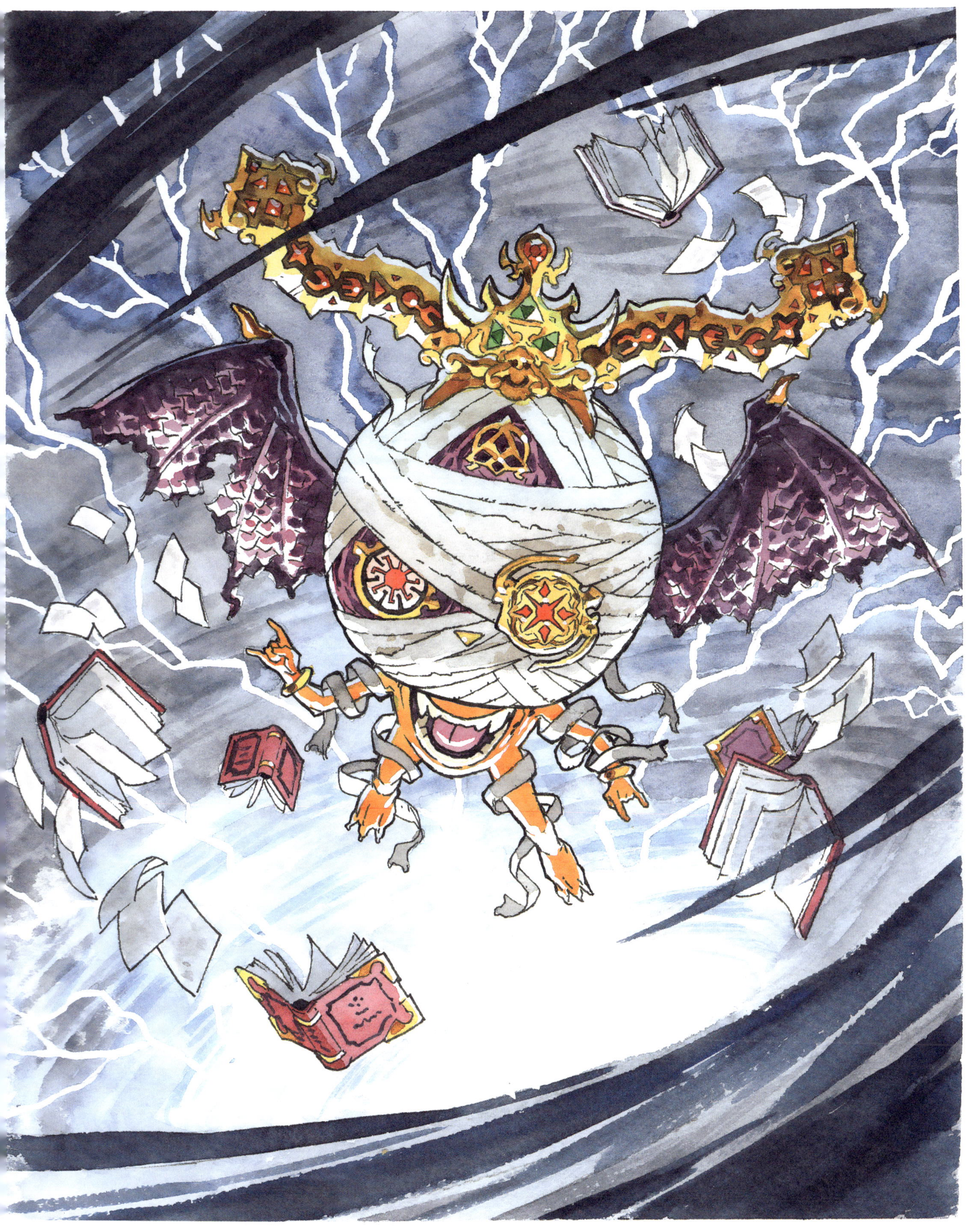

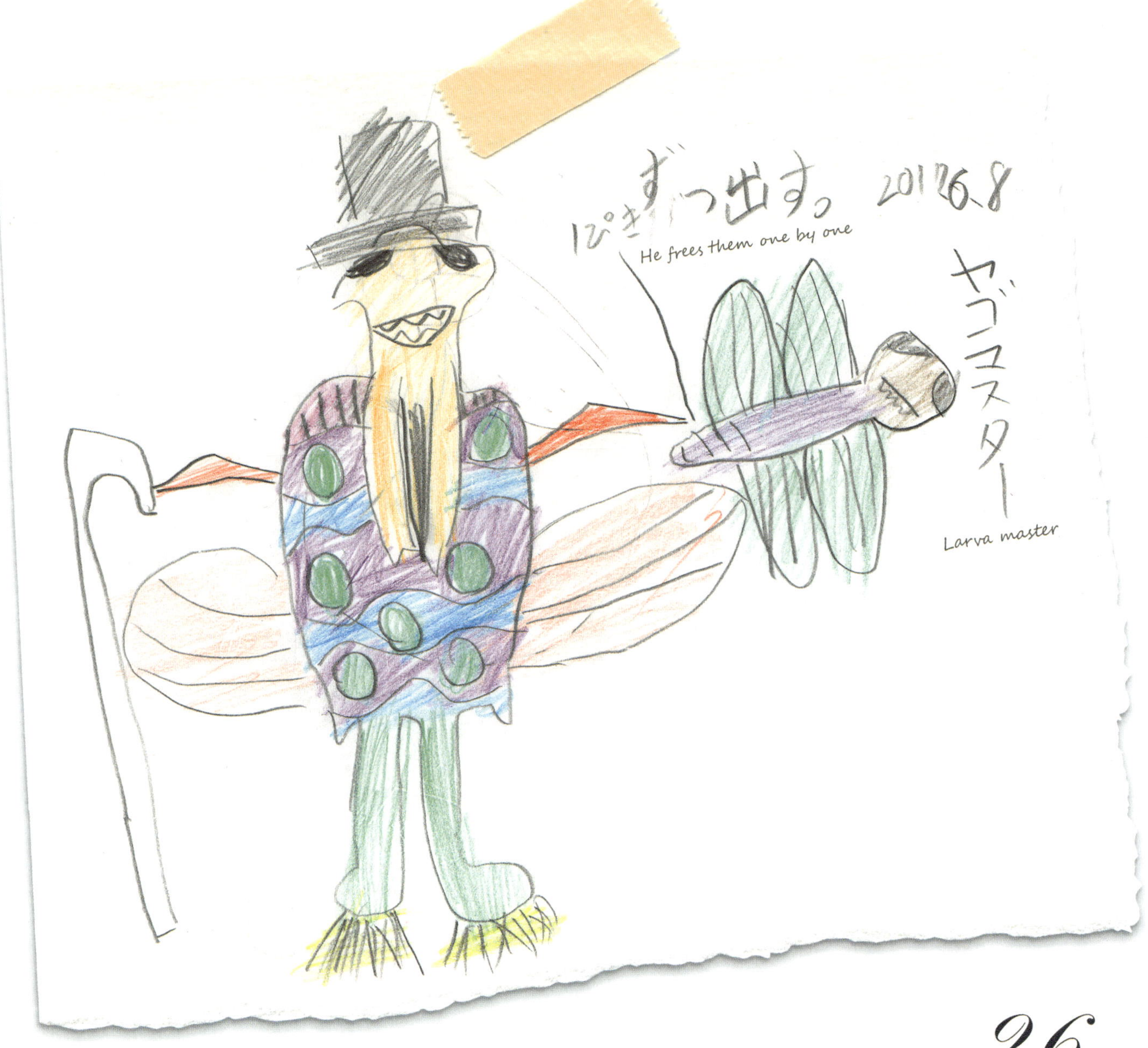

26

Yago the Apothecary

Thomas

I love the burlesque side of this creature that Itsuki imagined. The idea of combining an insect with an eccentric costume and that elegant hat was excellent, which quite quickly gave me this vision of a sketchy apothecary selling potions and remedies with the help of his young assistant. I found much pleasure drawing the numerous accessories that give the image more richness. Fun fact: the hairs under Yago's feet permit him to polish the floor while he moves around his shop.

Itsuki

During the month of June, the students help clean the pool that is on the roof of our school so that it'll be ready for summer. We always find dragonfly larva in the stagnating water. In Japanese it is pronounced *Yago*. We pick them up and we raise them in class inside an aquarium. I thought that it might be fun to base my drawing on these dragonfly larvae.

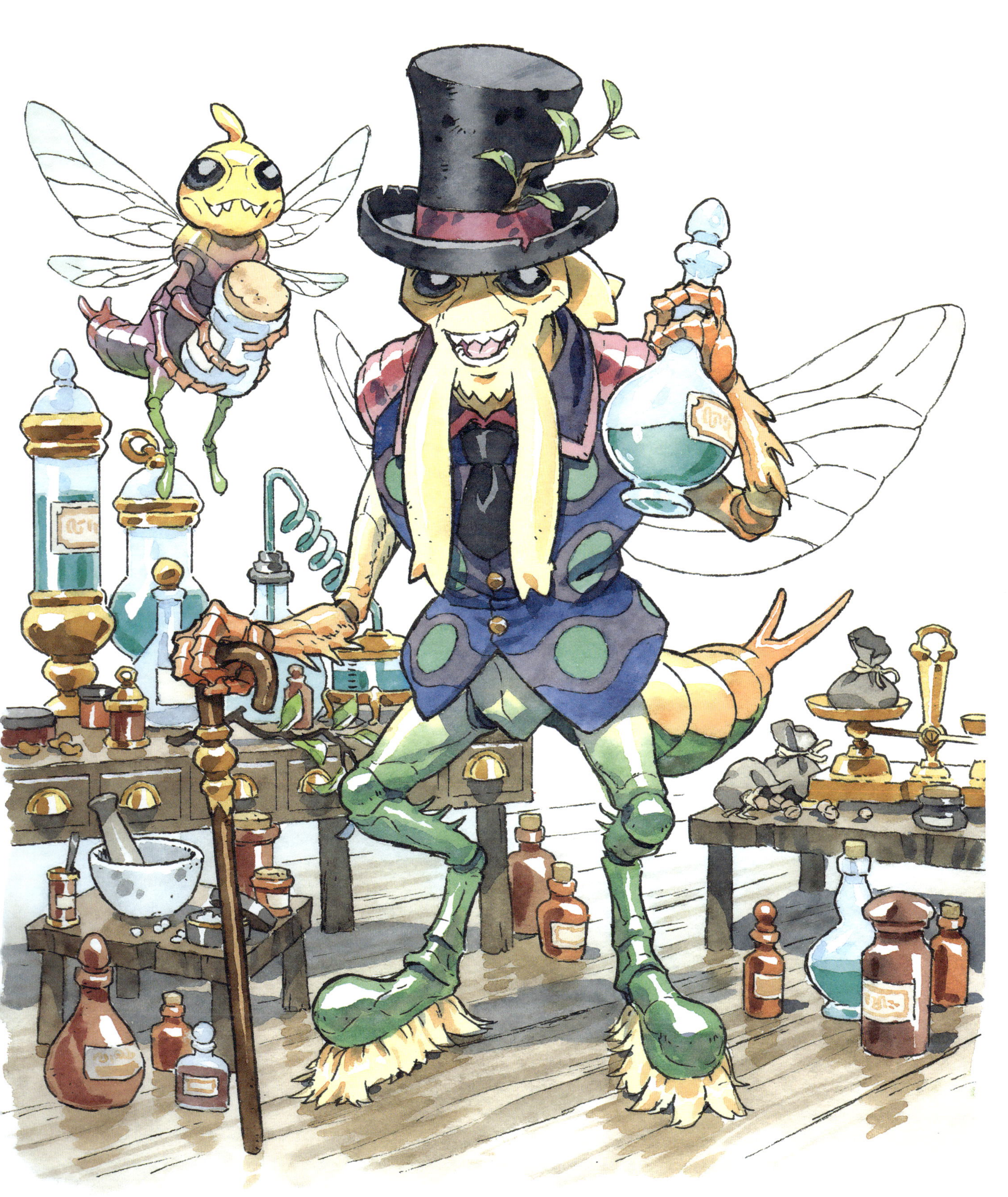

Bonus 03

The Mantamoth

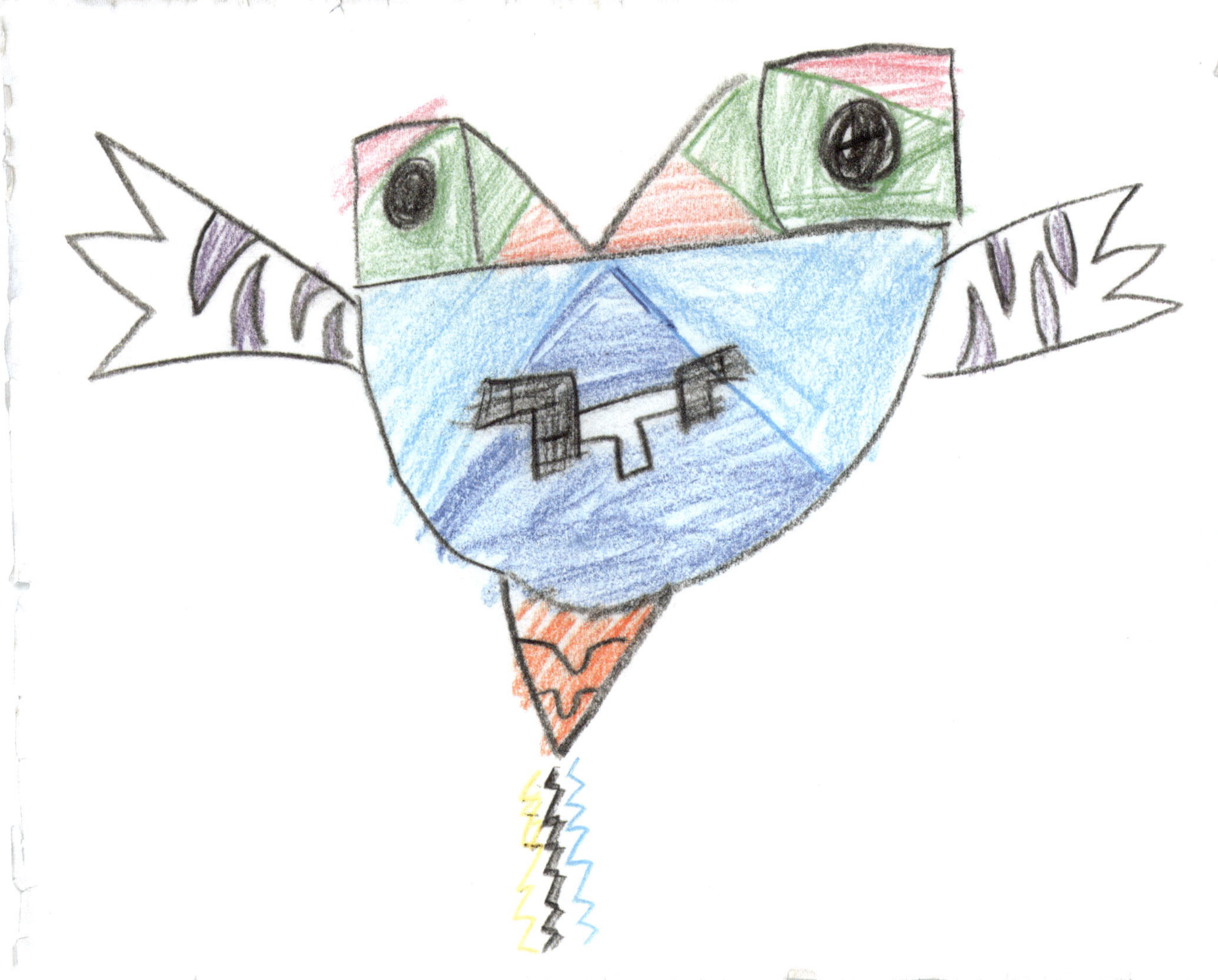

Thomas

I attempted to make this flying bug imagined by Itsuki more organic. I replaced the geometric forms with curves and roundness, which gives the Mantamoth a rather puffy aspect that's quite funny. But do not be fooled by its jovial looks! It is quite the formidable creature, capable of projecting waves of destructive energy from its abdominal stinger. This creature lives in a desert country littered with columns of petrified vegetation. It will let no one approach its territory, inside of which it raises its young. The Koomos will have to find another way to go across the region.

Itsuki

This is a drawing I made at my grandfather's home during summer vacation in France. I saw some birds through the window, which gave me the idea to draw a winged creature. I combined it with an enemy from *Space Invaders* that shoots lasers from underneath. What I like best about Dad's drawings is the background filled with large violet plants. Seeing images of an imaginary world like that is really dreamlike.

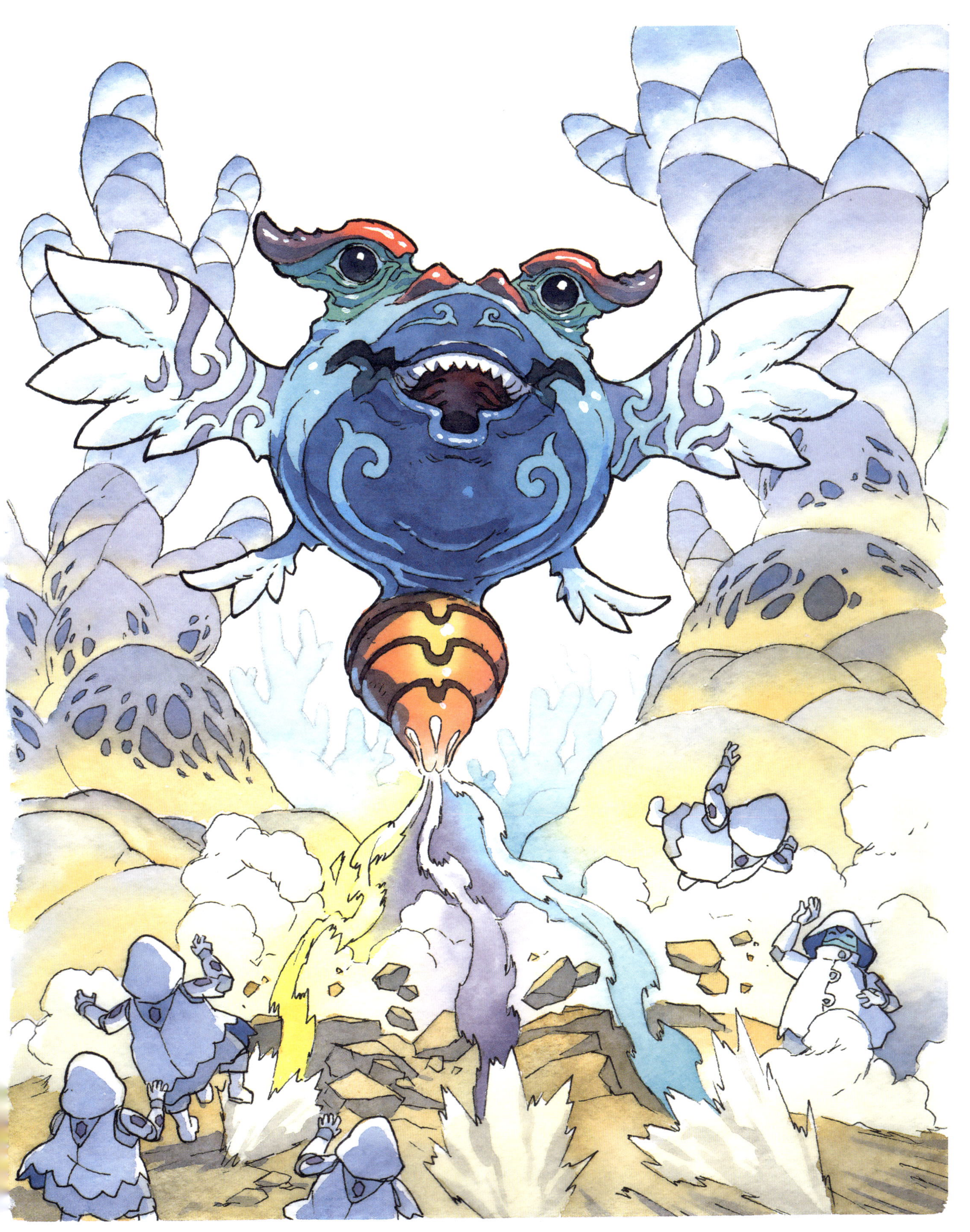

27

The Demon Lord of the Half-Dead

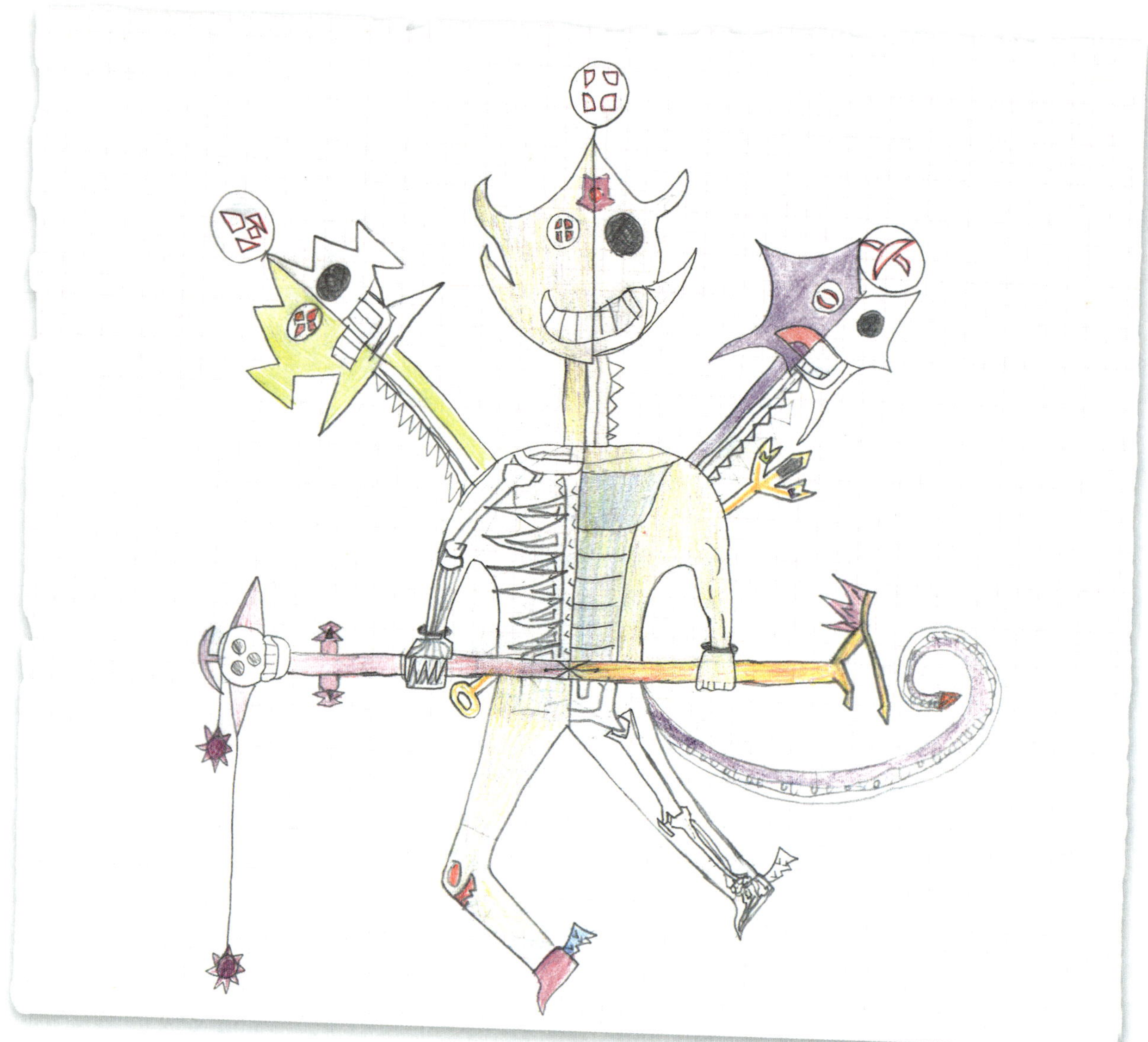

Thomas

Our most popular drawing on Youtube. I made a montage showing how we worked on this character. The video gained viral success! The quality of Ryunosuke's drawing has much to do with it. The semi-transparent body of the demon allowing the skeleton to be visible, its three differently-colored heads, and the details of its accessories are all elements I took great pleasure in recreating in my illustration. Even the colors of the skin, slightly dull, are well chosen, as they permit the golden accessories to pop.

Ryunosuke

In school, during art class, we had to draw a *Fuujin*. That's a Japanese wind god. He's very buff. We see him as statues in certain temples. At home I had the urge to draw a character with visible musculature, specifically the abdominals. For the skeleton I looked up references on the net. After that, Dad gave me a book on anatomical drawing, which is way more practical. What I love are the parts of the body with a transparent effect around the muscles, and the horns around the middle head that really make him look like a boss!

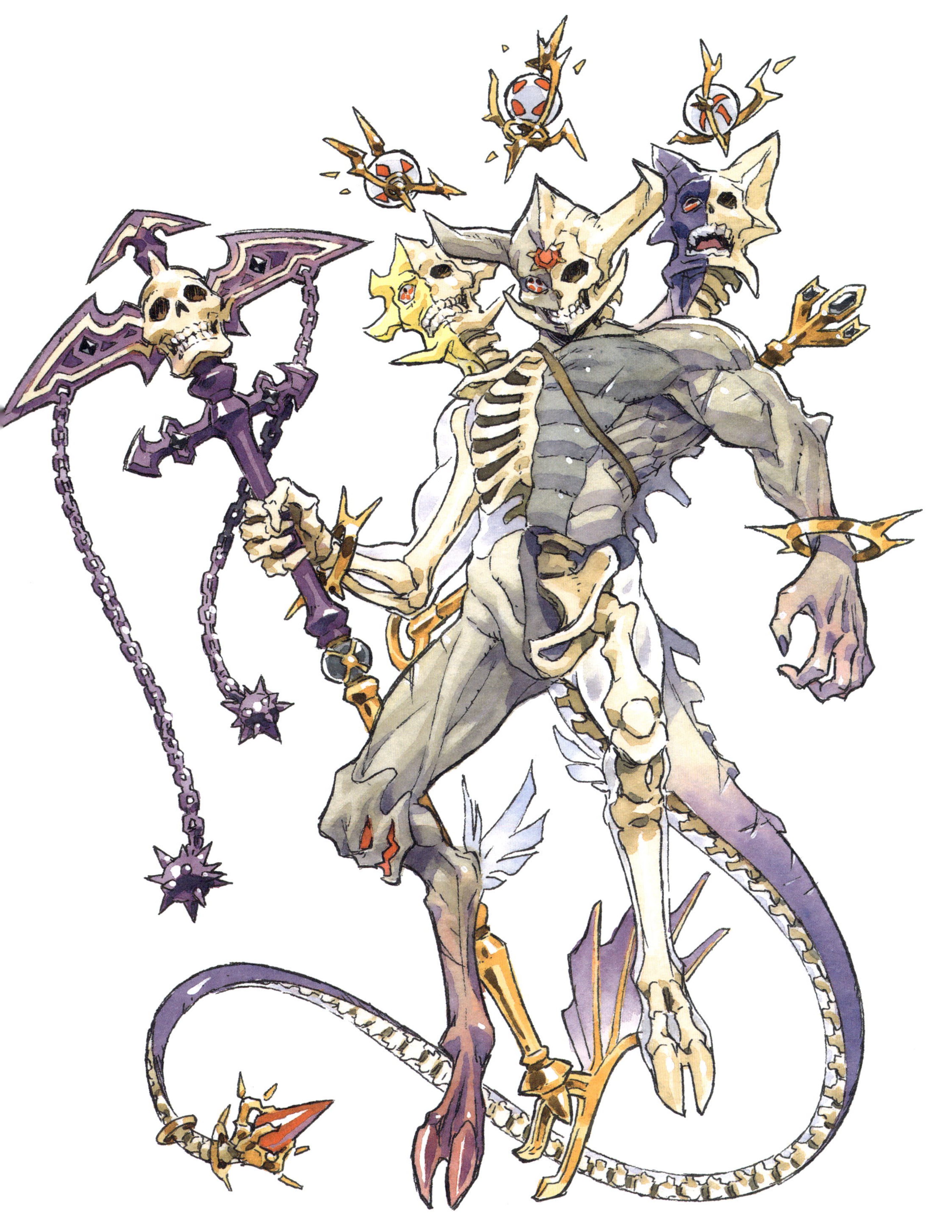

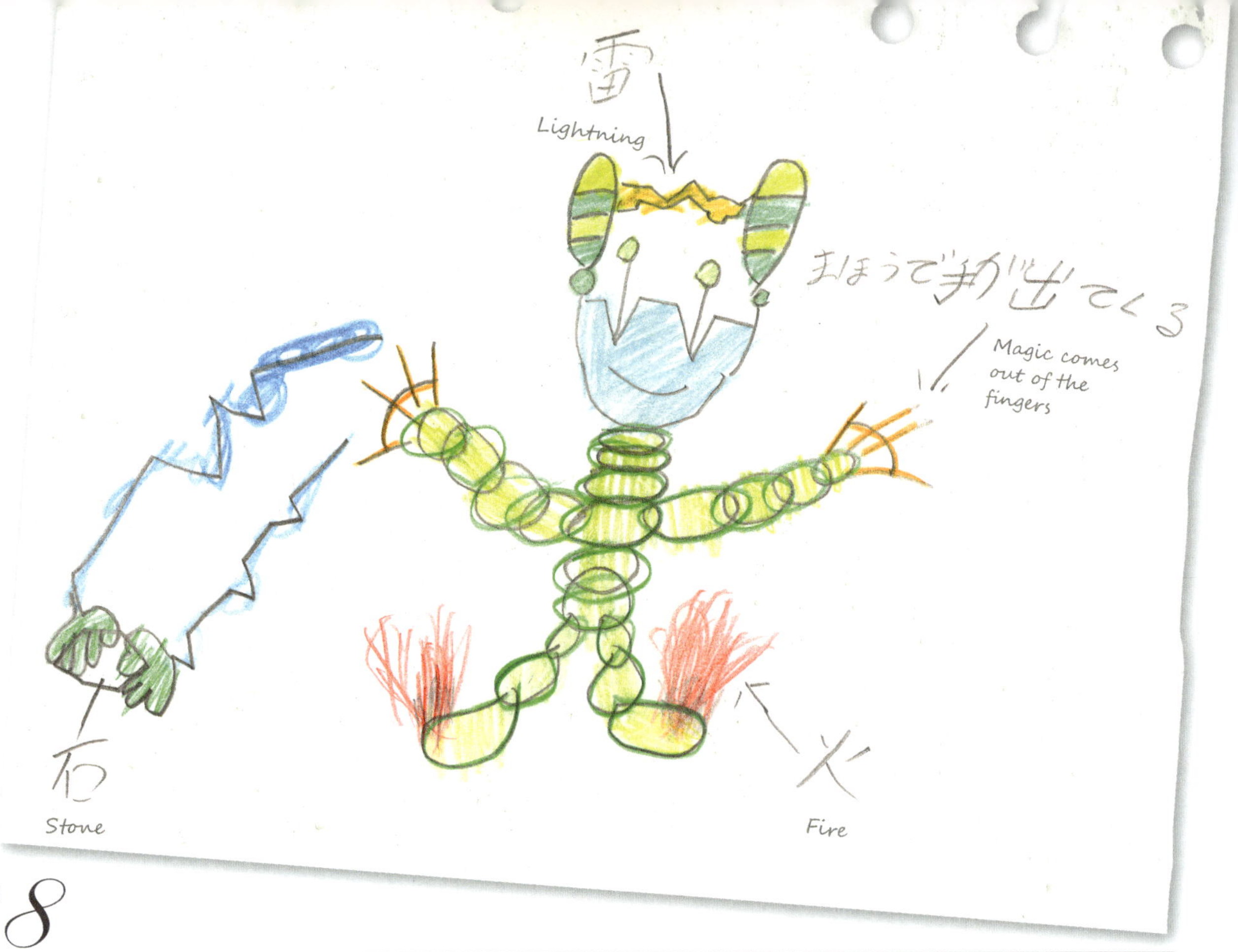

雷
Lightning

Magic comes out of the fingers

石
Stone

火
Fire

28

Sylveria Guardian of the Woods

Thomas

I let my imagination wander quite far on this drawing. I certainly conserved the principal characteristics of this vegetal creature, but I evolved it into something far more refined. Where Itsuki made rounded leaves, I went and found more complex shapes. I transformed the eye pistils to antennae and moved the eyes onto the blue petals to give Sylveria, the goddess of the forest, a far more malicious expression. Her natural presence is reinforced by the massive stone throne upon which she sits. With the goal of detaching her green silhouette in mind, I chose to paint it in red. The three tiny adventuring Koomos bow before her, making a request. Will she agree to help them? And at what price?

Itsuki

After imagining tulip characters, I felt like re-attempting a flower character. Her hands are like those of a scarecrow. Above her head there is an electric arc, and geysers of fire shoot from her feet. Dad did not carry them over. Maybe it's better that way because then the character would risk burning to cinders.

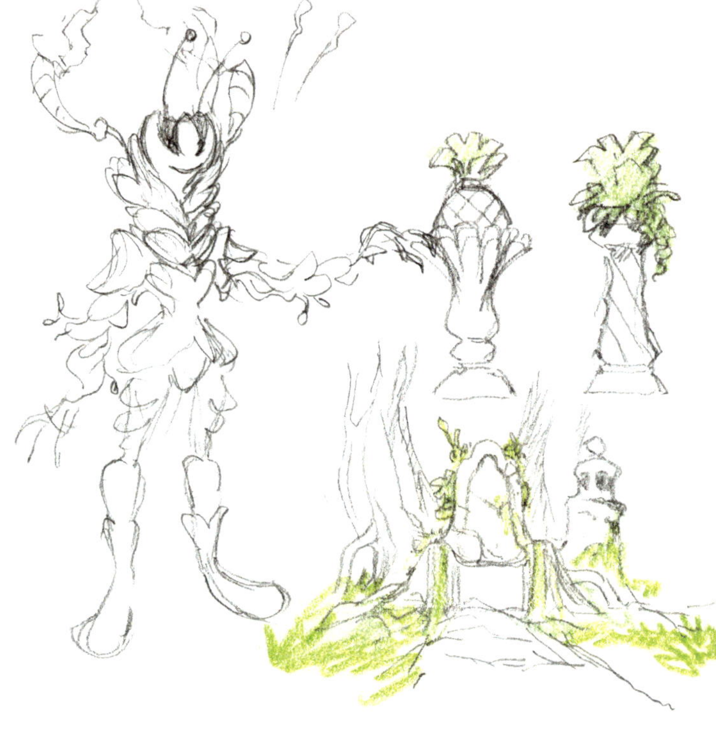

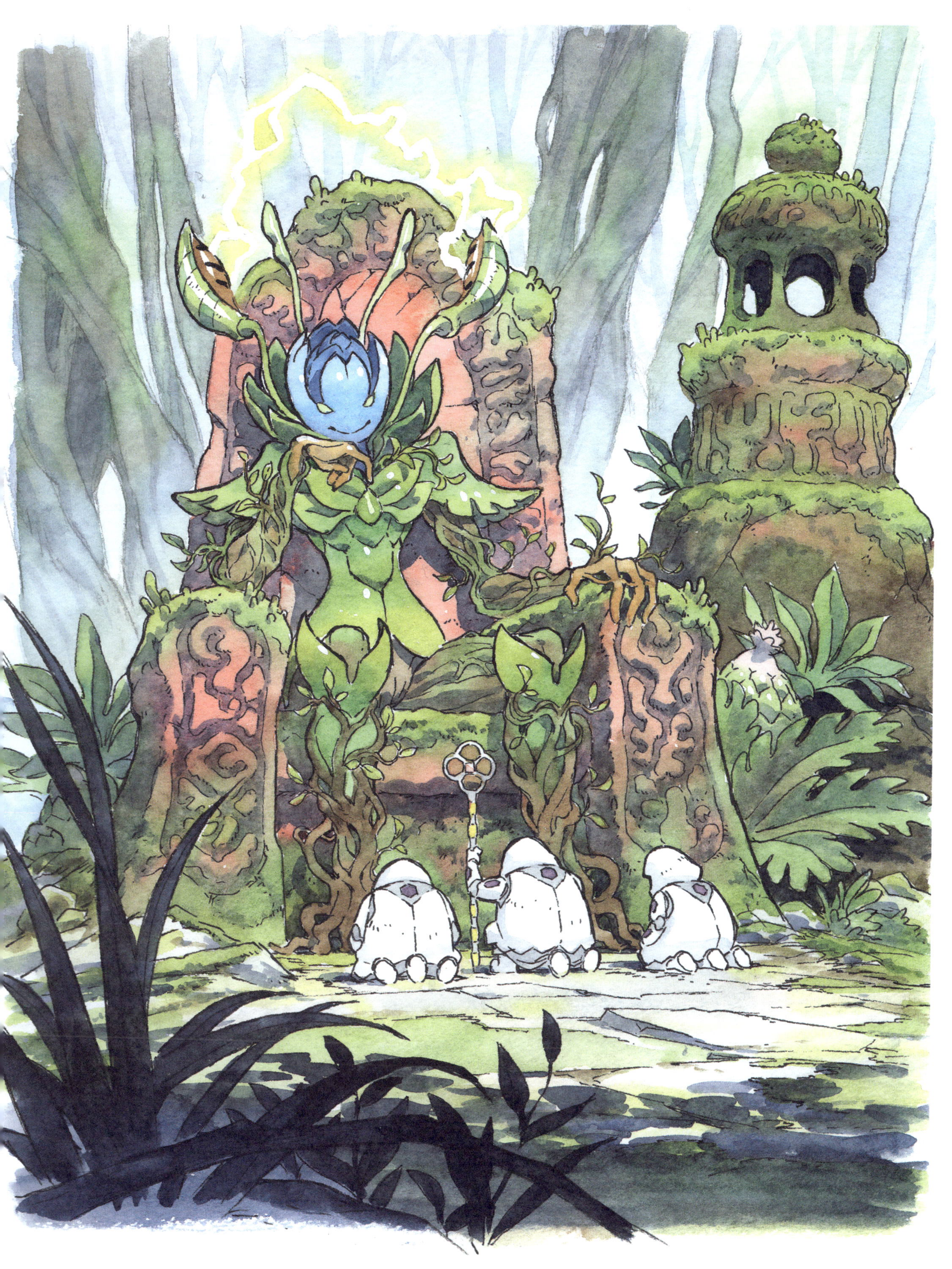

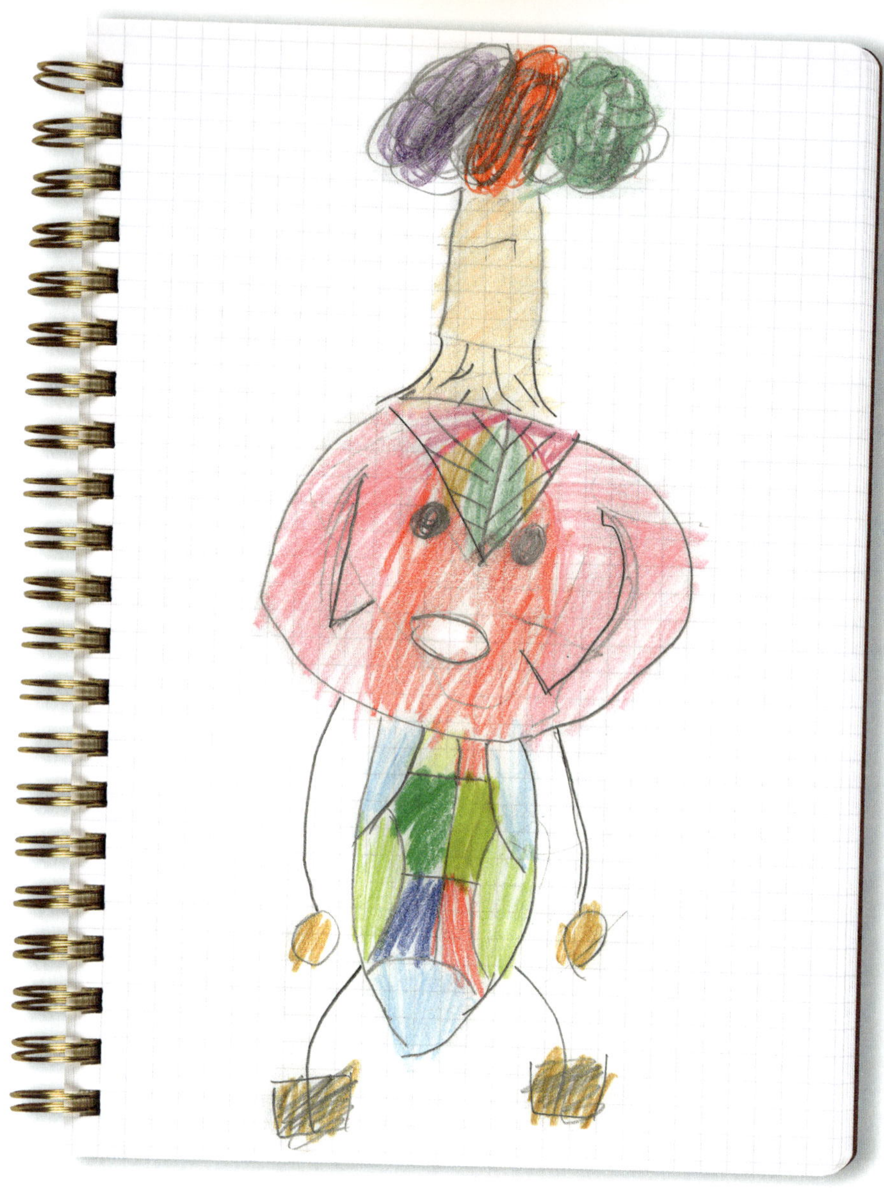

Bonus 04

The Wandering Forest

Thomas

Itsuki drew this friendly and colorful-looking character. His way of juxtaposing very different colors is his personal touch. The tree that grows on the head of the character gave me the urge to create on a gigantic scale. If it wasn't just one tree but an entire forest on his back, would that not make him even more impressive? This is the idea that oriented my drawing. This is a pacifistic and migratory creature that travels untamed lands in search of a more favorable climate. No one knows exactly how it feeds or reproduces itself; it could be that this organism is capable of photosynthesis, as it seems to appreciate sunlight.

Itsuki

I wanted to draw a nature-like character, a kind of god, maybe? I colored the tree multiple colors, as green would have been too simple and not very interesting. Dad's drawing, thanks to the background, shows off an entire universe. He makes us want to climb on the creature's back and wander this supernatural forest.

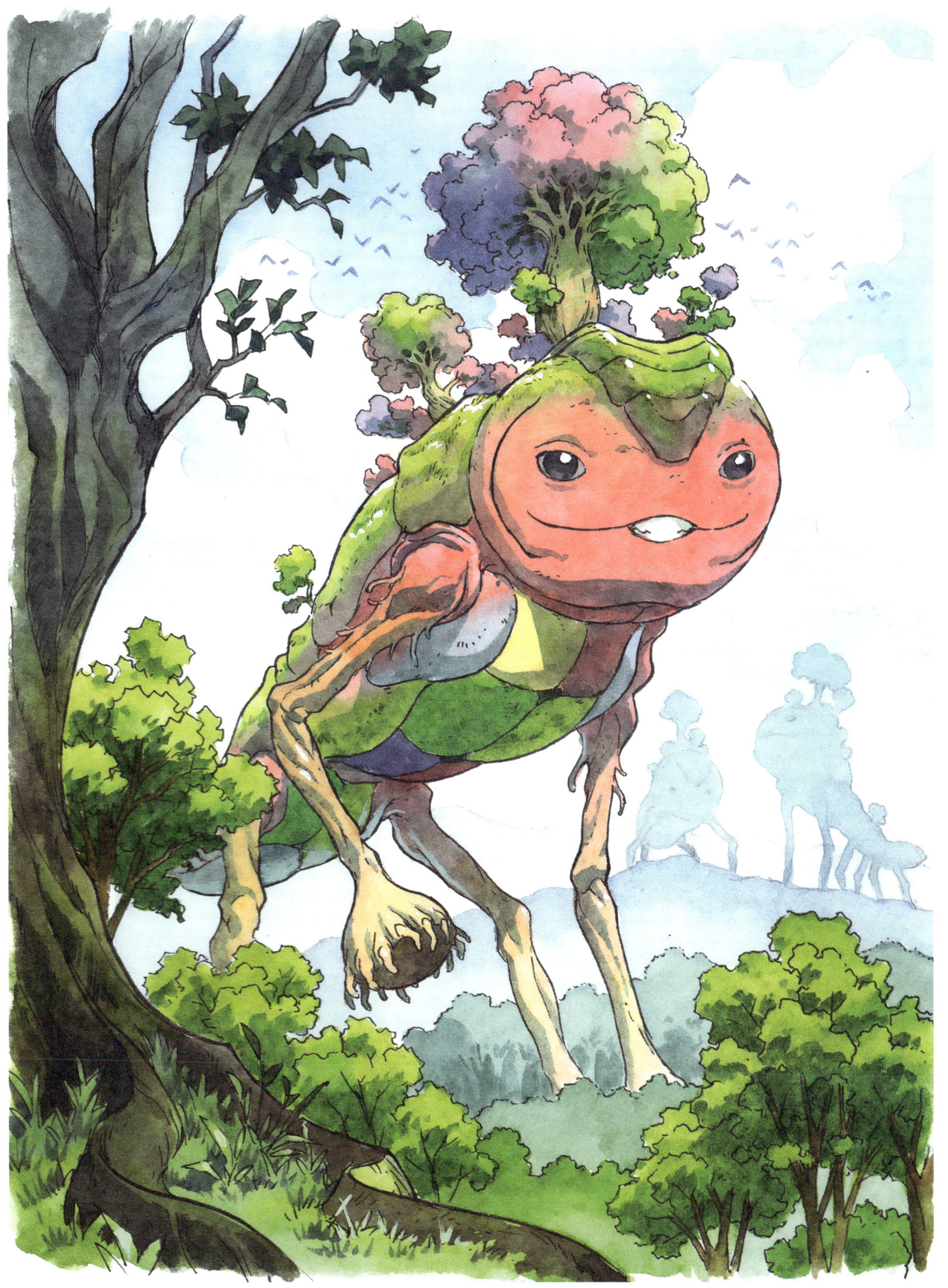

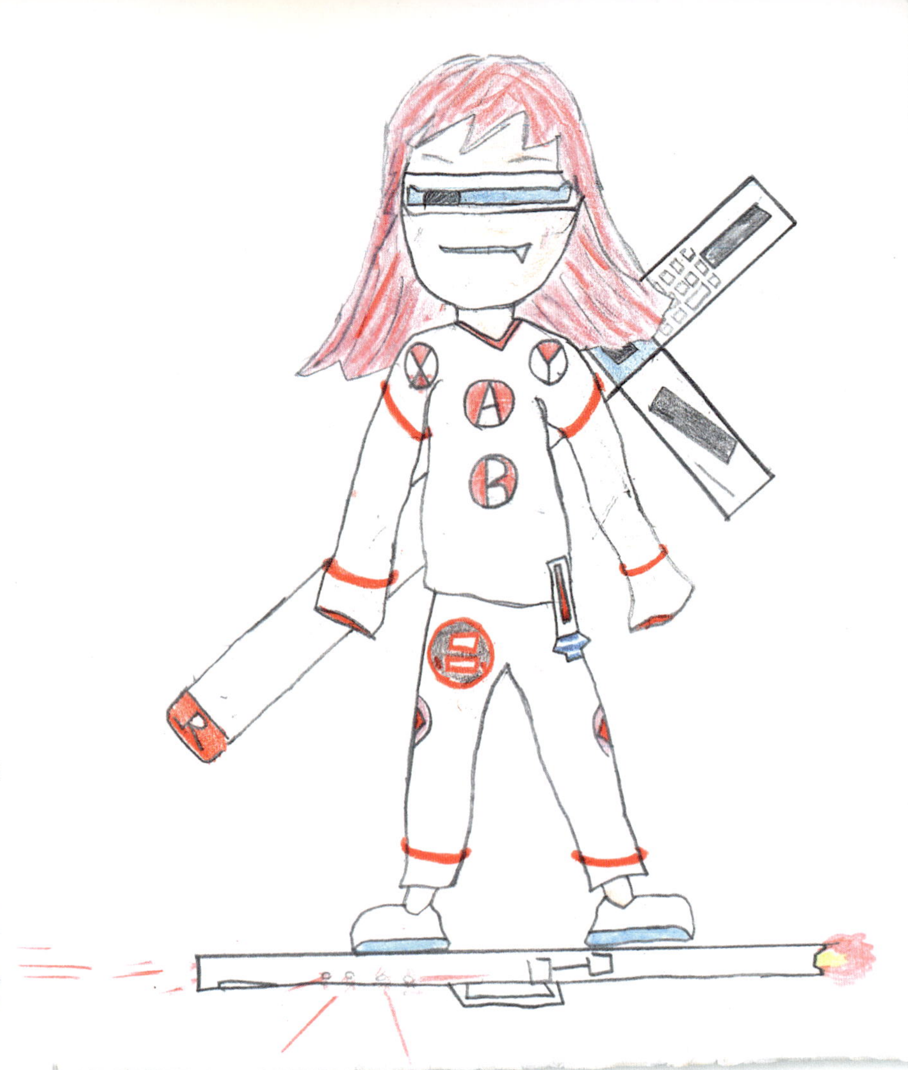

29 Justice

Thomas

This drawing was in part a suggestion that I made. “And what if you drew a girl character?” This is what I proposed to Ryunosuke. To give him a more precise idea, I told him he could draw a hacker, or at least a girl living in a futuristic world, one very at ease with technology. I was not disappointed! The design is a little tomboy and the hairstyle reminded me of Molly from *Oban Star-Racers*. The straightforward colors, particularly the white highlights in the pink hair, are very efficient. The illustration evokes some good memories of the golden age of anime that was the 90s.

Ryunosuke

I inspired myself with smartphones, computers and videogame consoles. The very square and clean design of the sword, the touches of blue that make you think of a computer keyboard, the red motifs on Justice's clothes: it all comes from that. Dad made the character far more dynamic by giving her a surfing pose. I really like the deformed shadow on the ground that truly gives the impression of super speed.

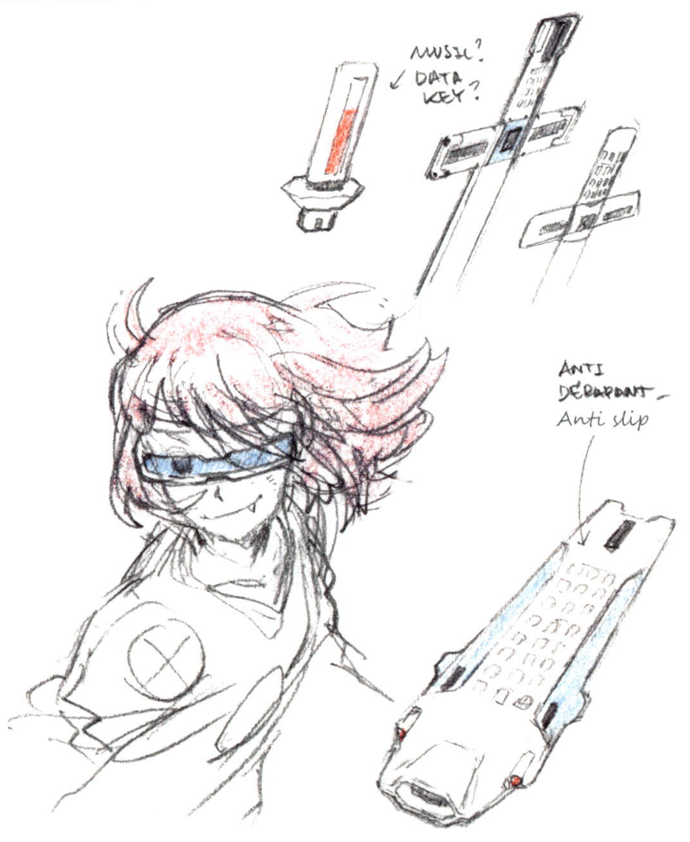

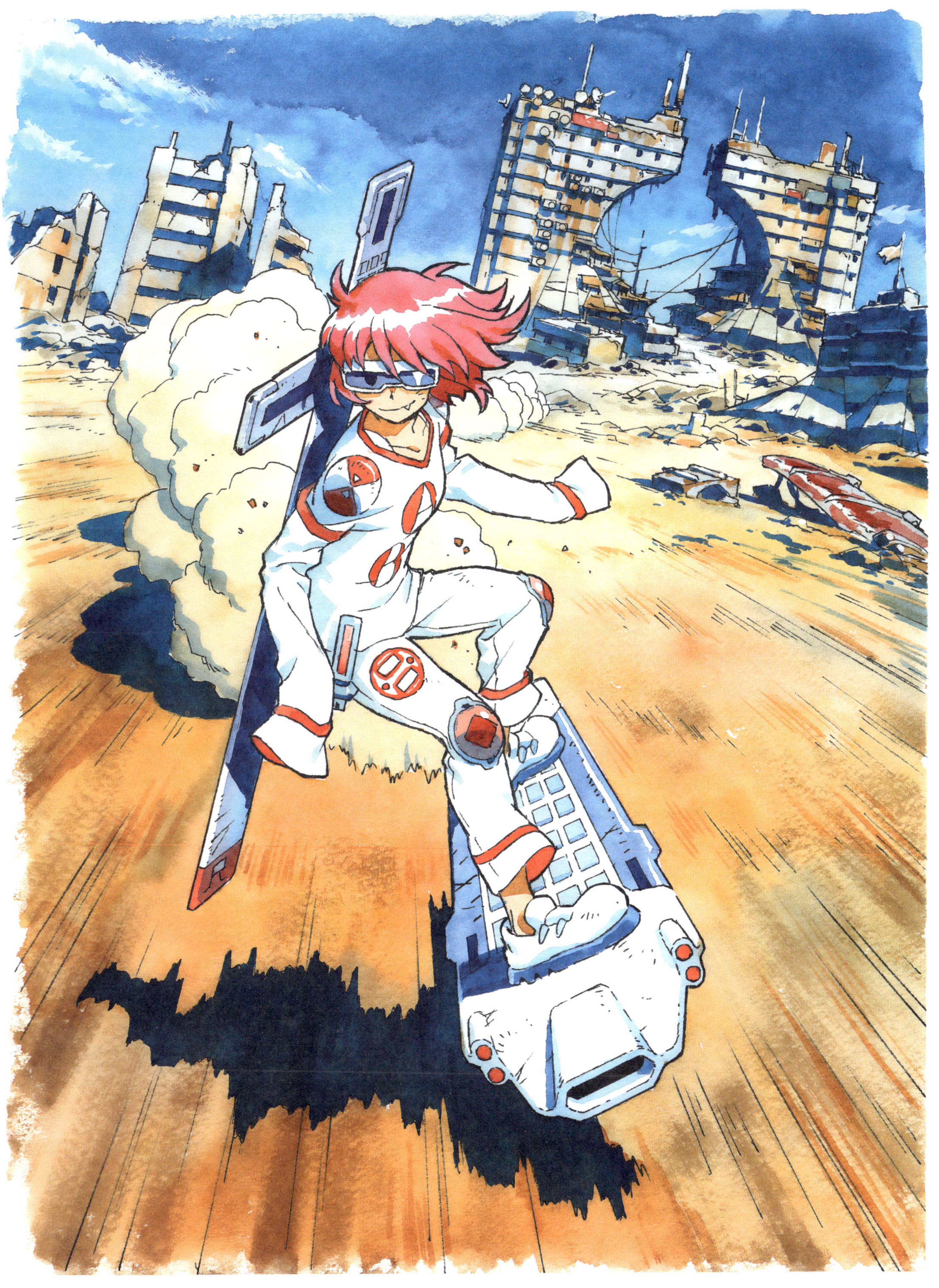

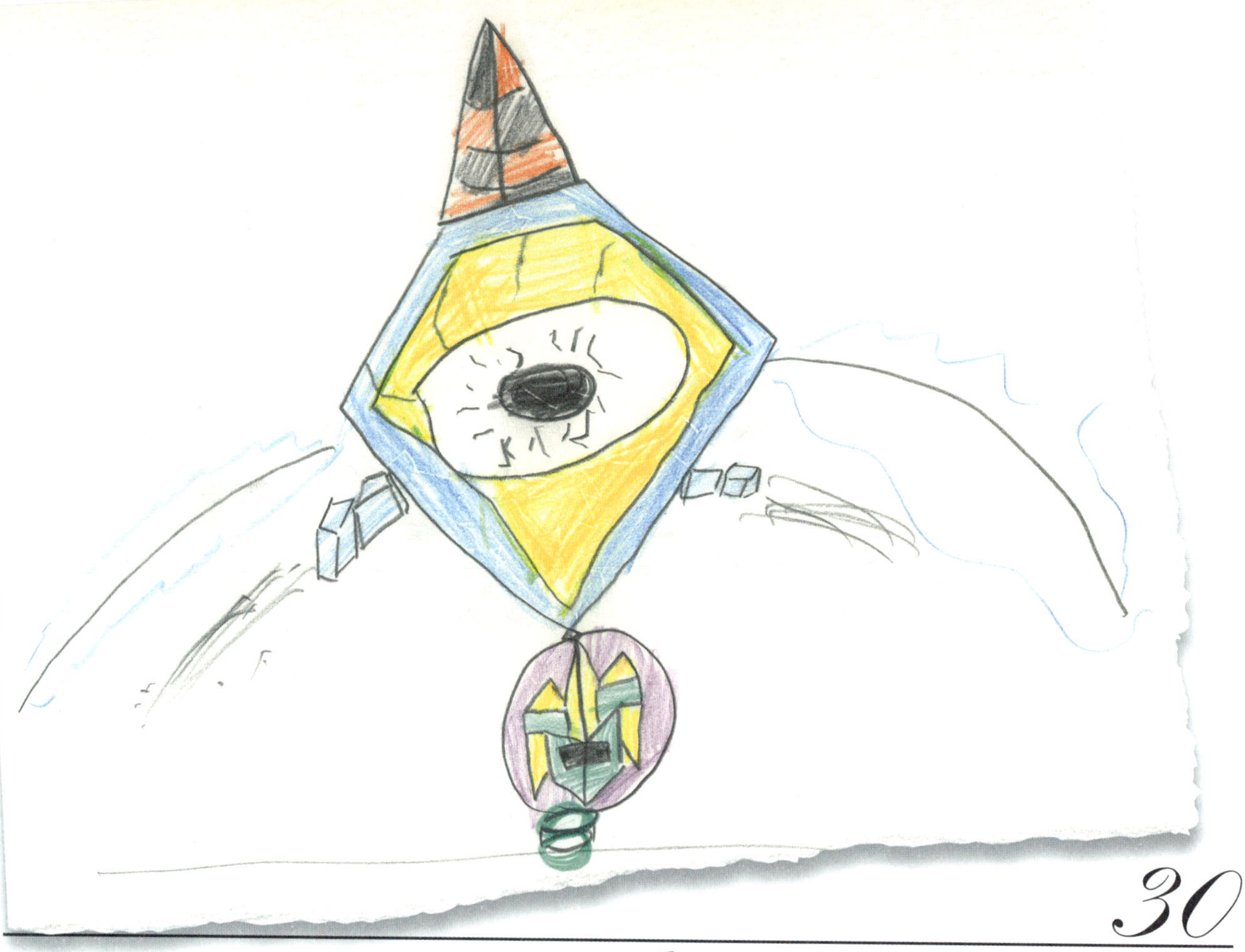

30

The Eye of Ice

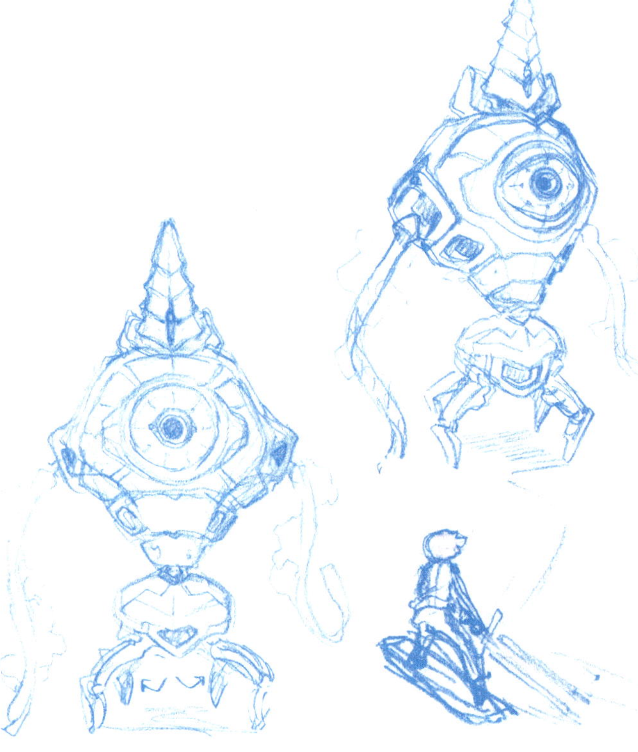

Thomas

I liked the character of Justice so much I simply had to draw her again right away. In this scene, I am confronting her with a bizarre robot. Itsuki's drawing was a little difficult to interpret on account of the abstract forms and the number of different colors used. But, in the end, the originality of his choices was a good thing, as the design became even more surprising. The small changes that I made to it include transforming the sphere beneath its body into bendable mechanical legs and changing the color yellow to a much colder green. This robot, having ice attacks, pushed me to bathe it in a blue ambiance.

Itsuki

I didn't have too many ideas for this one, so I started off with a diamond shape. I added a giant eye, and since it was a little sad-looking I added a kind of horn hat and a ball on the bottom. This robot has the ability to fire ice attacks. We can see that on the final drawing with the frozen buildings in the background.

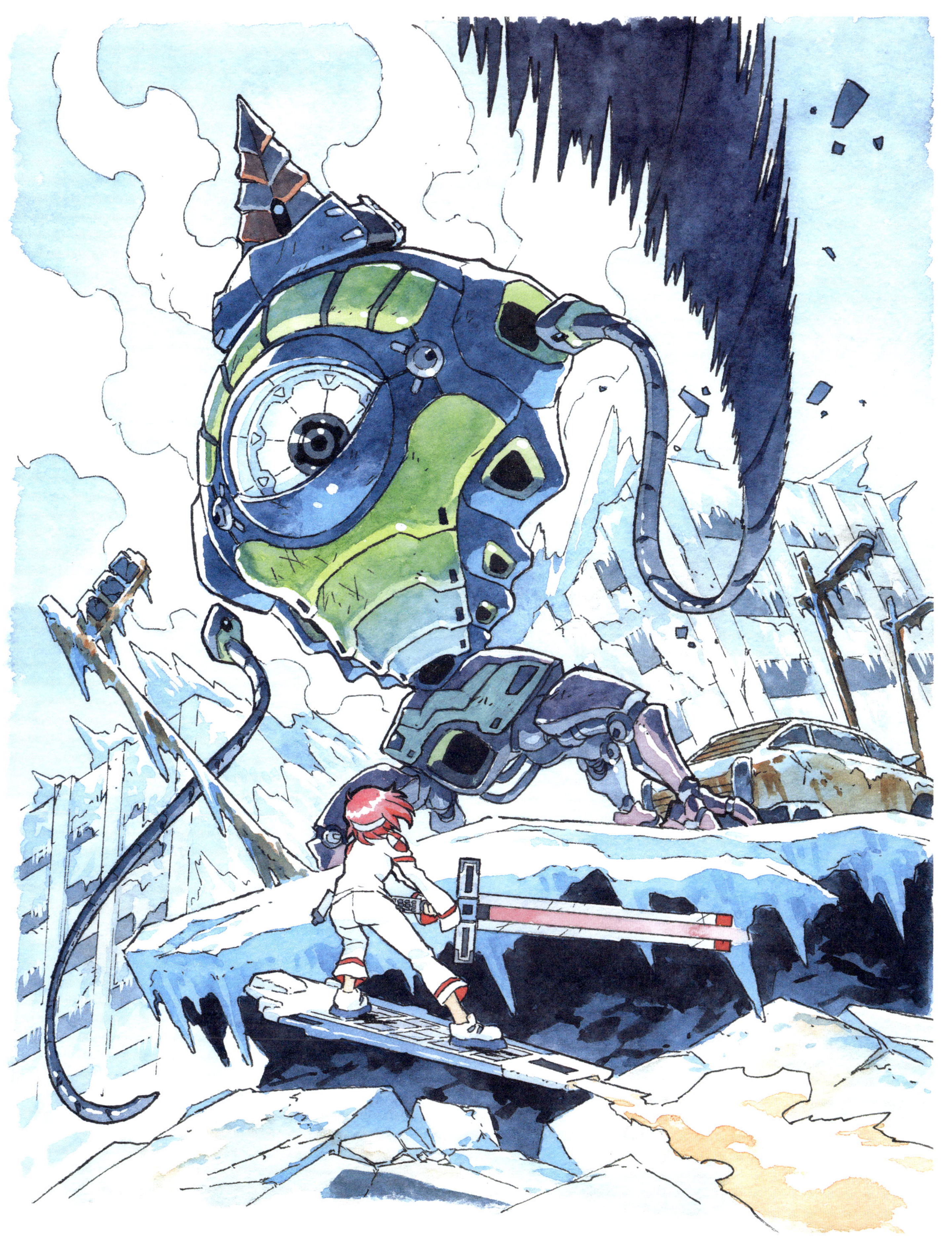

31 The Pompaa's Boutique

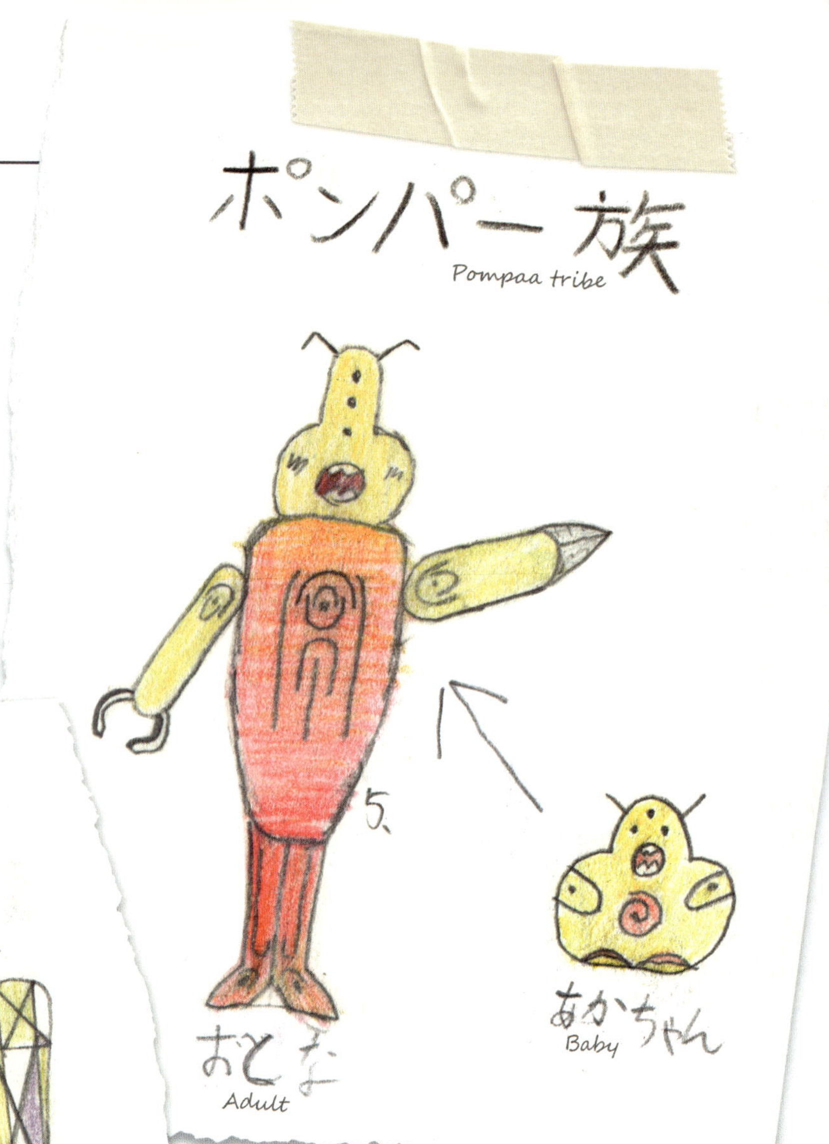

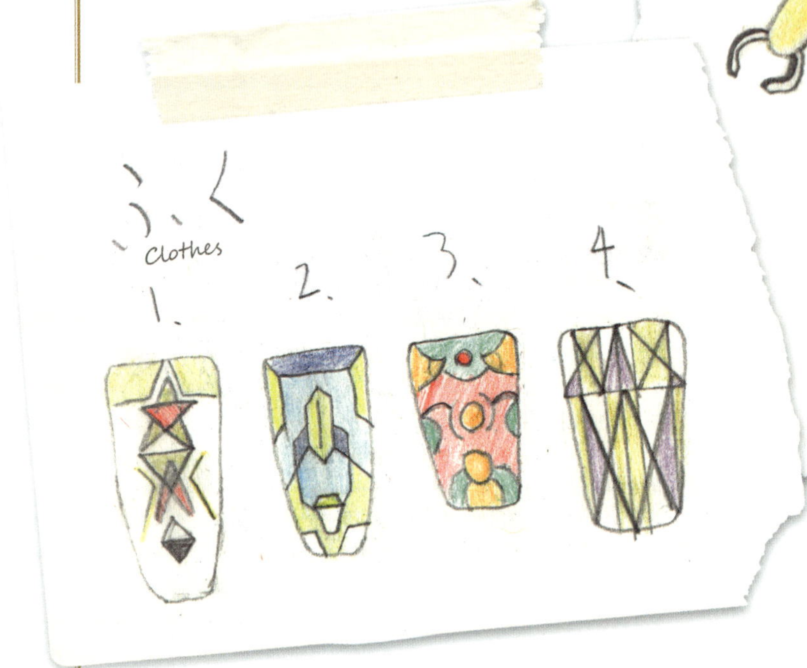

ポンパー族
Pompaa tribe

ふく
Clothes
1. 2. 3. 4.

5.

おとな
Adult

あかちゃん
Baby

Thomas

To showcase this character and the different costumes that Ryunosuke drew, I had the idea of making him a merchant. This Pompaa and his wife run a small bric-a-brac boutique highly popular with adventurers. Wishing to equip himself for a quest, a Koomo has come by to do some shopping. This is one of the richest illustrations in the series - I have no doubt that it took me more time. I was determined to give it a credible atmosphere and add some depth to the room so that the spectator would want to explore it with his eyes. The use of wood in this architecture gives off a familiar warmth, while the unique forms of his beams and windows transport us into an imaginary universe.

Ryunosuke

This character is a Pompaa. This is a race from the same universe as the Koomos. I haven't really thought about their way of life and their customs, but what I can say is that they are elegant; they love to dress in clothes with multicolored motifs. The fact that Dad made him a merchant was a good idea because he was able to show off the different clothes that I drew. I love the reflection in the mirror - that detail is my favorite.

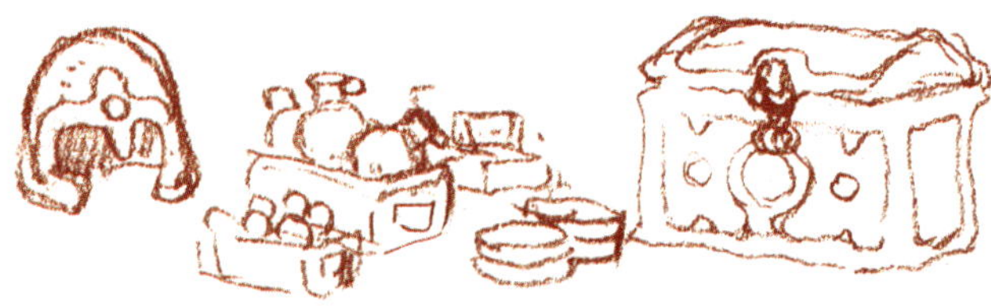

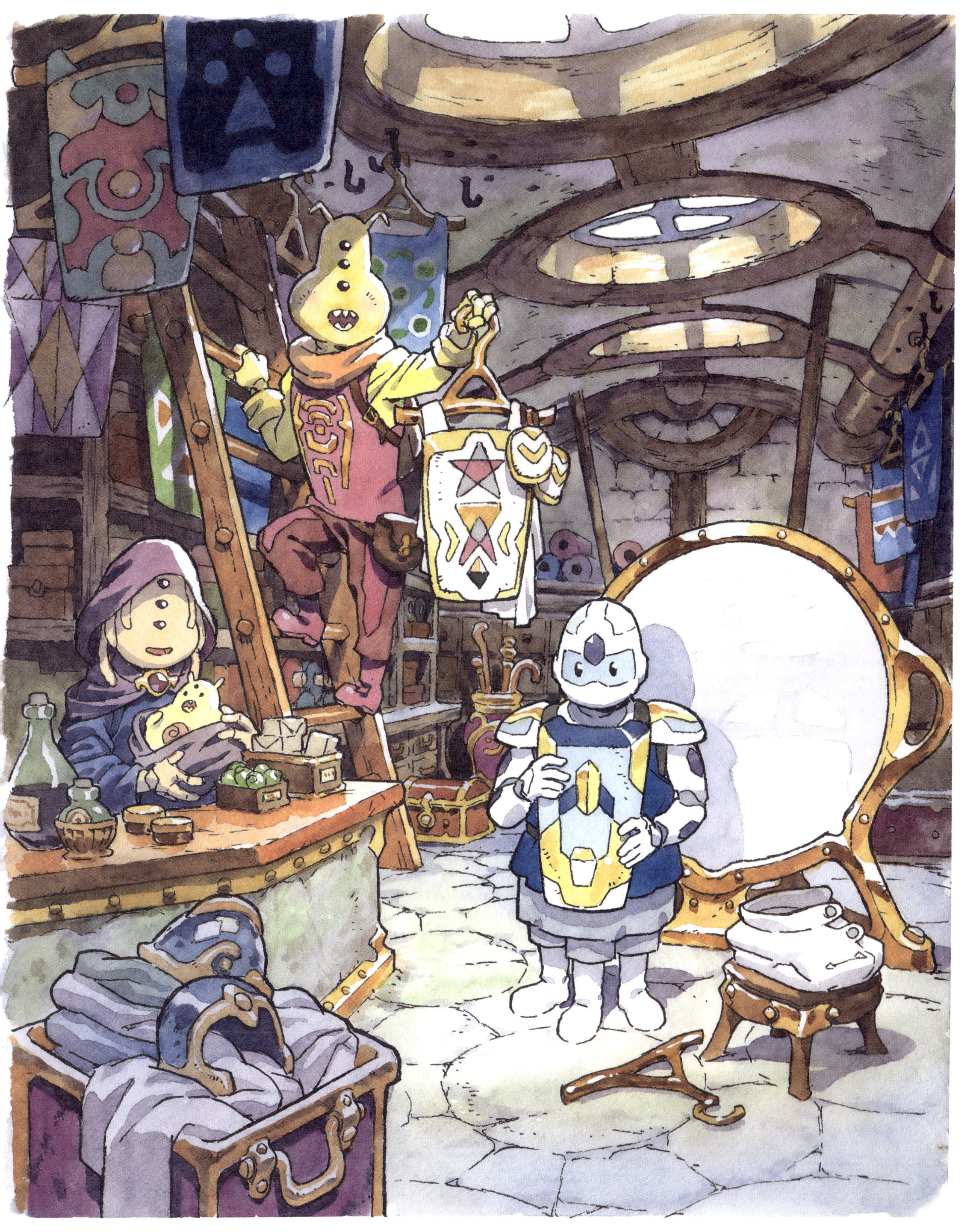

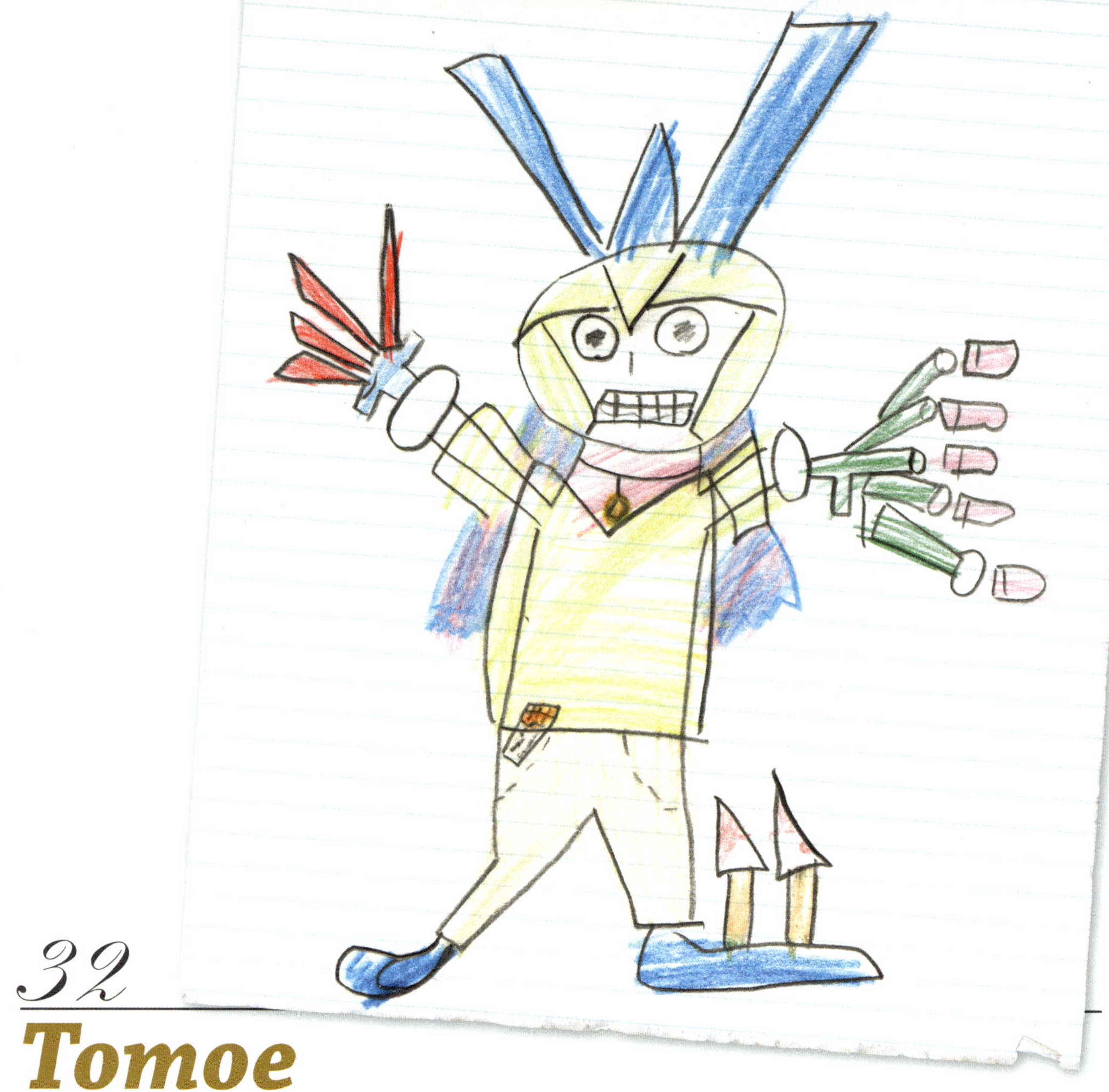

32

Tomoe

Thomas

After asking Ryunosuke for a female heroine, I proposed to Itsuki that he do the same. He then created this female warrior. The use of simple colors, with blue and yellow being dominant, and the jagged silhouette of the helmet evoking a samurai's armor really allowed me to pull a coherent design out of it. I freely interpreted the green stick as a kind of magic scepter with the ability to project small crystal stars. The points that seem to pierce her foot gave me a clue towards my background: a floor filled with traps. The detail from Itsuki's drawing that was true genius was the chocolate bar in her pocket, which I didn't forget to faithfully reproduce. There's no better way to regain your strength when up against formidable adversaries than to bite into tasty chocolate.

Itsuki

Up until now I had only done robots and weird creatures, so it was really hard to draw a human character. Actually, at the beginning, I only had a warrior in mind; it was only halfway through that I transformed her into a girl by adding long hair. To make her look young I added the chocolate bar in her pocket; that's her snack. What I like best about Dad's drawing is the golden armor that's really well-made.

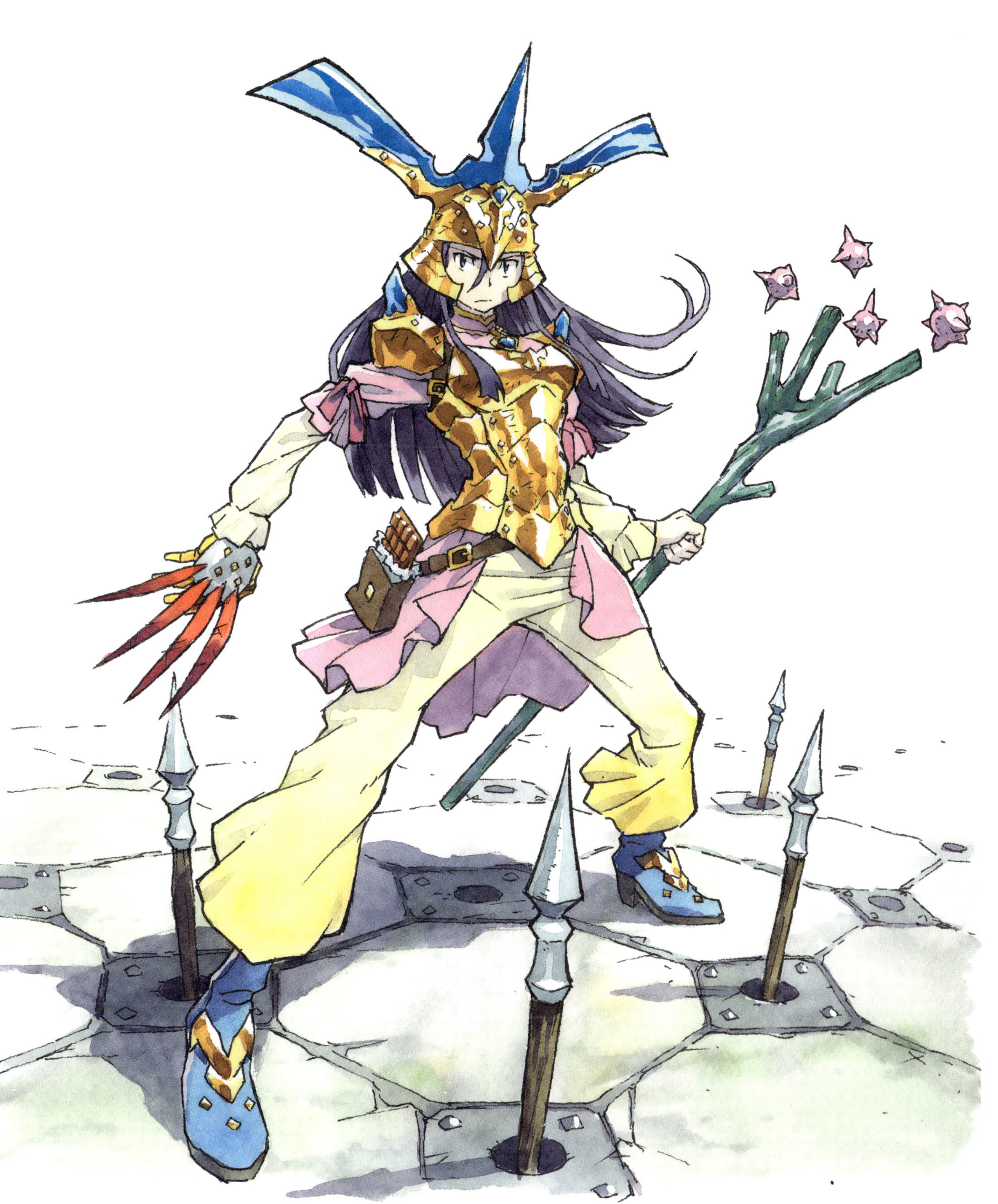

33

Narwhagon

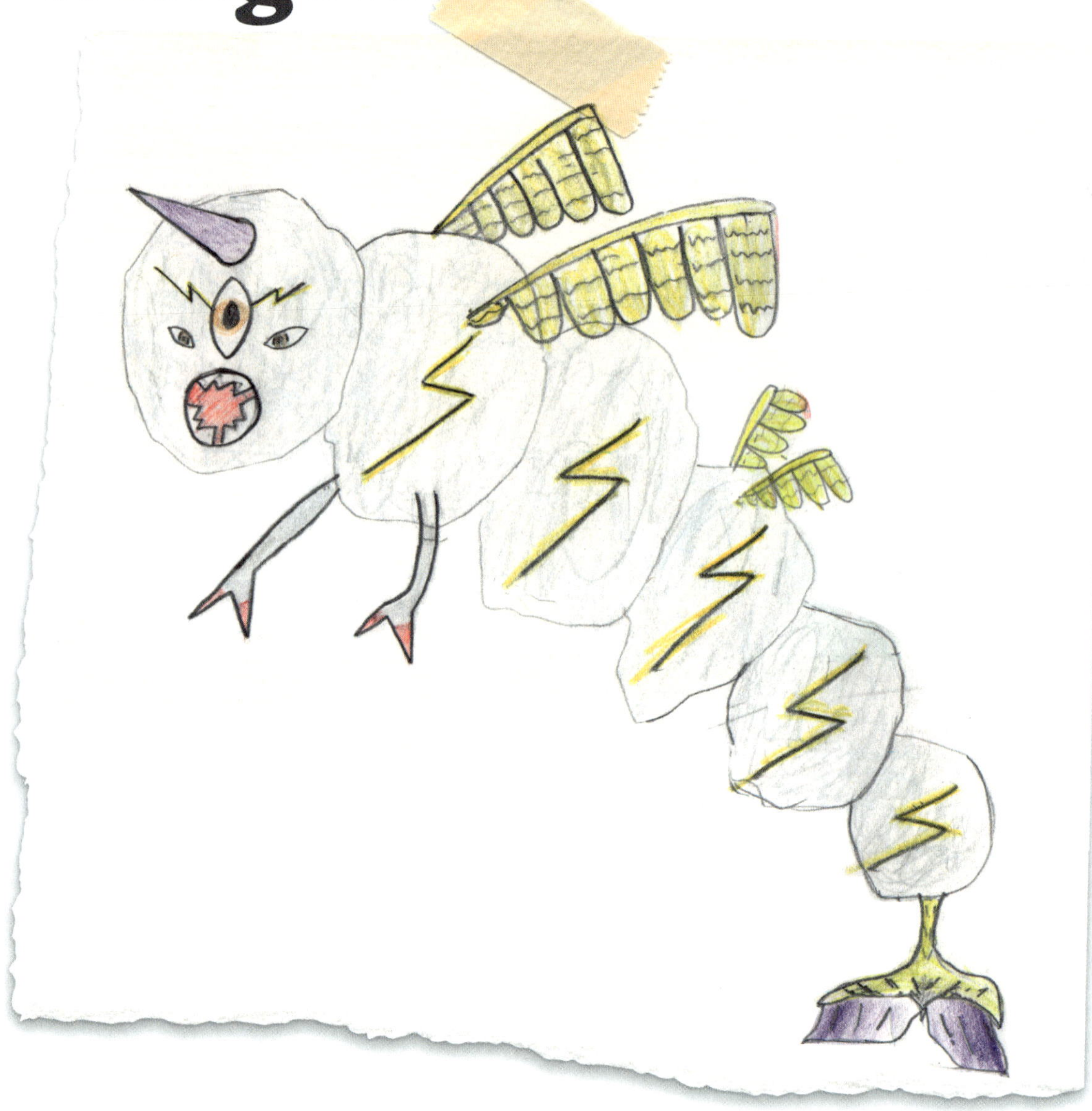

Thomas

The name Narwhagon is the combination of 'narwhal', a fascinating aquatic mammal that possesses a single horn, and 'dragon'. I transformed Ryunosuke's drawing into a mount for Scal, the trainer we had previously created. Crossing over characters between one another in order to build a universe, drawing after drawing, is one of the more passionate aspects of this project. The drawings take on a whole other dimension; they become windows onto another world, one that's rich with its own culture and ecosystem.

Ryunosuke

Dad inspired himself with this drawing long after I had done it. It was the first one in my sketchbook. At the base, I was inspired by the design of a rock Pokémon, but I wanted to make it into a far more impressive creature, a kind of dragon, so I added eight wings. I think Dad had a good idea by adding these two characters together. They both have violet horns on the forehead, which gives them a common visual point. The drawing of the rocky cavern evokes ancient legends. I find that the backdrop really adds to the general atmosphere.

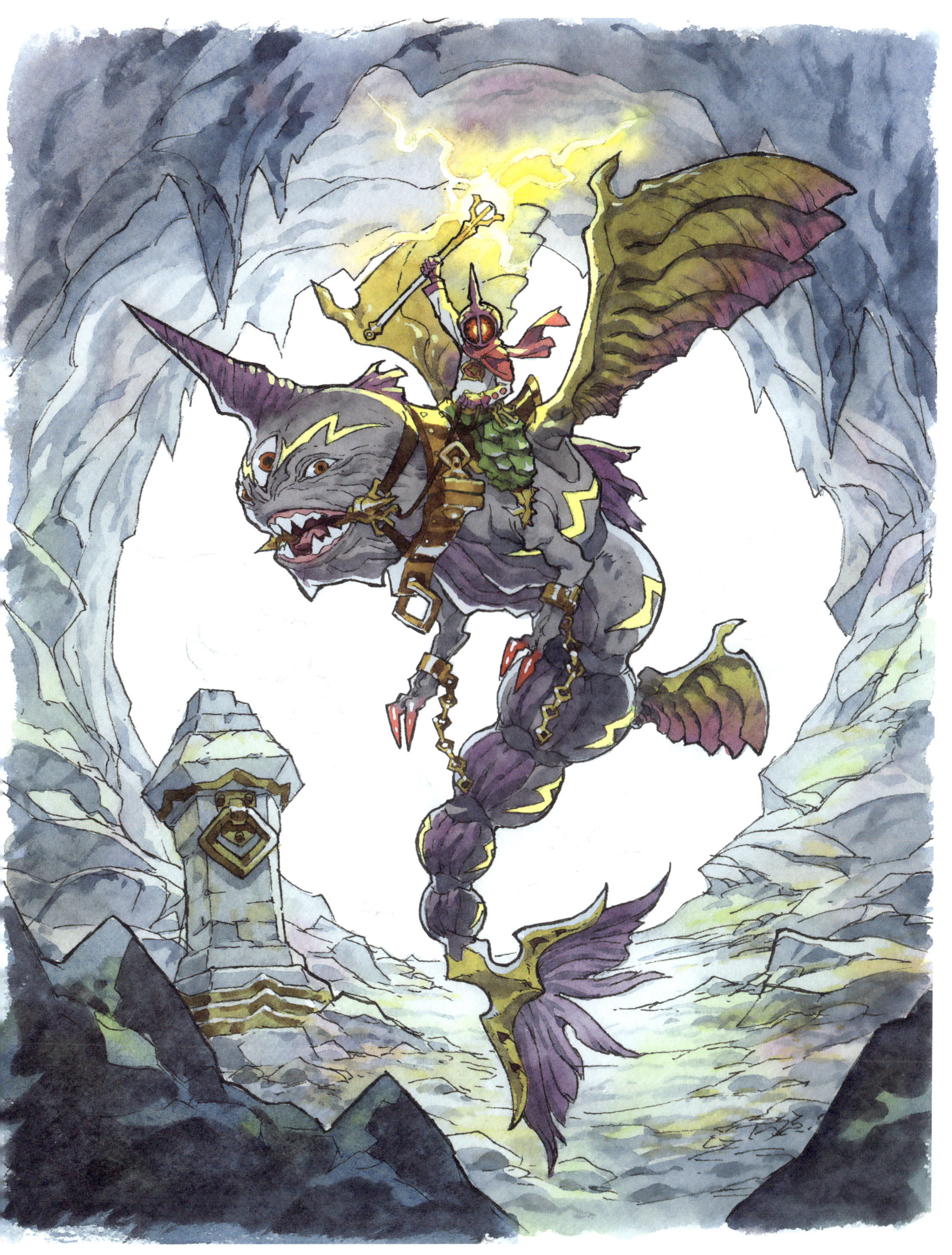

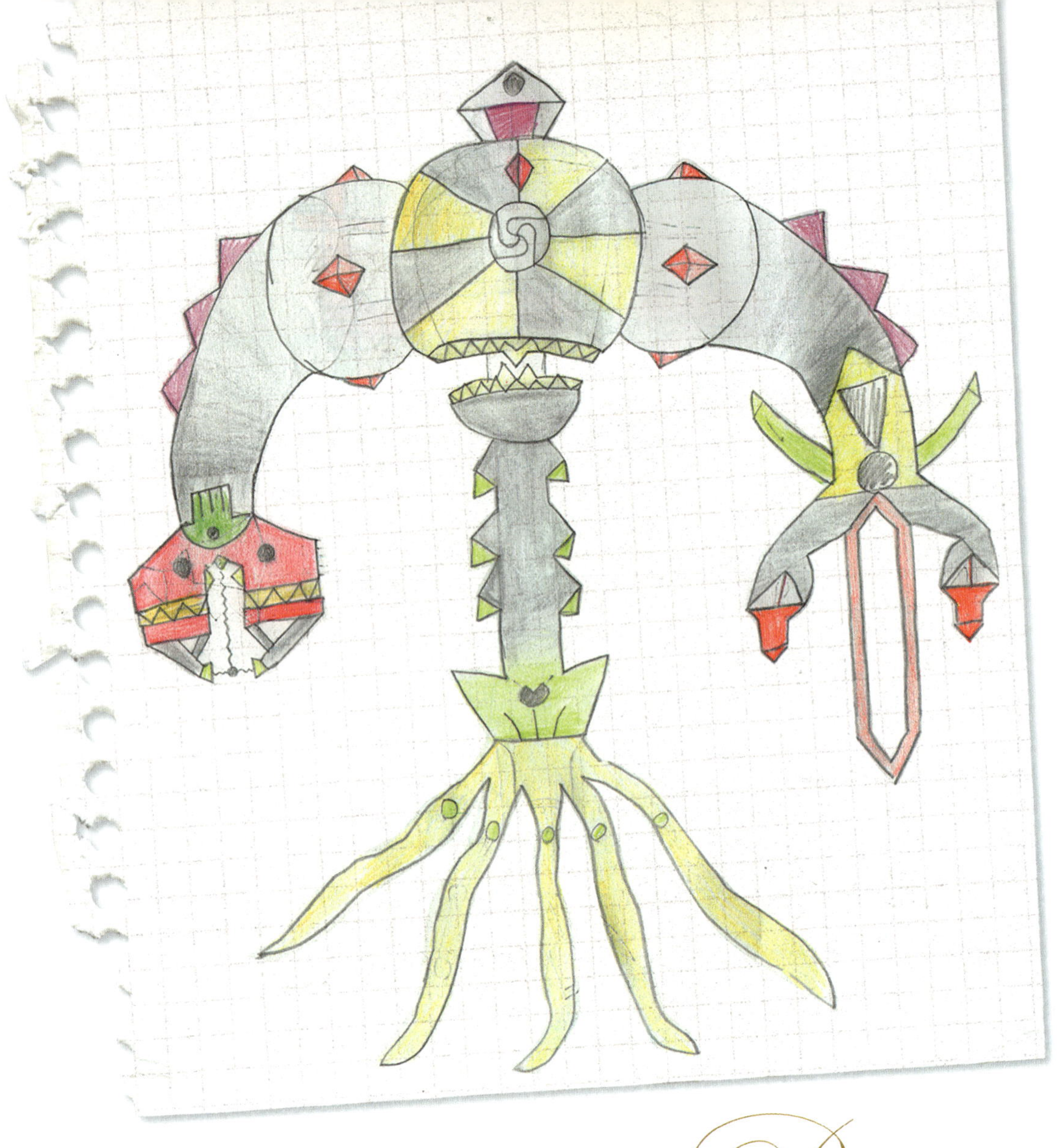

Bonus 05

Heavy Combat Unit SK-02

Thomas

Is it a robot? Is it a hybrid creature created with genetic modification? What is certain is that the technology behind this combat unit is very advanced and particularly formidable. Ryunosuke drew it as a variation on the Skulloids. I then naturally included it in the same scene with them. Drawing small ones around him allows me to give the viewer the idea that unit SK-02 is gigantic. The worrisome Skulloid army is on the march - who can protect us from it?

Ryunosuke

This character is a boss - he has massive weapons at the end of each arm. When I started, the massive skull was meant to be his head, but Dad suggested making it its torso and adding a smaller head up top. I find this makes him far more impressive. He created articulations on the arms and legs to give it a more robotic aspect. He's also way bigger than I had imagined; next to him, the soldiers are so tiny! I also like the background; the destroyed buildings really give a great ambiance to the drawing.

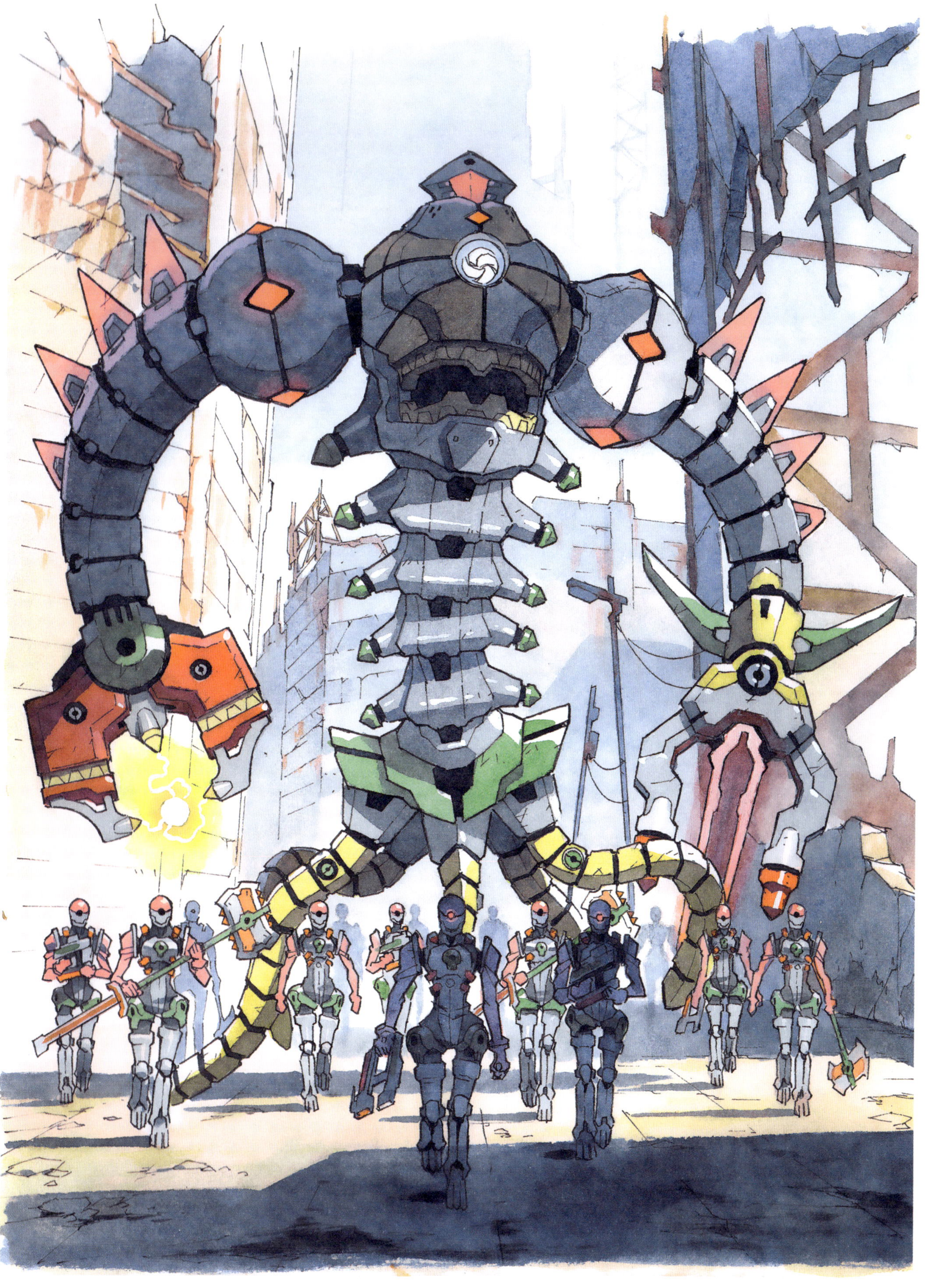

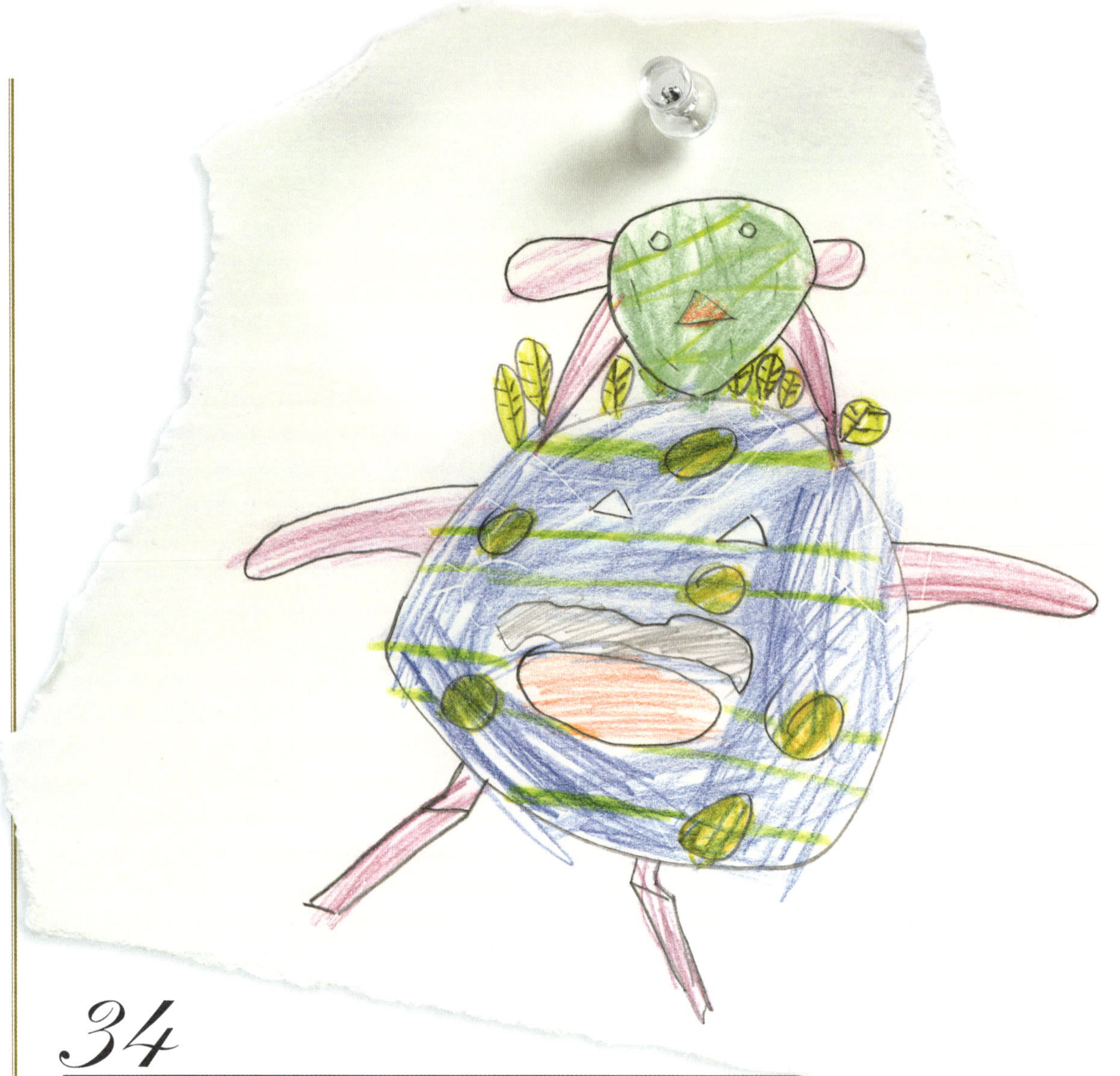

34

The Rockthieves

Thomas

I took a long time before creating this illustration. I mulled over the idea for several weeks, while I was working on other drawings, before throwing myself at it. My first idea was to make it into a strange totem in the Koomos' world. In the meantime the character of Tomoe had been created and Itsuki's drawing gave me the opportunity to show her off in a different situation. The rockthieves are veritable polymorphs. Much like a hermit crab that uses a seashell to protect itself, they use blocks scavenged from ancient ruins as makeshift armor. The chiseled faces are used to scare off their predators. They are in fact totally pacifistic and love to eat fruit and other sweet-tasting foods. They have been attracted by the sweet smell of the chocolate bar that Tomoe carries around in her small satchel.

Itsuki

I was a little bored that day, so I told myself I could pass some time while drawing. However, I didn't have too many ideas other than a creature that was a little plant-like, with squishy arms and legs. I'm glad Dad brought back the samurai girl, since it makes the drawing really interesting, even if I don't want to be in her shoes.

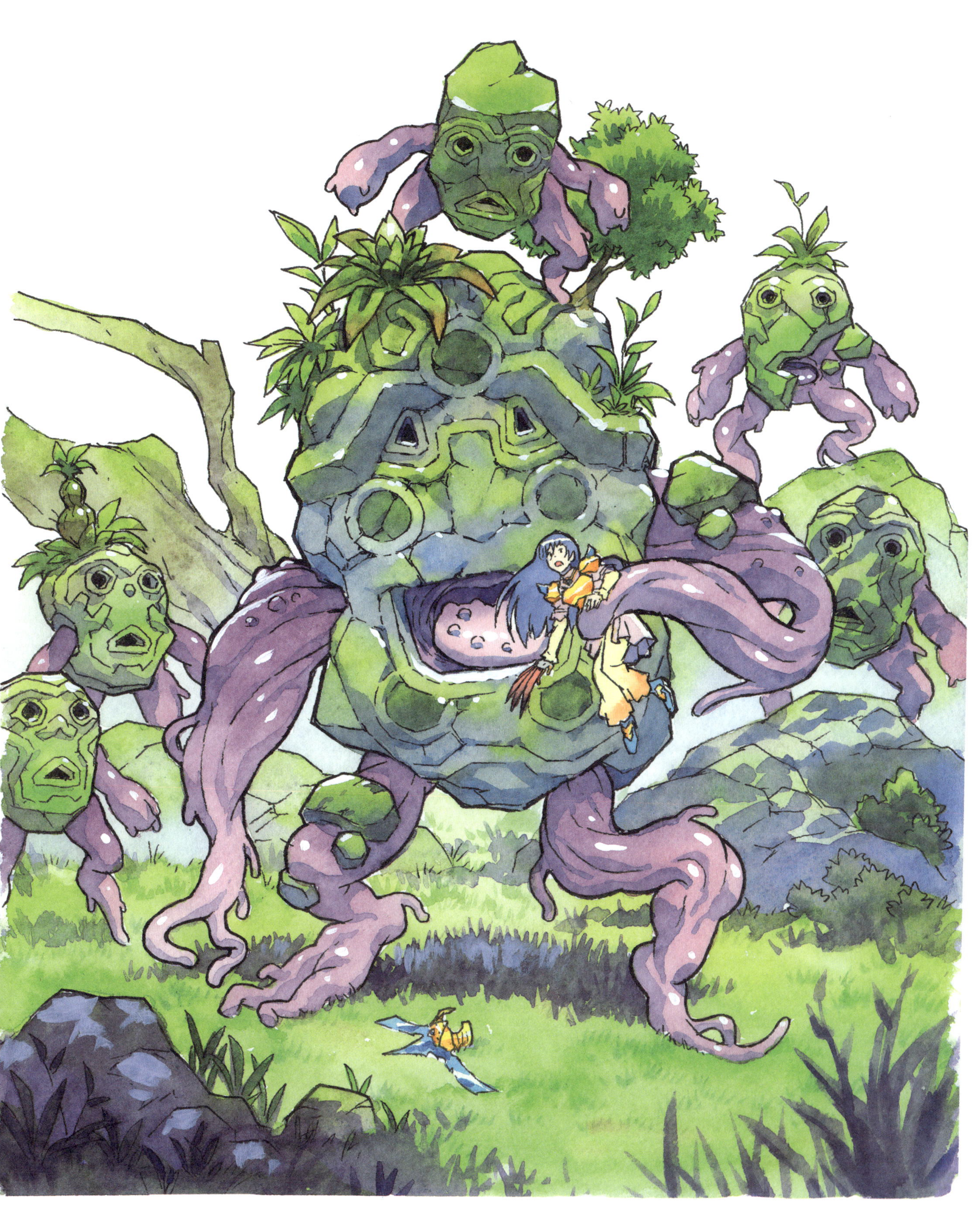

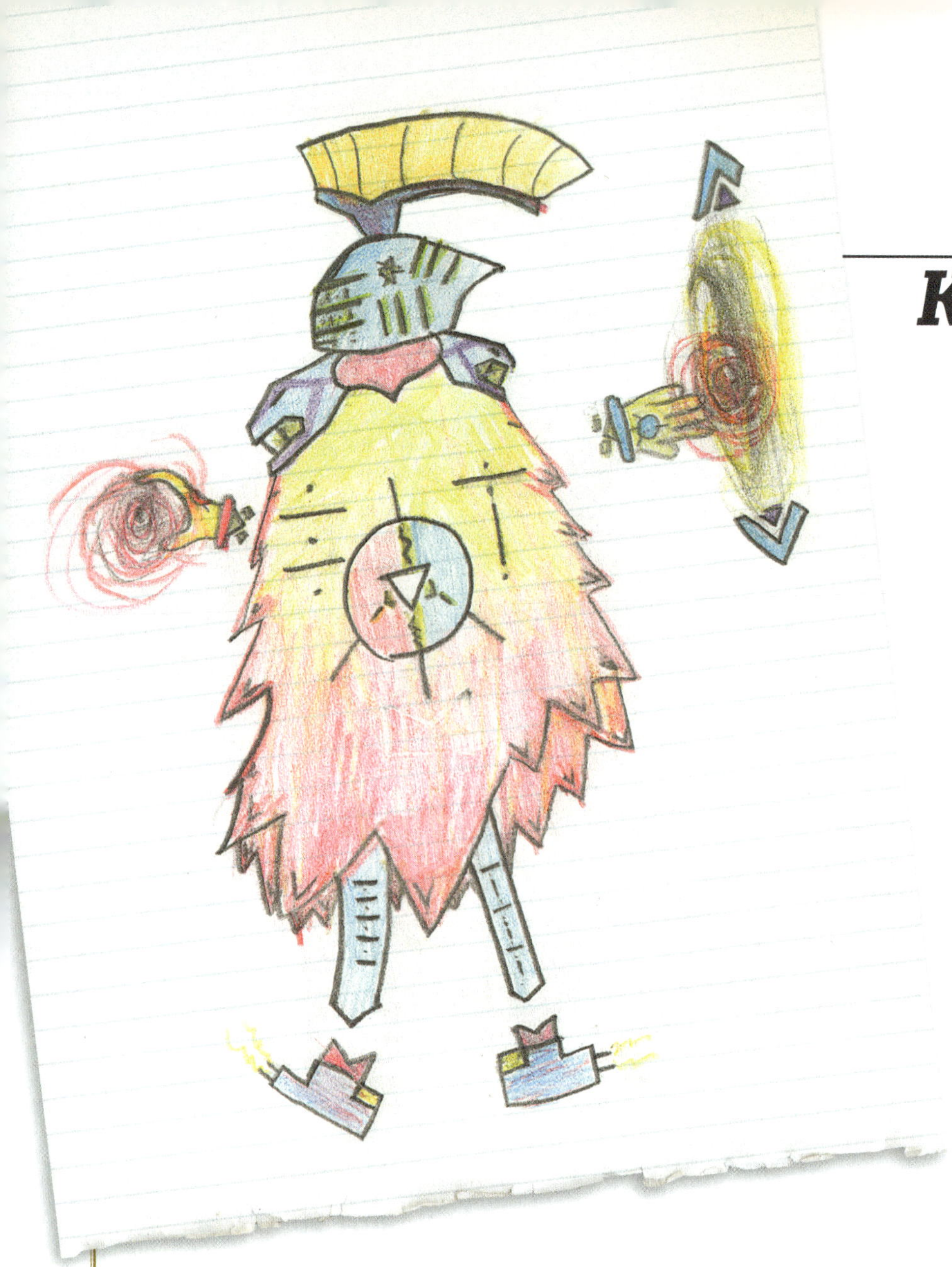

35

Knight of the Royal Garden

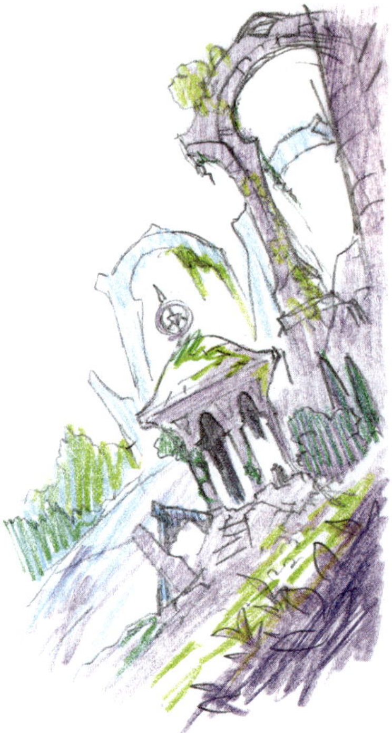

Thomas

This mysterious silver knight is naught but a shadow of his former self. Once the captain of the royal guard, he failed in his mission to protect his sovereign and witnessed the fall of his kingdom. He continues to wander in the sumptuous garden which was his final battlefield, dragging his cold and empty armor, animated solely by the will of his tormented soul, searching for a second chance. This is the kind of legendary tale I attempted to evoke through my interpretation of Ryunosuke's drawing, notably by putting the accent on the backdrop. The choice of the classic form for the helm clearly evokes the Middle Ages, an ideal time for tales of epic combat. But certain details, like the fact that his hands and feet are separate from the body, indicate that this is not an ordinary knight, but a magical being.

Ryunosuke

I drew this knight without looking at any references while trying to remember the shape of medieval armor. I added a touch of magic that I find is reinforced in Dad's drawing. The snake heads on his shoulders make him look like a powerful sorcerer. I love the stone kiosk in the background. At its top we find the same symbol that is on the character's chest, which is the emblem of the fallen kingdom.

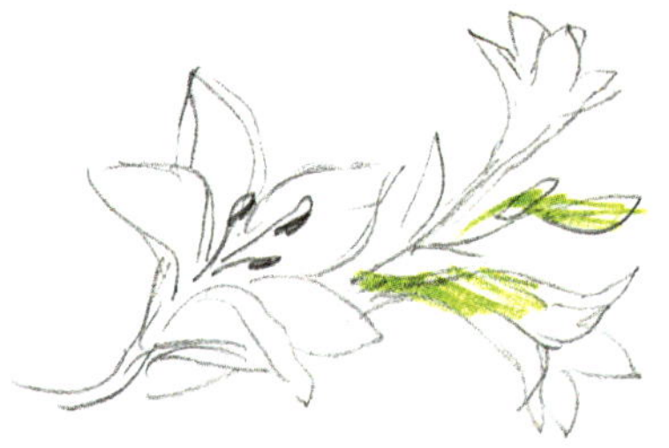

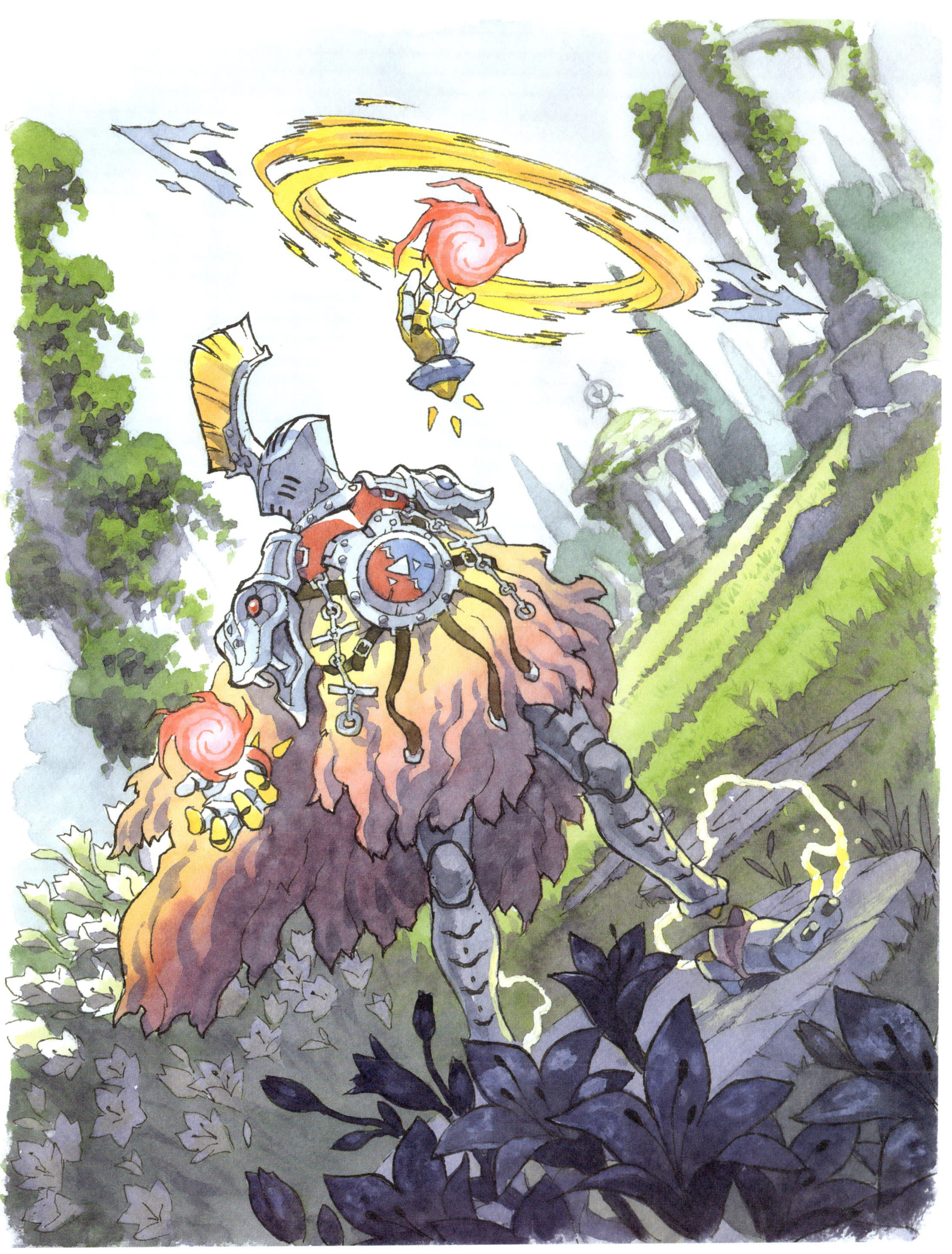

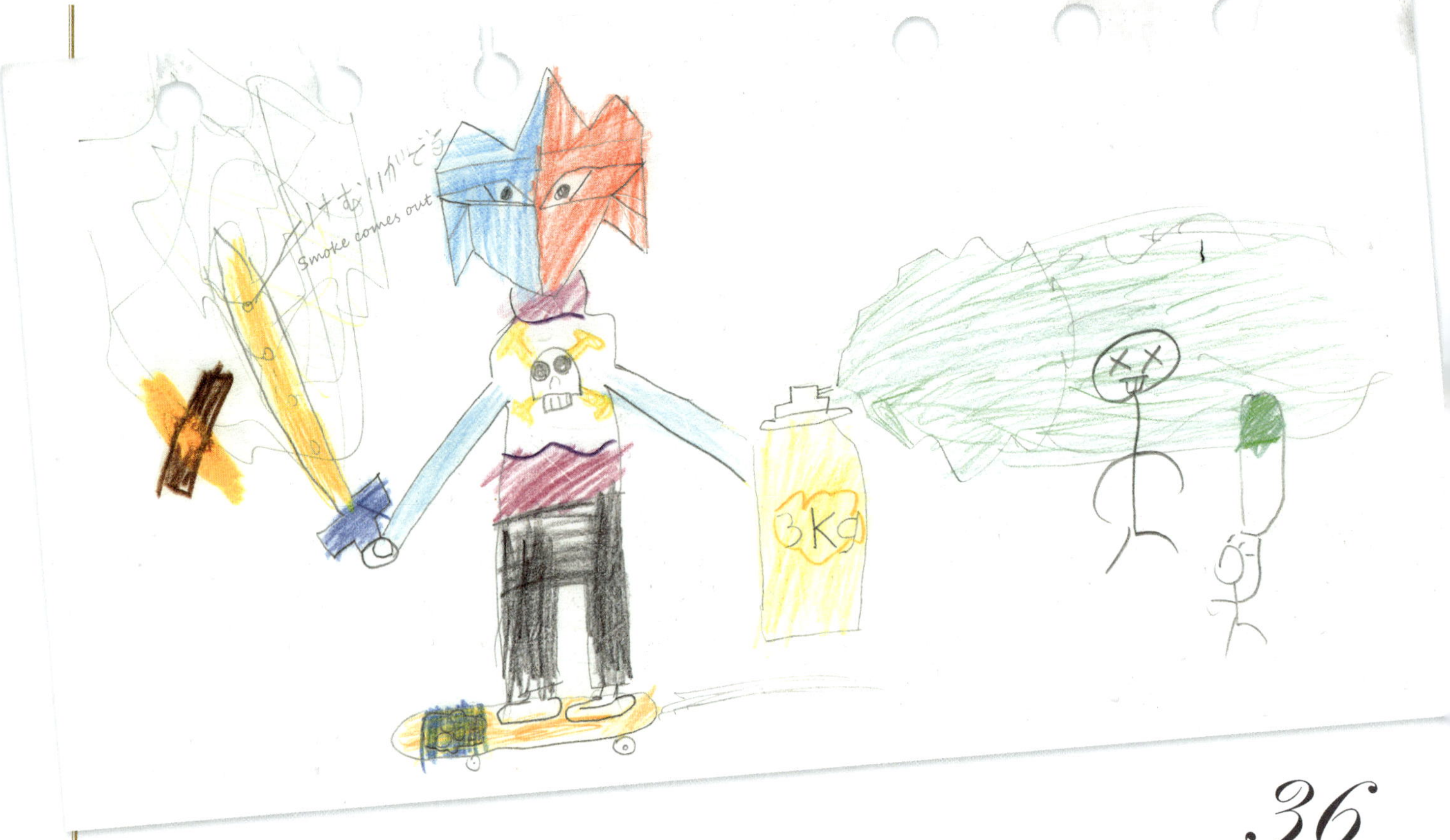

36

Noah
the Toxic Surfer

Thomas

This character, drawn by Itsuki, is one of my favorites. I find the idea of a sword that diffuses a toxic cloud absolutely brilliant. I danced around this concept, tying the yellow canister to the knob by a tube and adding a small meter to indicate pressure. I also drew some filters on the mask to give a gasmask effect. The initiative to replace the wheels on the skateboard with small reactors came from my desire to make him a friend of Justice, the pink-haired girl. They can then surf together on the arid expanses of a post-apocalyptic world. I can imagine them fighting side-by-side against robots with a menacing A.I. or going on long expeditions searching for valuable artifacts.

Itsuki

For this one, I let myself be guided by what was going through my mind. I wanted a hero that looked cool - but the idea of the smoke that comes out of the blade, I have no idea where that came from! I mixed together the 'poison' symbol, the skateboard, and the mask, thinking it would make the character cool. I never thought of turning the wheels into reactors the way Dad did, but it adds a little more to it. It's super dynamic.

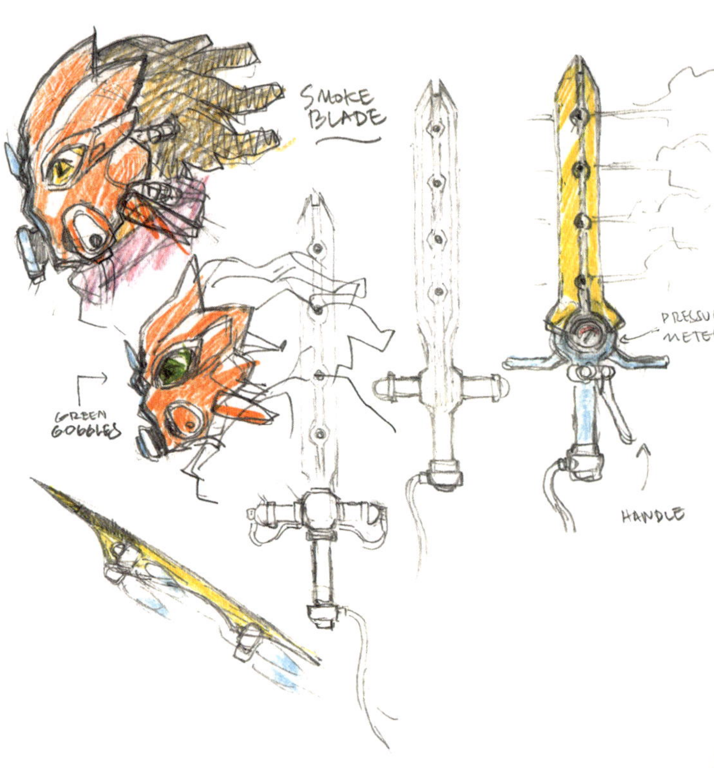

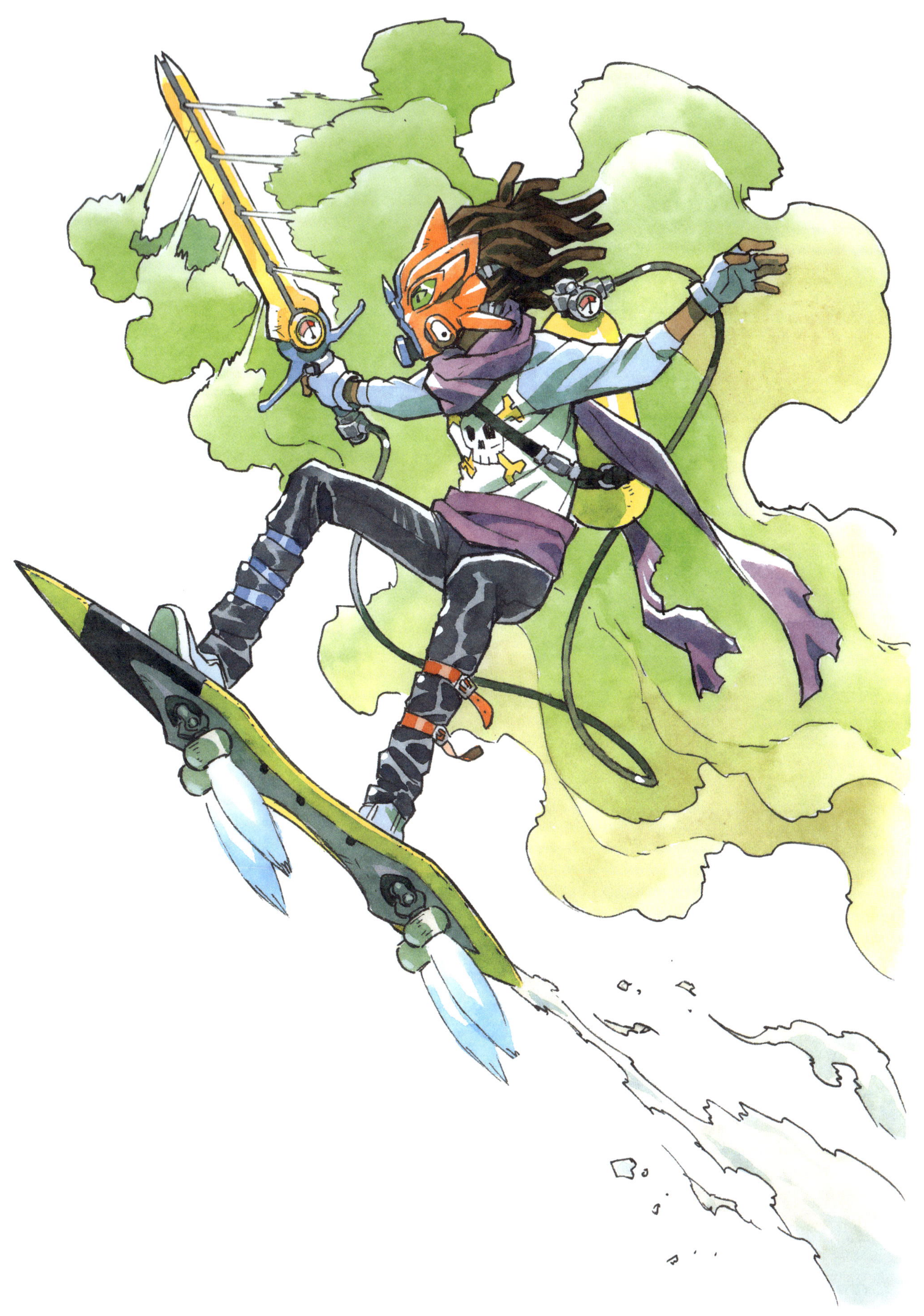

Bonus 06
Cyber Pursuit

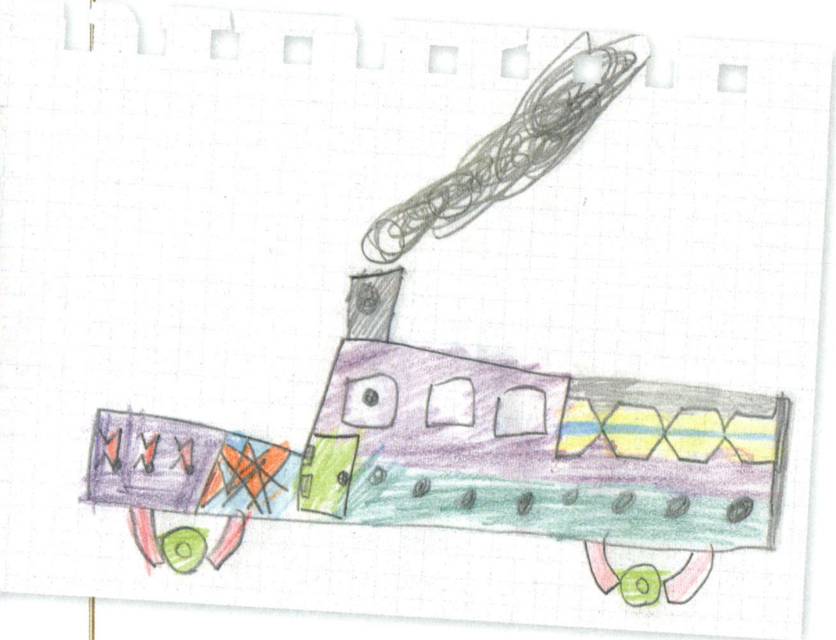

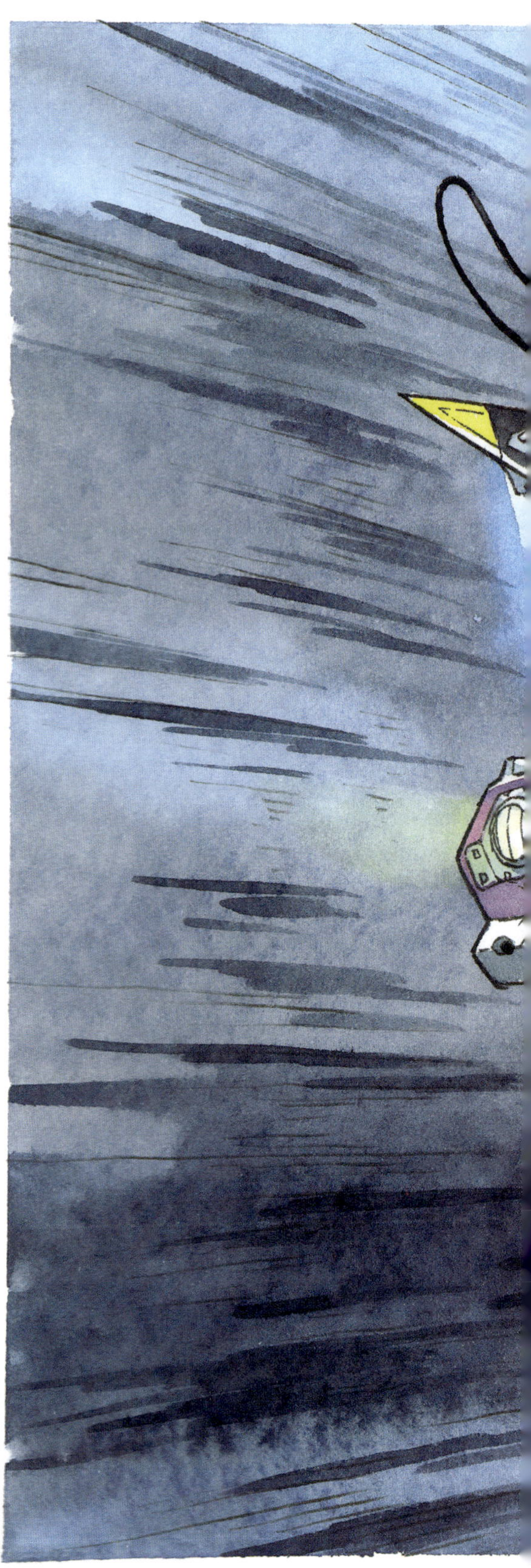

Thomas

Itsuki's drawing surprised me. I wasn't expecting him to draw a vehicle. This is one of the most stimulating aspects of this project: I never know what to expect. I must then adapt myself and be creative to best exploit the original idea. It would have been a little sad to draw a lonesome vehicle, so I chose to bring back some of my favorite characters, Justice and Noah. The pilot is none other than Offline Max, the cyborg from one of Itsuki's old drawings. I tried to keep the angular shapes of the car. This gives it a retro look, which makes you think of the mythical DeLorean from *Back to the Future*.

Itsuki

To make a change from drawing characters, I had the urge to draw a vehicle. I inspired myself with a limousine I saw in Shinjuku, one of the major districts of Tokyo, where we often go for walks. I crossed this car with elements from trains. My drawing is pretty simple but Dad managed to turn it into something more realistic. The car looks good with its green reactors that look like light sabers, but the coolest thing is having lots of characters come back, especially the cyborg, which was my first drawing.

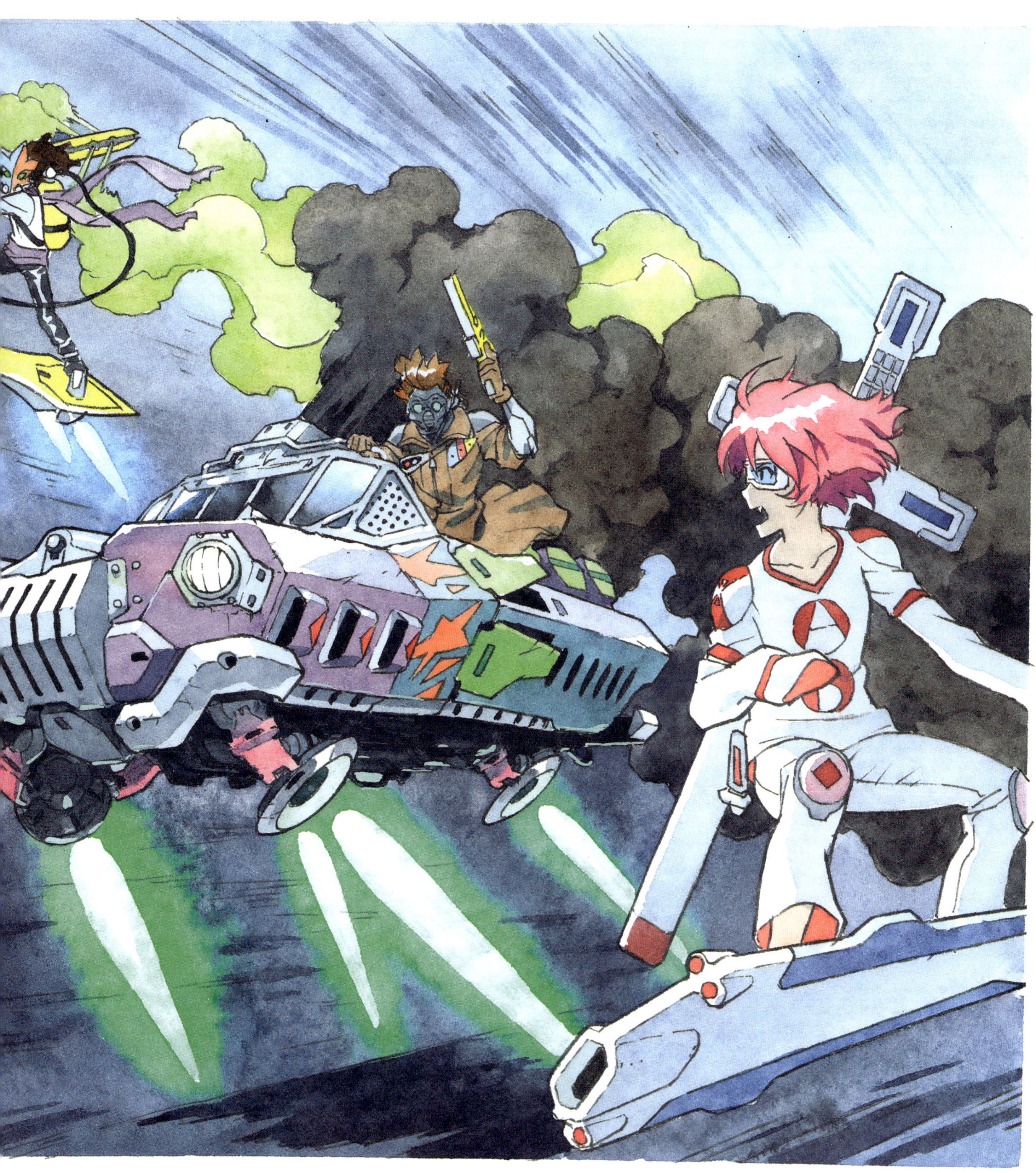

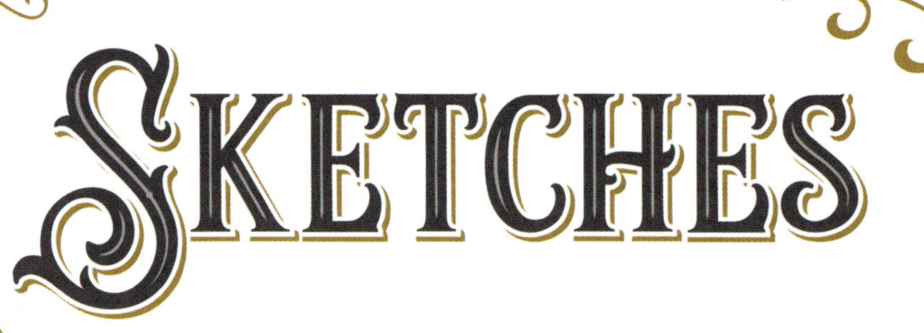

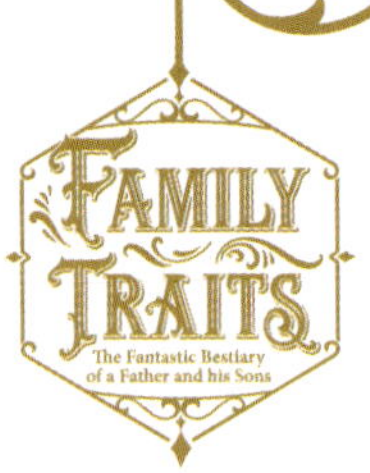

After the fifth character, I got into the habit of creating a few research sketches before beginning the definitive illustration. These sketches allow me to work in a more relaxed manner, without worrying about the quality of the drawing itself, as they are not meant to be shown. These roughs help me to define the details, the character's pose and the composition of the final image.

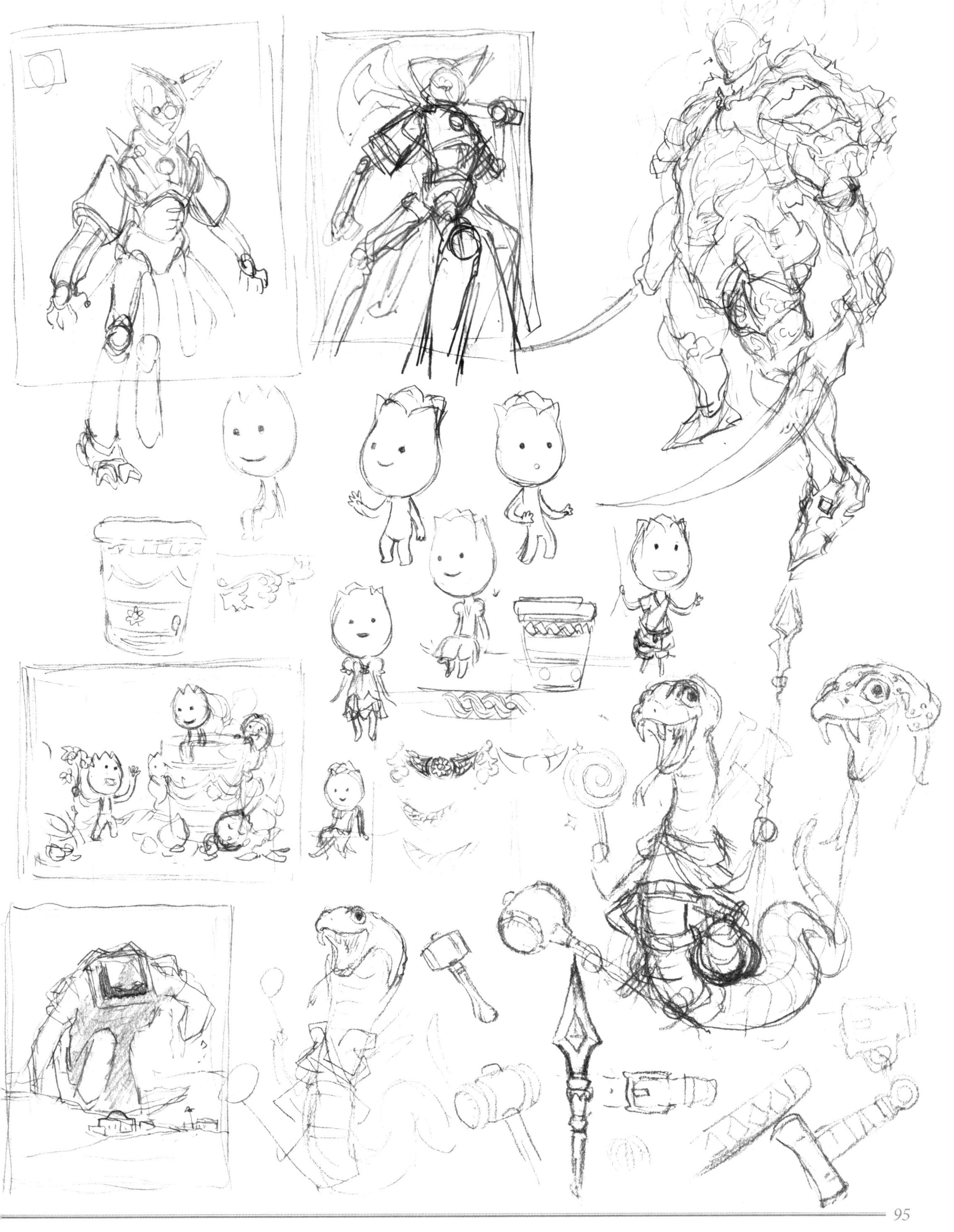

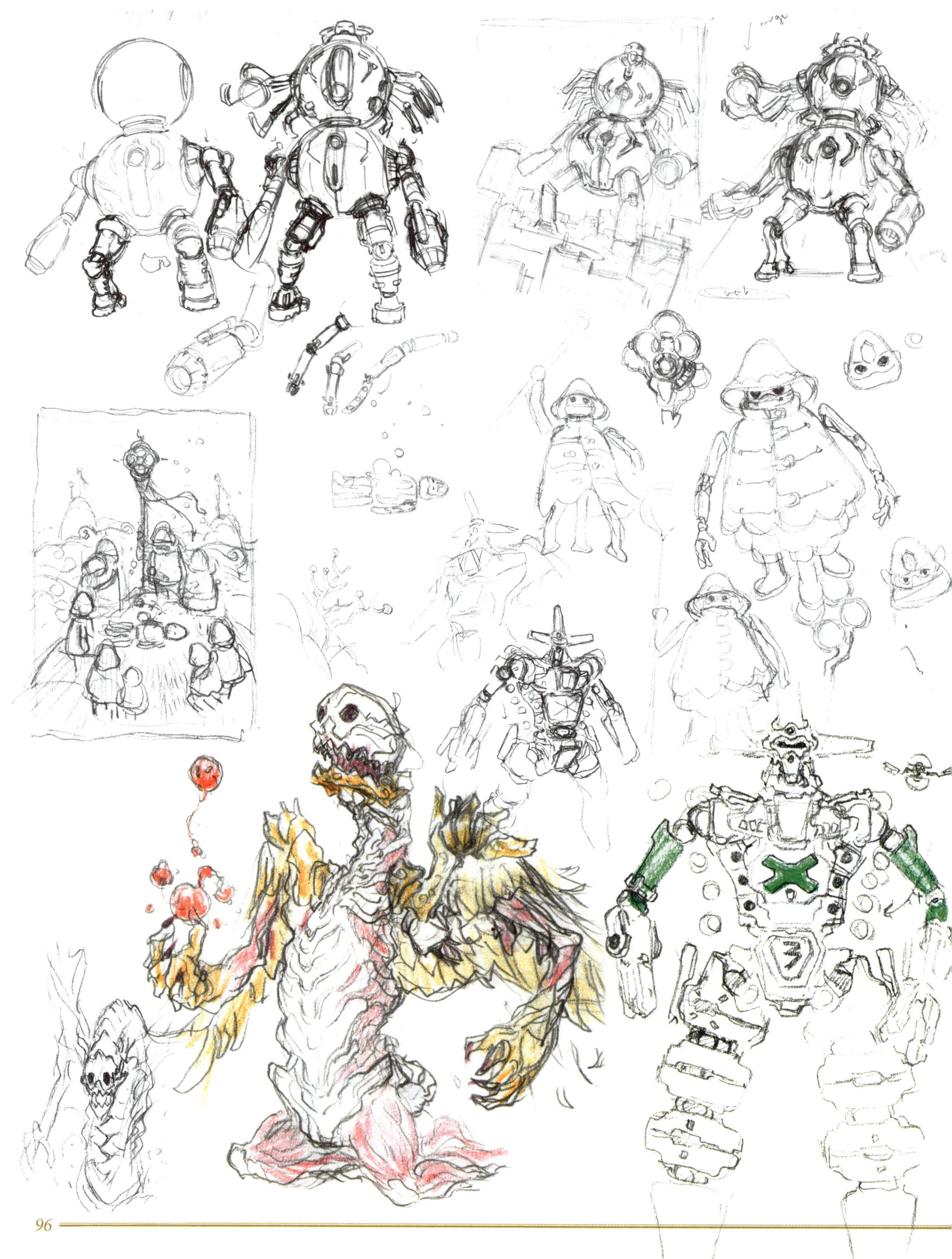

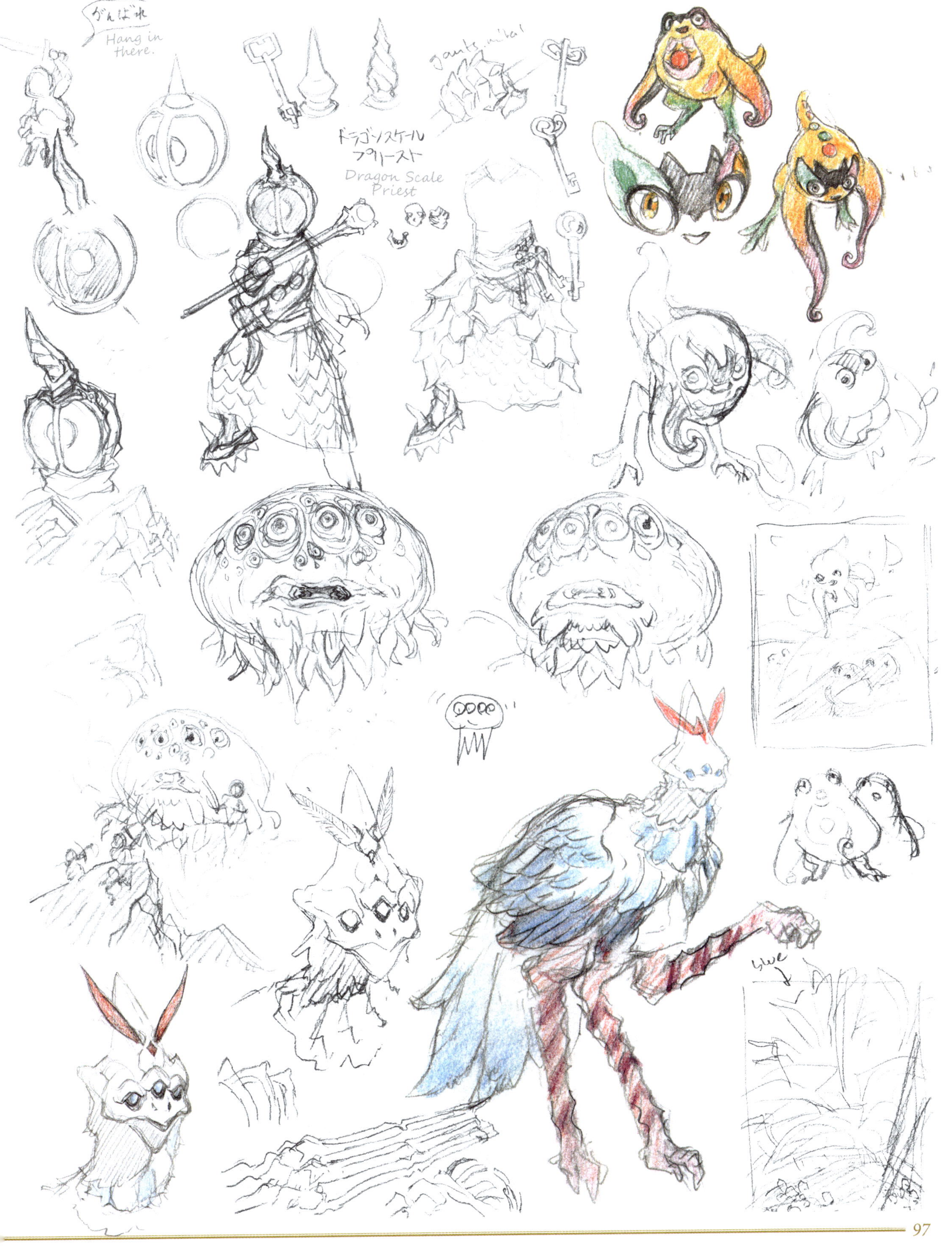
がんばれ
Hang in there.
ドラゴンスケール
プリースト
Dragon Scale
Priest

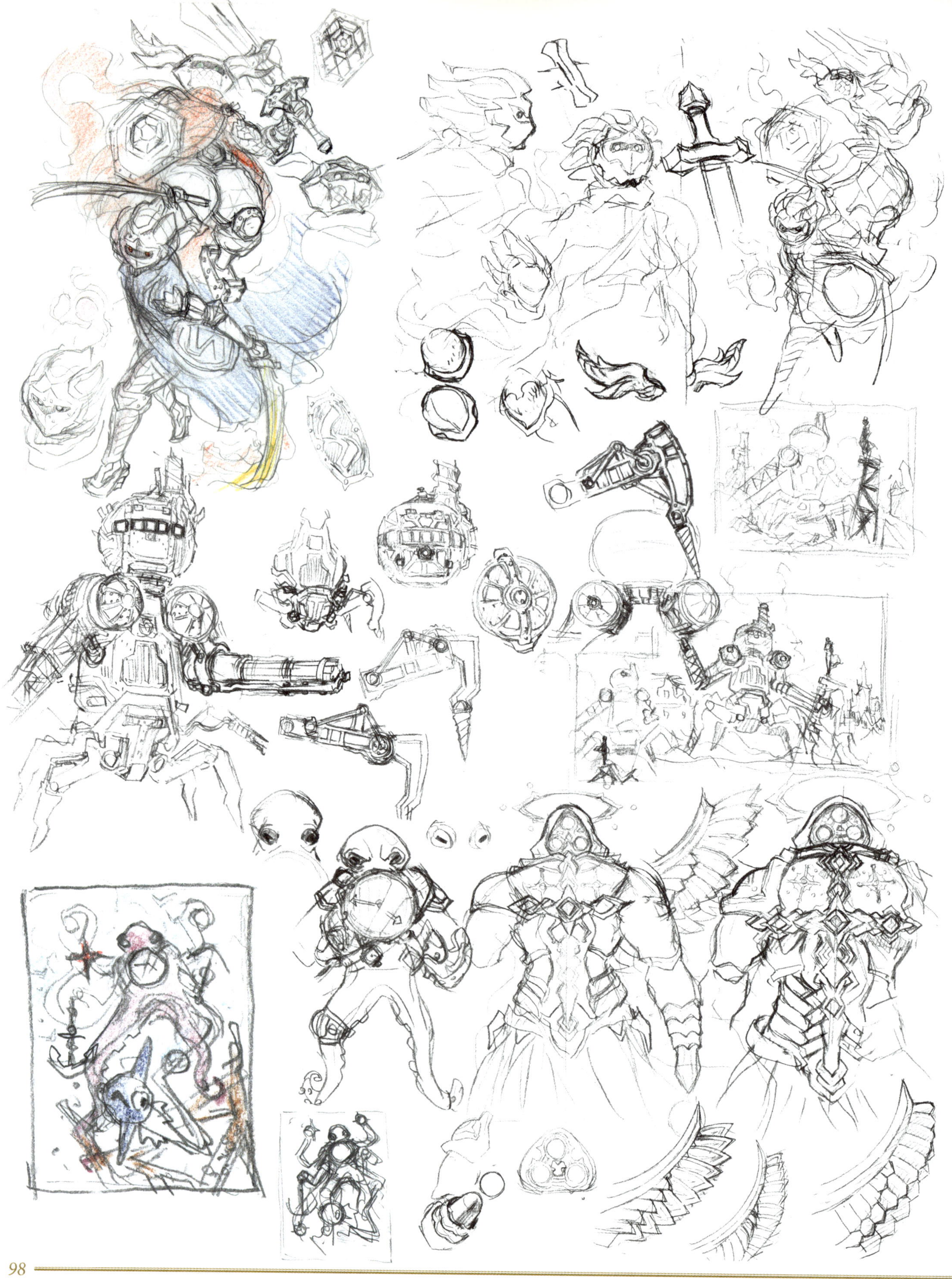

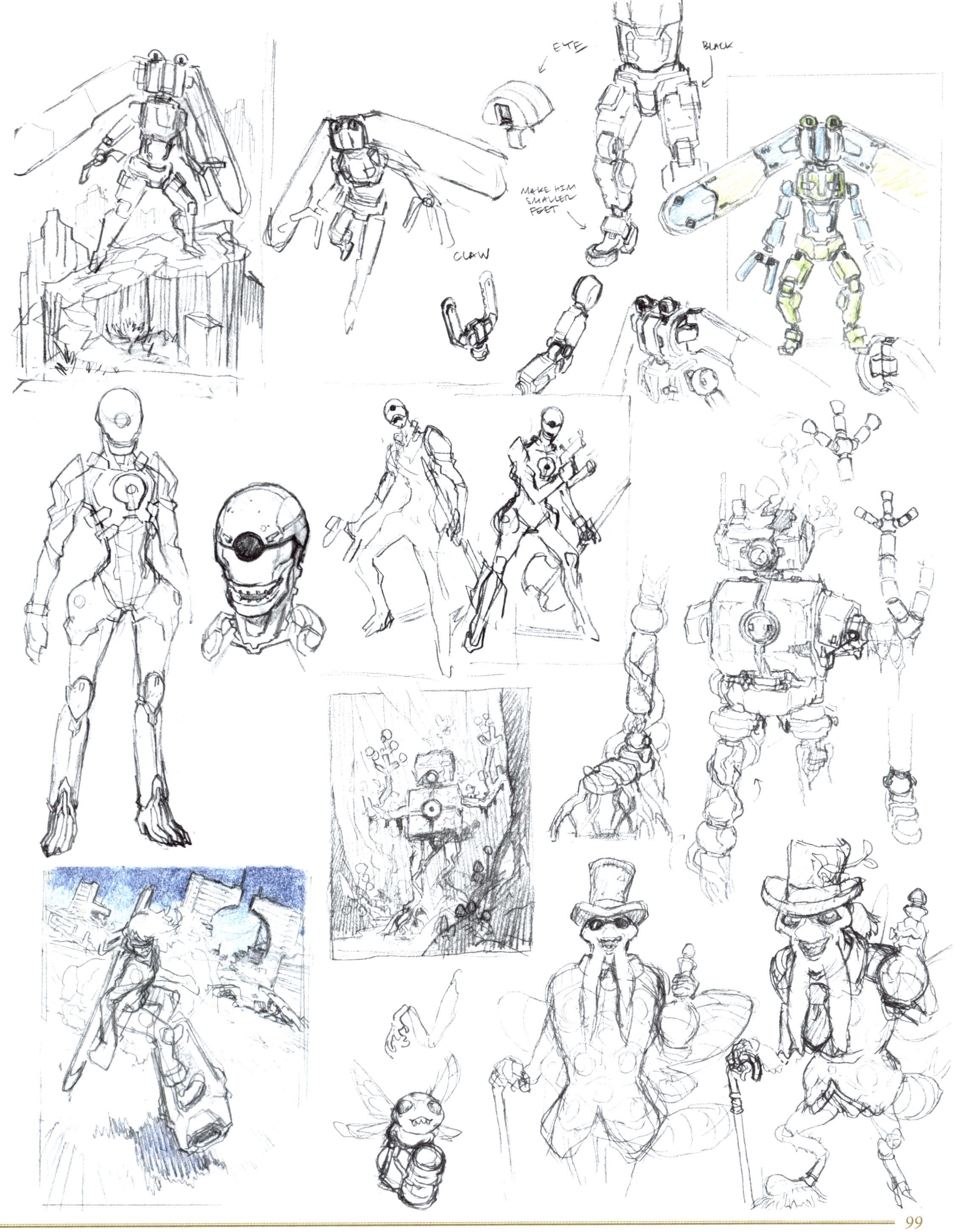
EYE
BLACK
MAKE HIM SMALLER FEET
CLAW

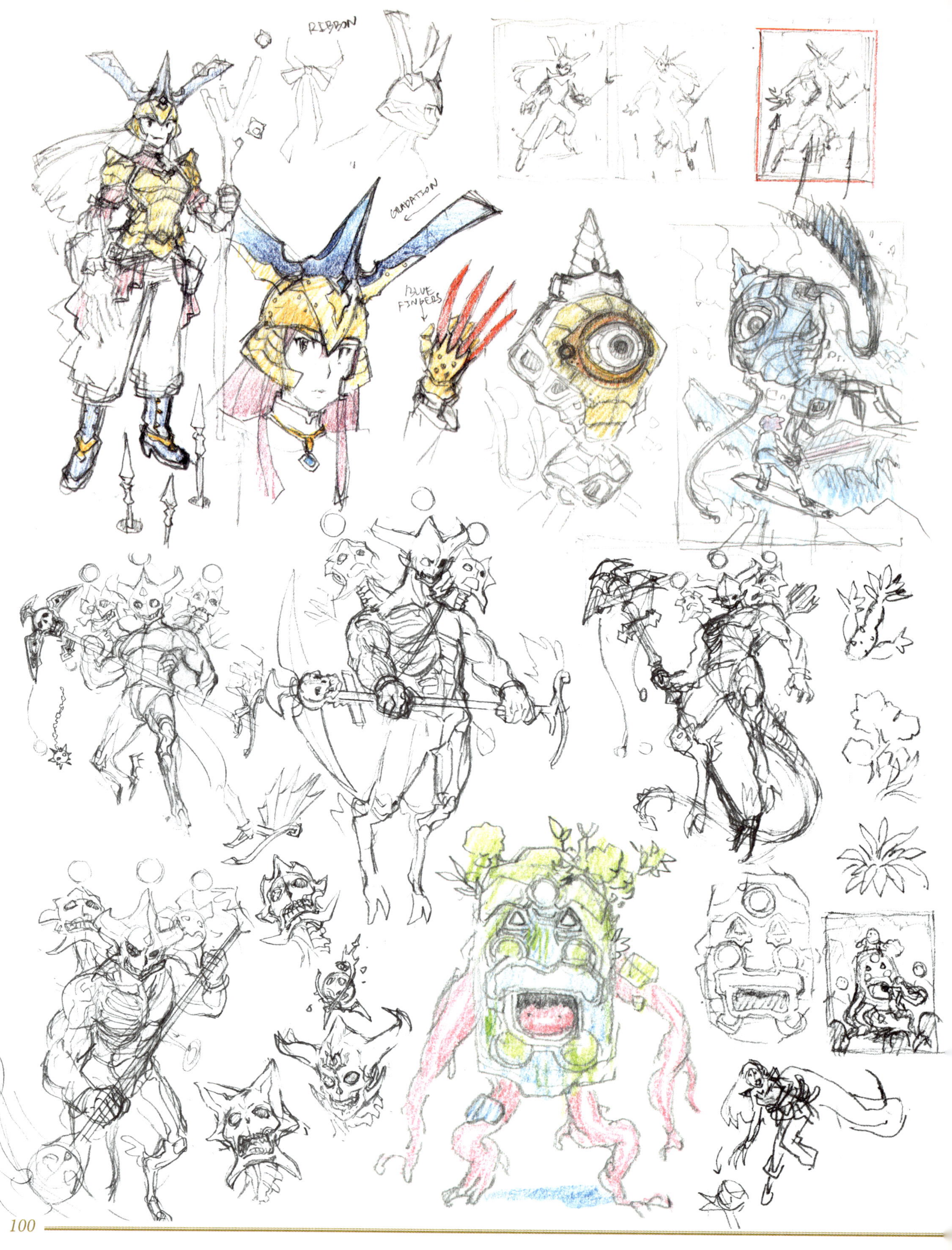
RIBBON
GRADATION
BLUE FINGERS

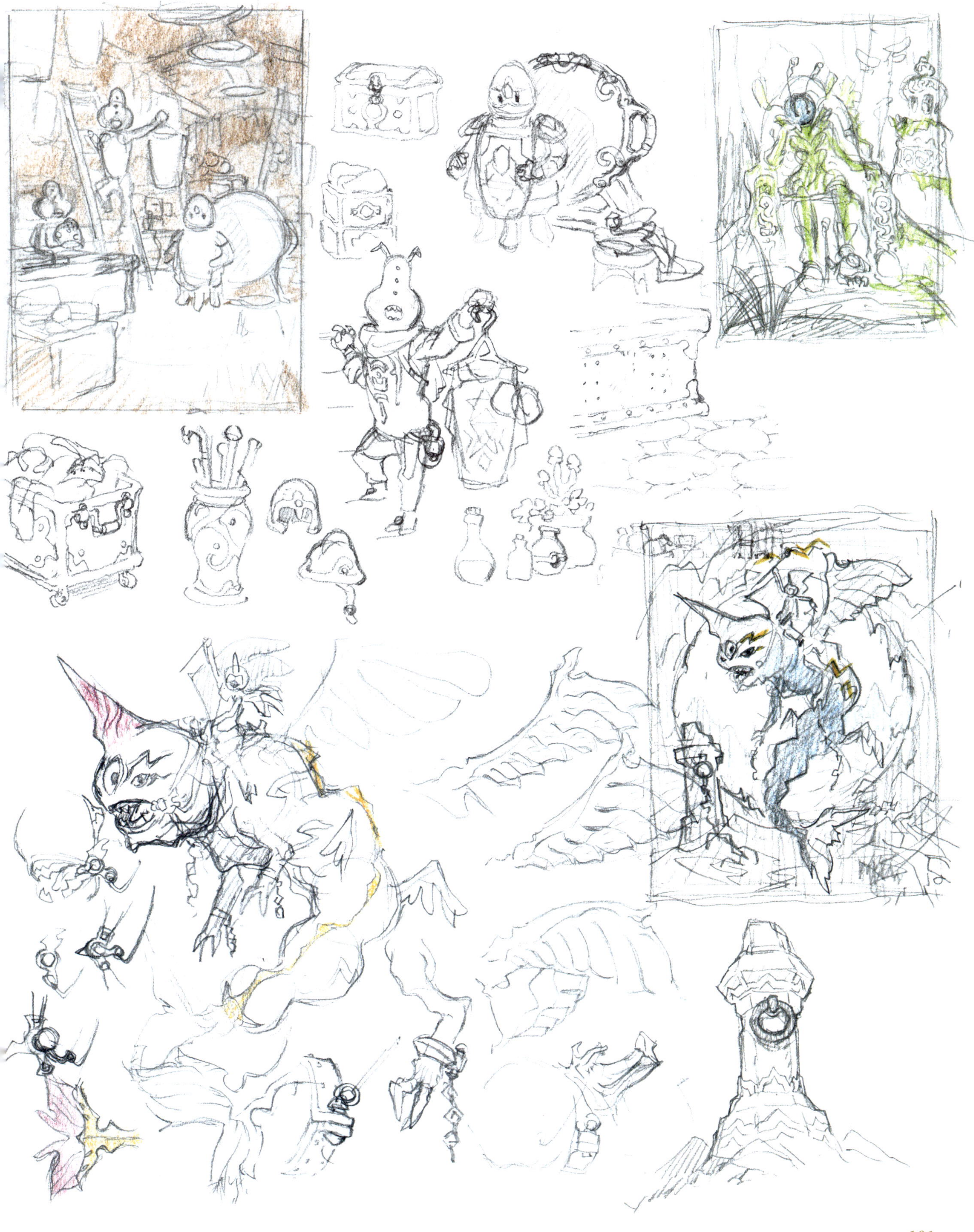

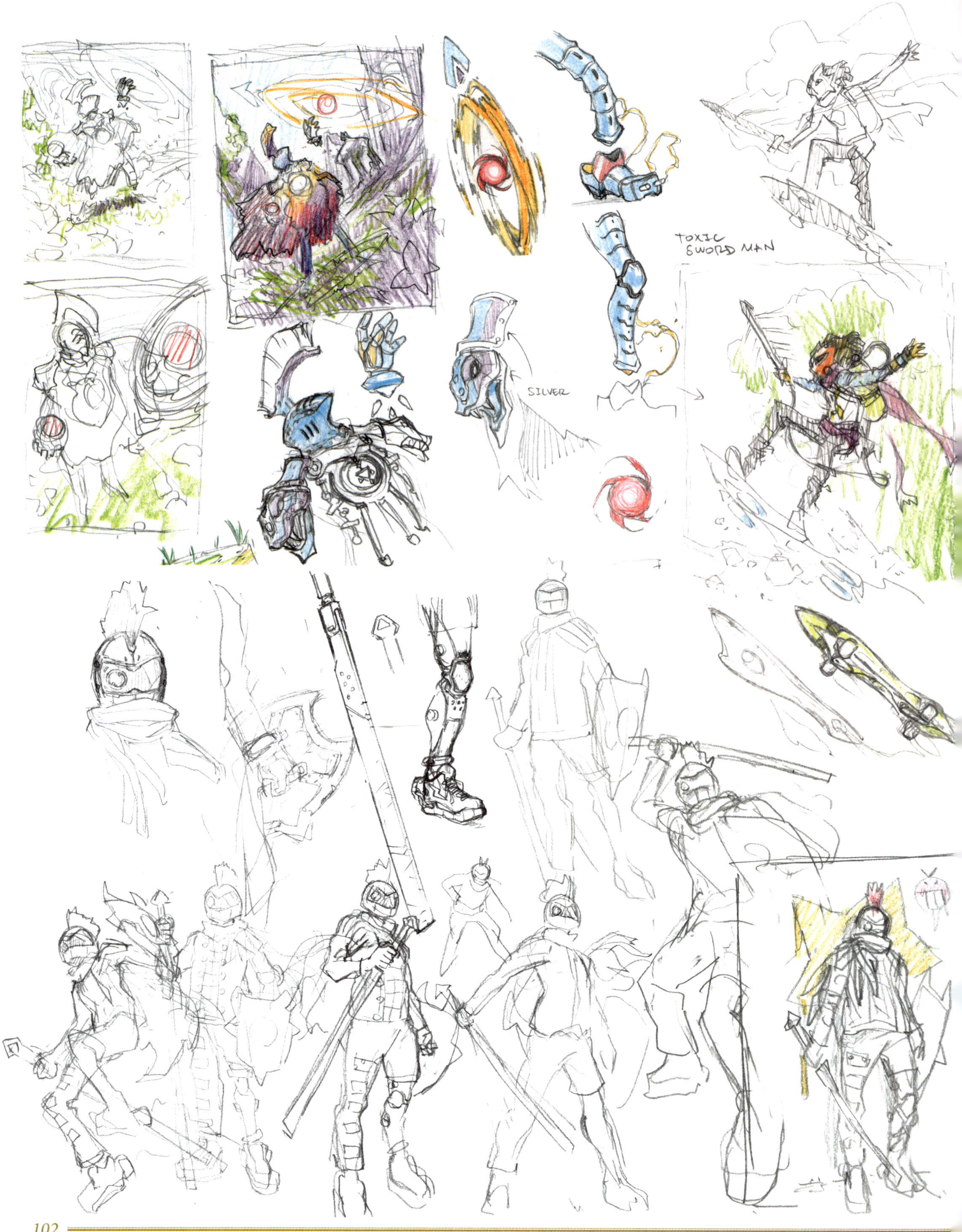
TOXIC
SWORD MAN
SILVER

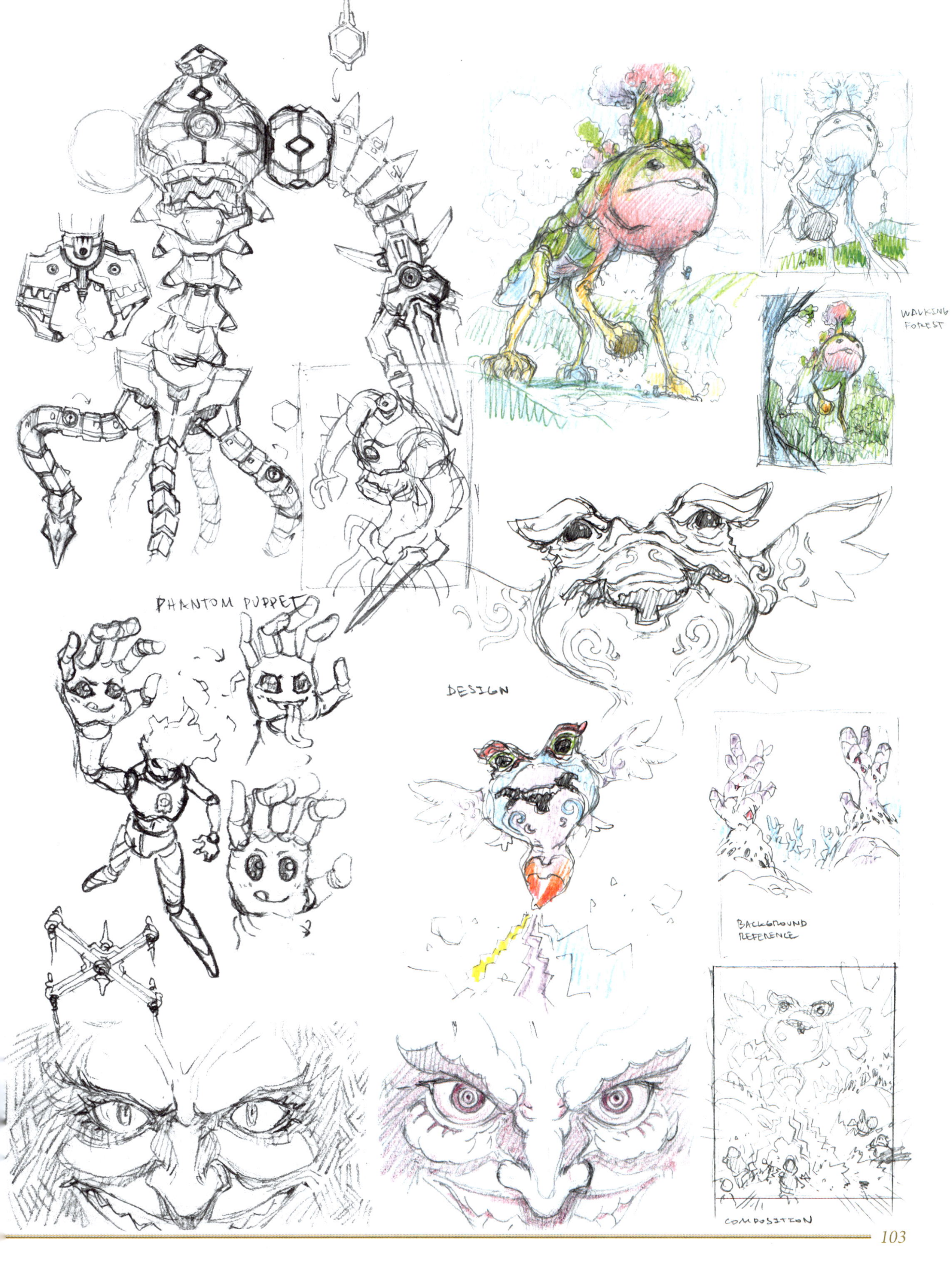
WALKING FOREST
PHANTOM PUPPET
DESIGN
BACKGROUND REFERENCE
COMPOSITION

Behind the Scenes

With these production steps, let's discover together the creation of the 28th illustration: *Sylveria, Guardian of the Forest's Entrance.*

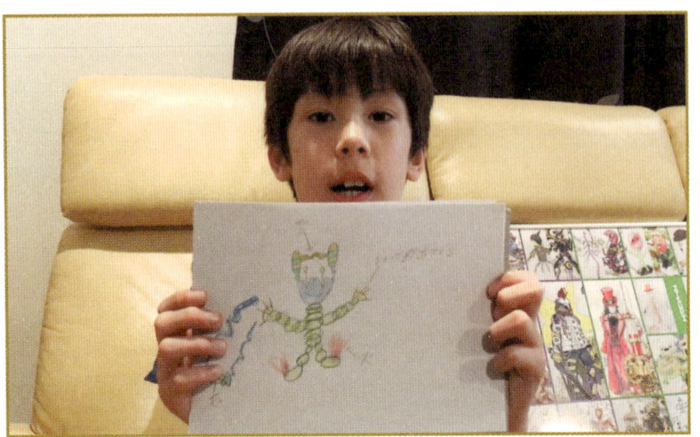

1 Everything begins with a drawing by Itsuki in his sketchbook, of a character composed of leaves and vegetation. As you can see on page 70, I started with a few research sketches on the character and the background.

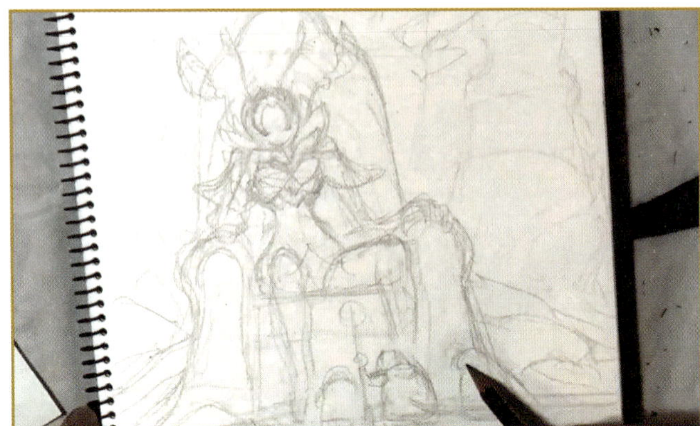

2 Once I have sufficiently defined the image I want to do through the sketches, I make an initial pencil rough. I use a special paper designed for watercolors.

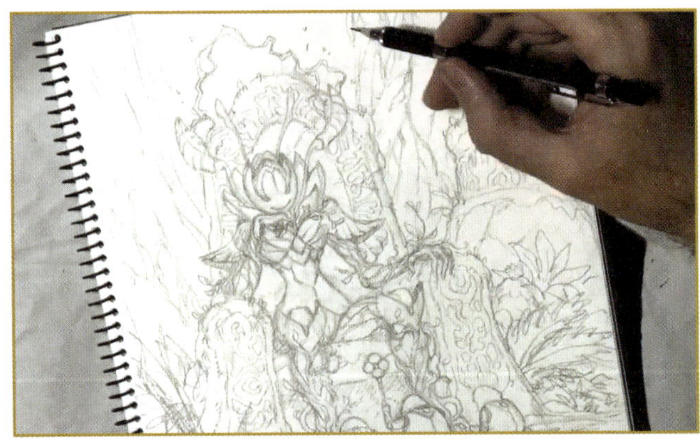

3 After finishing this first rough drawing, I add some details using a sharper mechanical pencil. I also draw the background with more precision. I have worked for over ten years as a background artist in animation, so I know from experience that their atmosphere can evoke numerous emotions in the spectator.

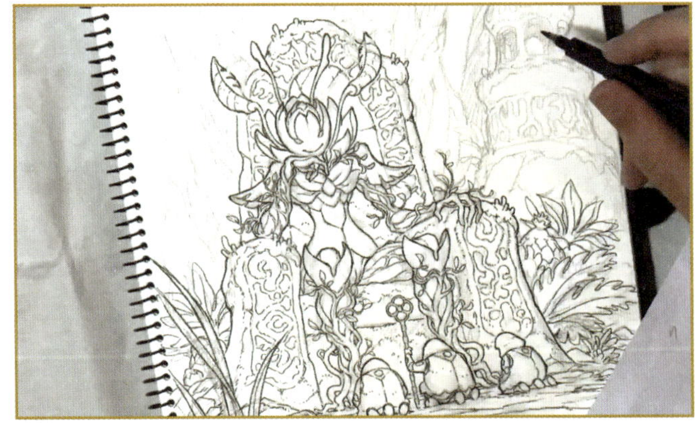

4 It is time to move on to the inking. I use a fine permanent ink brush pen. Please note that I do not use fill shading like they do in comics. I prefer creating the shading directly with watercolors. It's my favorite technique, one that comes from my pronounced taste for animated works.

Here is the pen I use for inking:
Zebra brush pen Brush sign superfine B-WFSS4

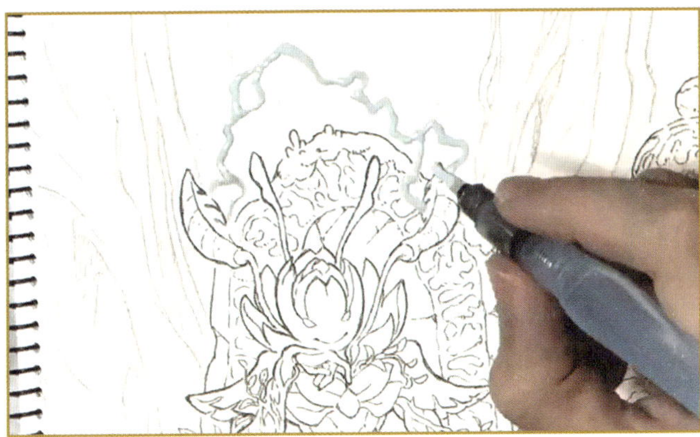

5 In order to create the electric arc above the head, I use a special drawing gum for use with watercolors. It will later be removed, leaving behind the white emplacement giving the impression of a luminous effect.

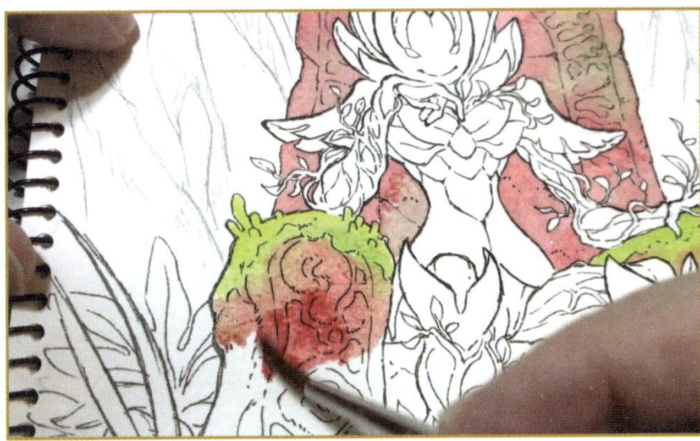

6 Here is how I painted the gradient on the throne. I prepare my different colors on the palette. Then, before the paint dries, I progressively change colors: first the light green, then a slightly darker green, then the red and brown which give an aged aspect to the stone.

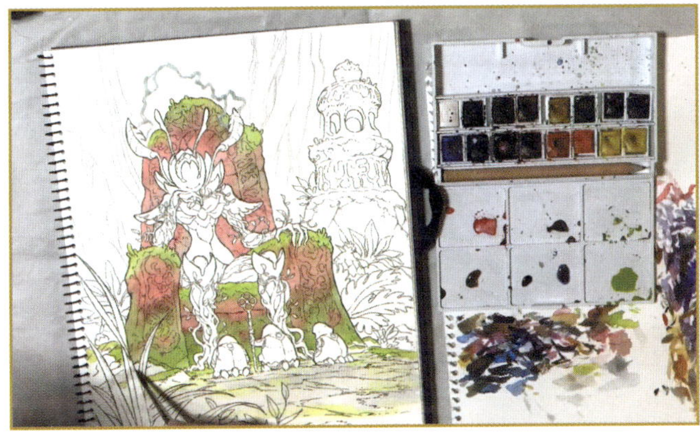

7 I then add a little more green to simulate the moss. As the watercolors slowly dry, the colors will mix together in a natural way.

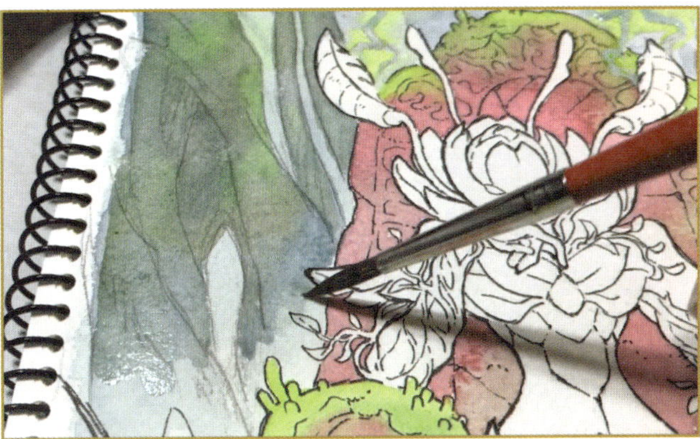

8 I use the same technique for the forest in the background. Sometimes I'll even finish off the gradients with help from water. In this case, it permits me to better show off the throne, as the background is lighter.

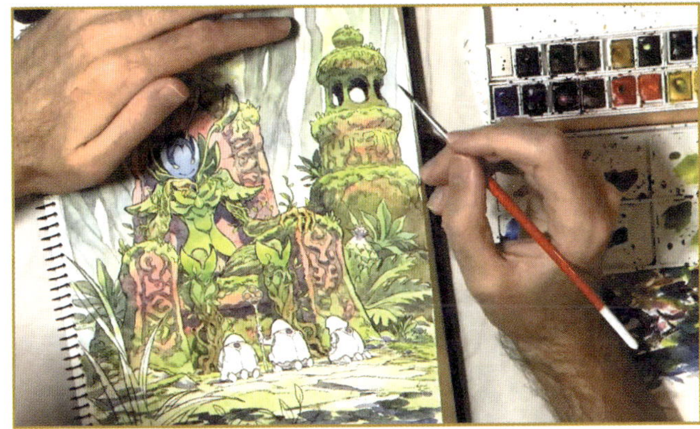

9 Once the colors are well placed, I add shading using dark blue tones. It is at this moment that the illustration takes on volume.

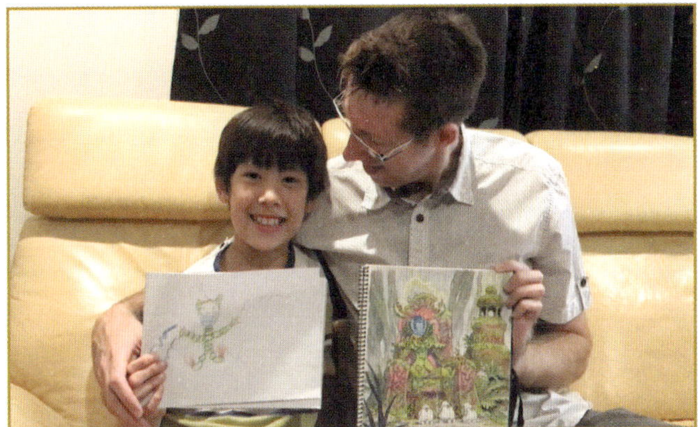

10 And there we have it!

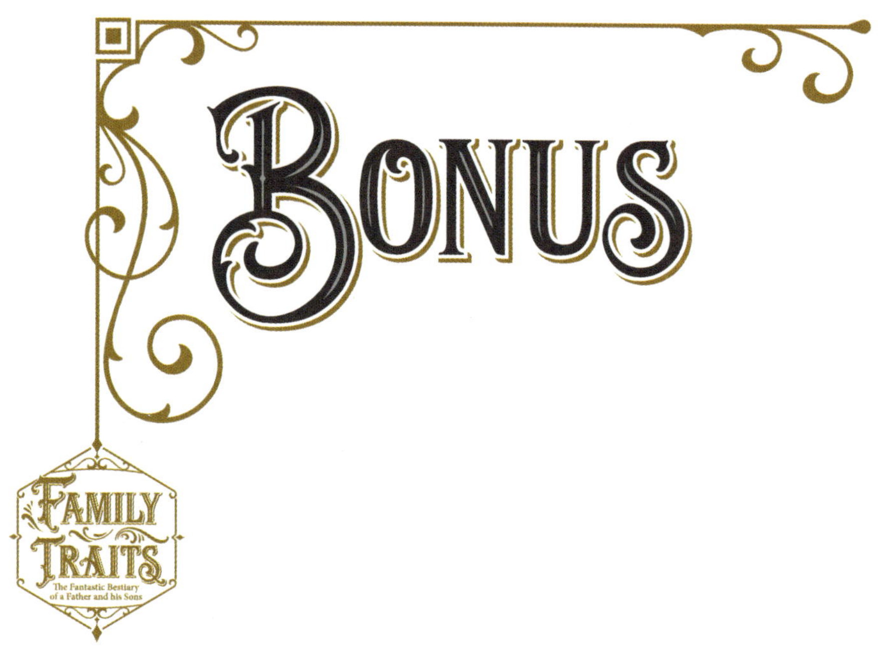
BONUS
FAMILY
TRAITS
The Fantastic Bestiary
of a Father and his Sons

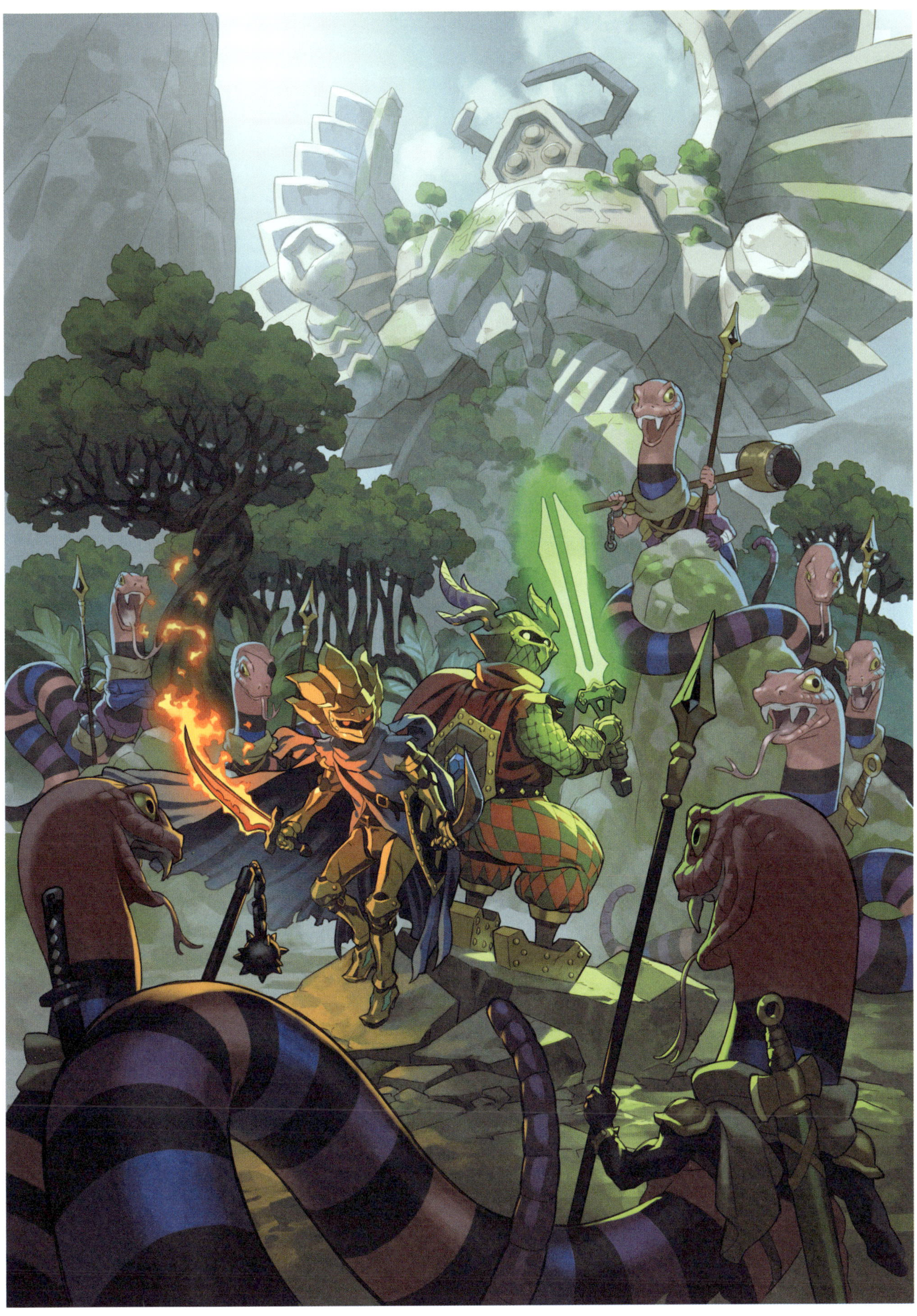

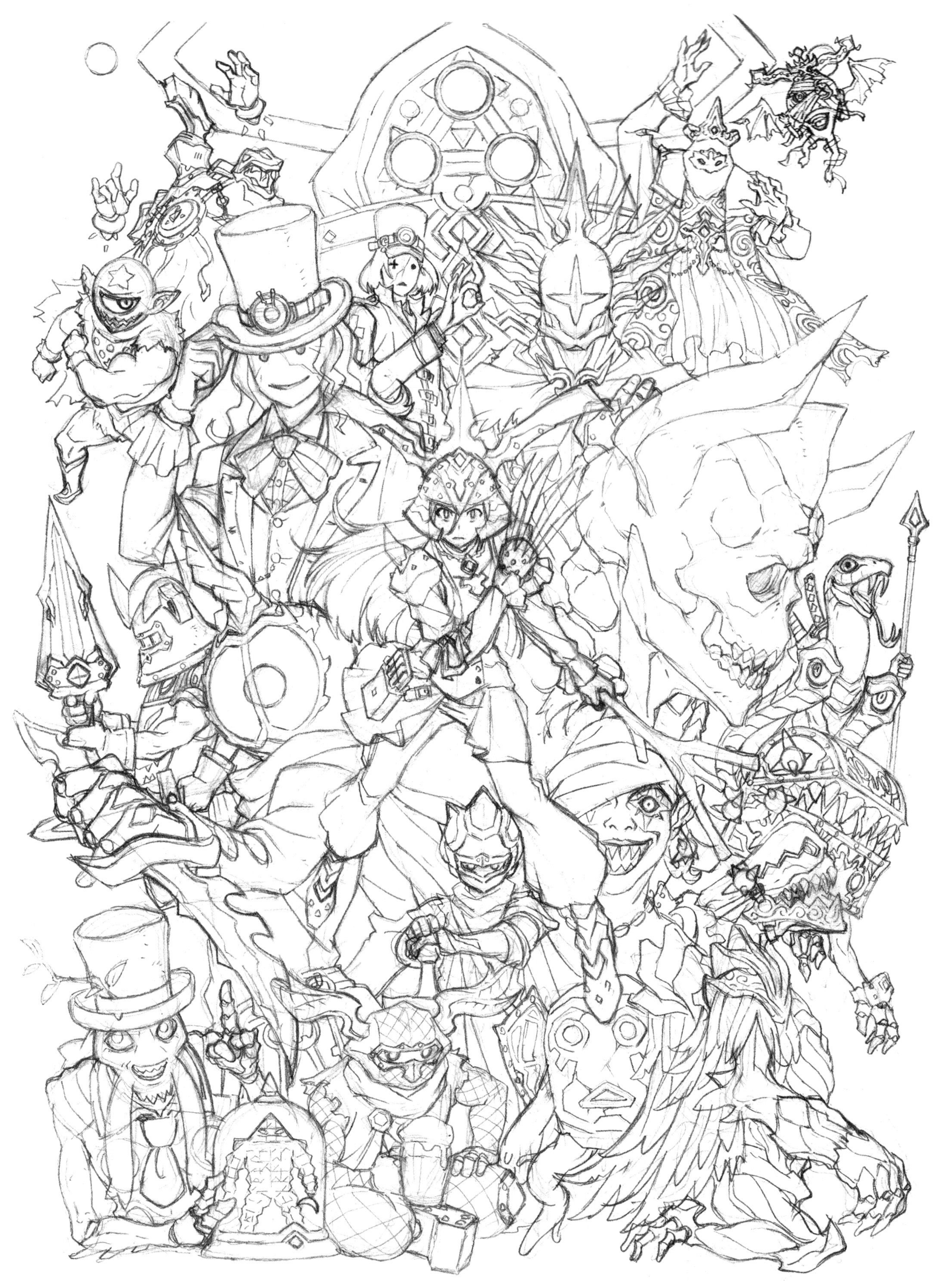

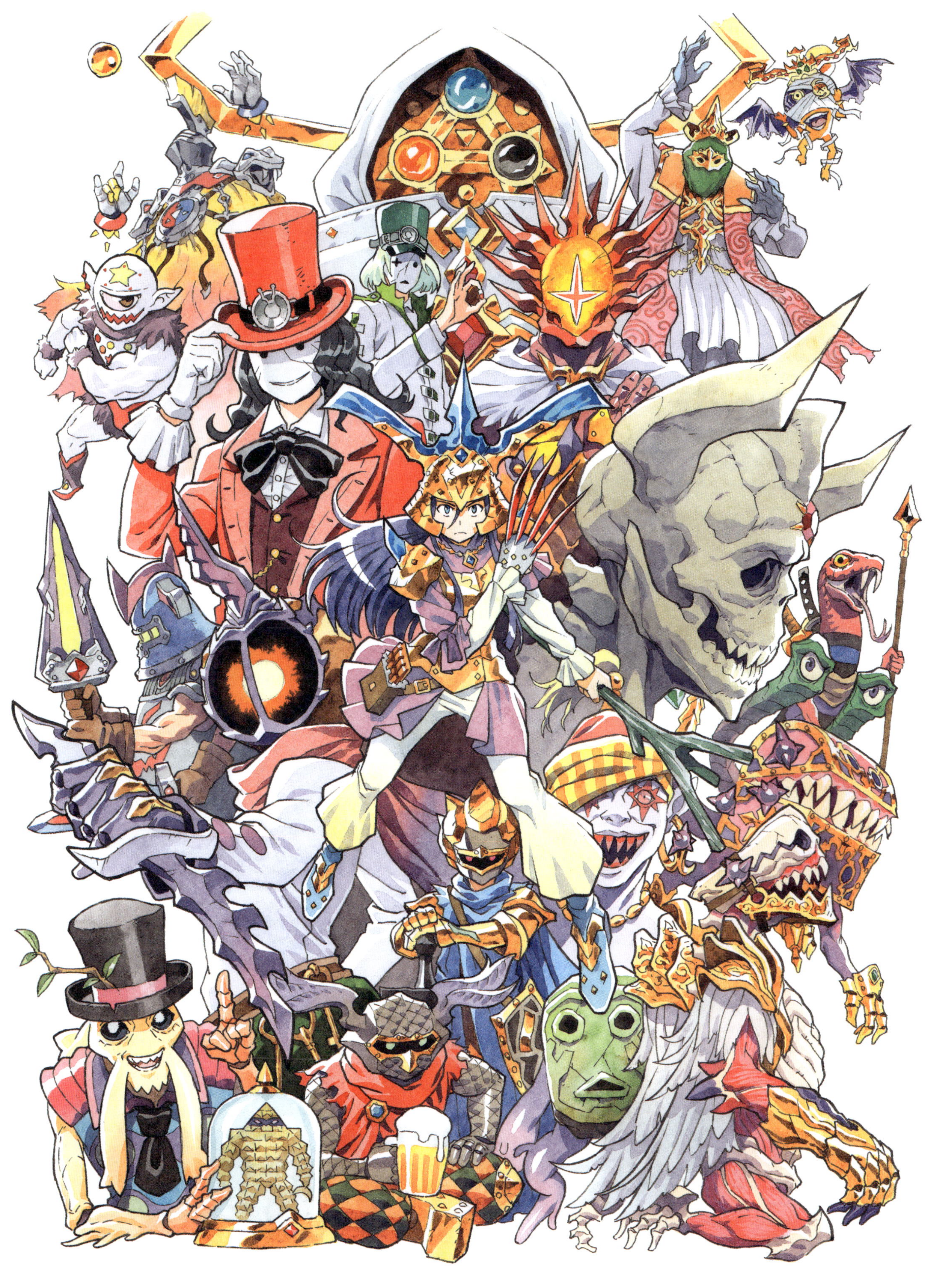

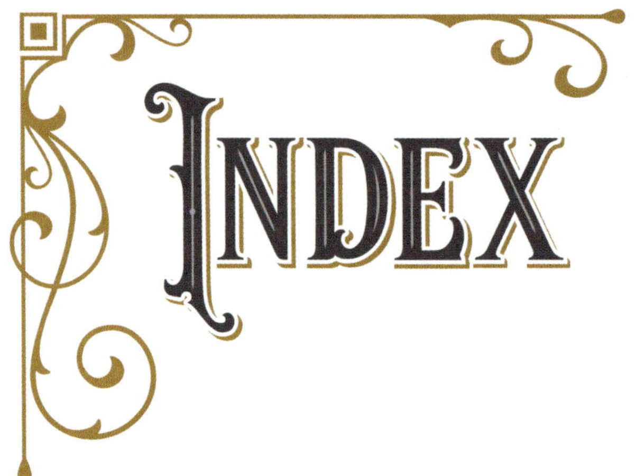

INDEX

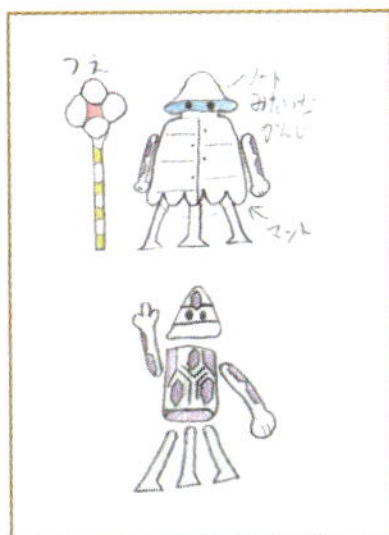
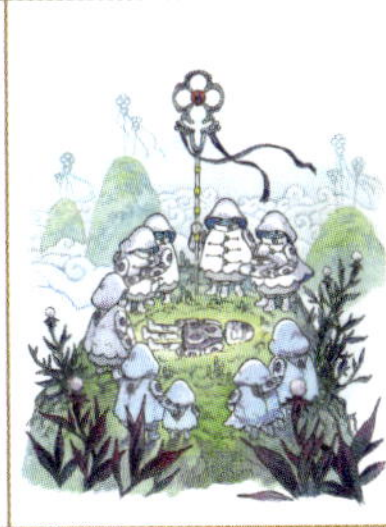

11 p30~31

The Koomos, Inhabitants of Cloud Hill

Ryunosuke & Thomas
12/03/2017

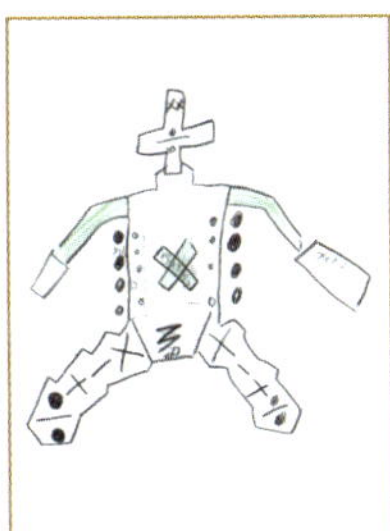
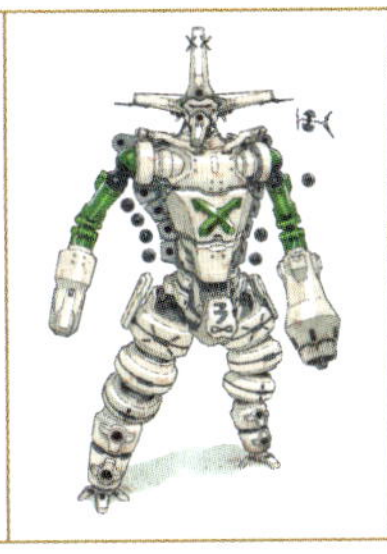

12 p32~33

K-3

Itsuki & Thomas
19/03/2017

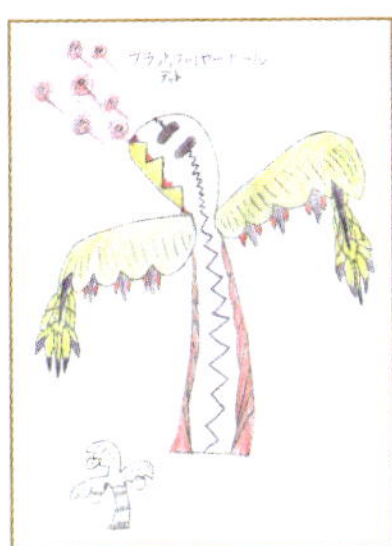
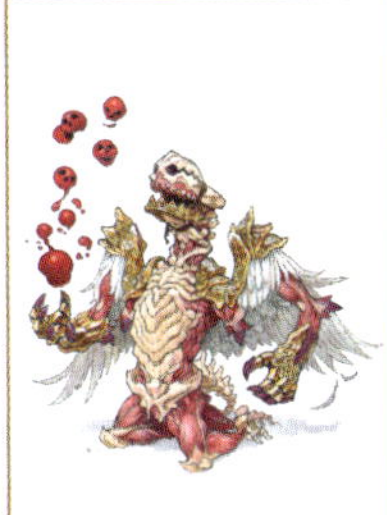

13 p34~35

The Cursed Blood Prince

Ryunosuke & Thomas
26/03/2017

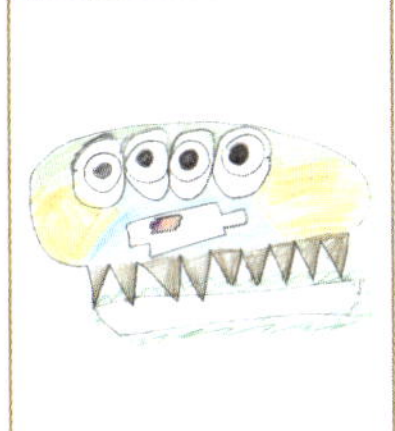
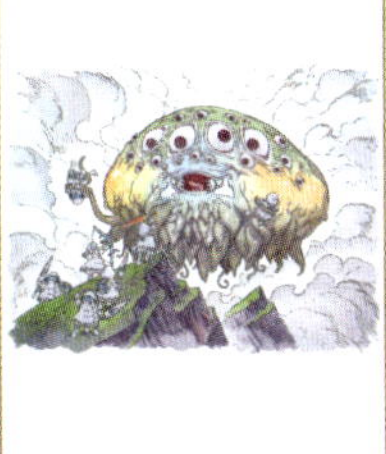

14 p36~37

The Royal Tentaduse

Itsuki & Thomas
02/04/2017

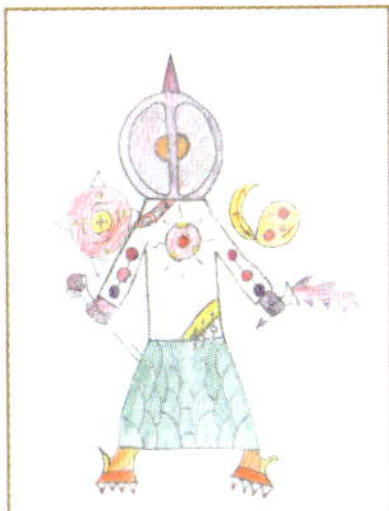
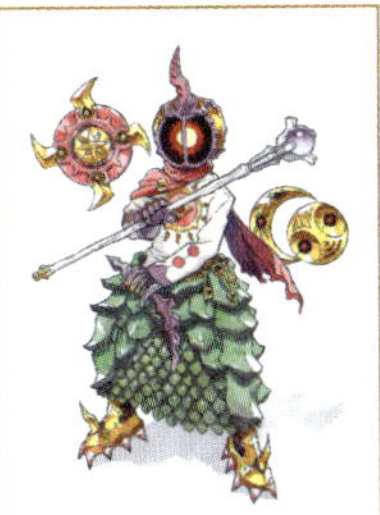

15 p38~39

Scal the Dragon Trainer

Ryunosuke & Thomas
10/04/2017

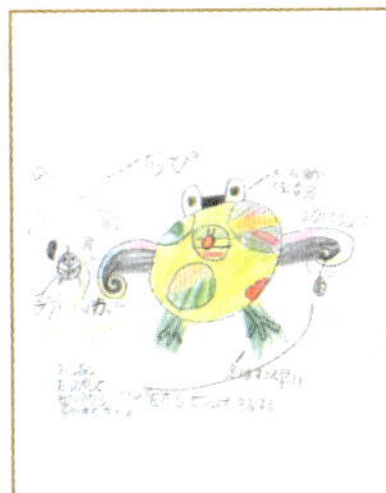
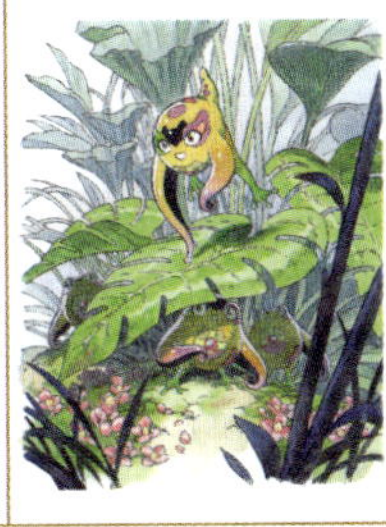

16 p40~41

The Leafrogs

Itsuki & Thomas
16/04/2017

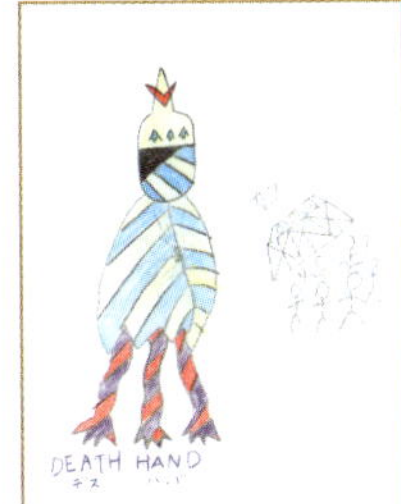

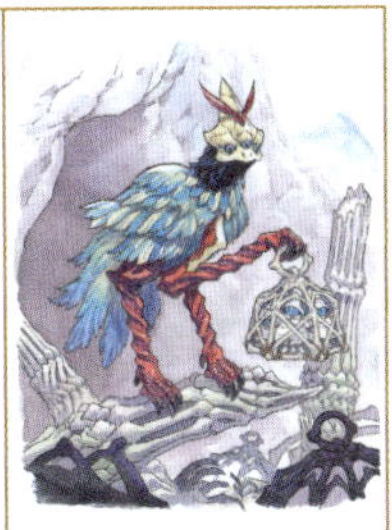

17 p42~43

The Wings from Bone Mountain

Ryunosuke & Thomas
23/04/2017

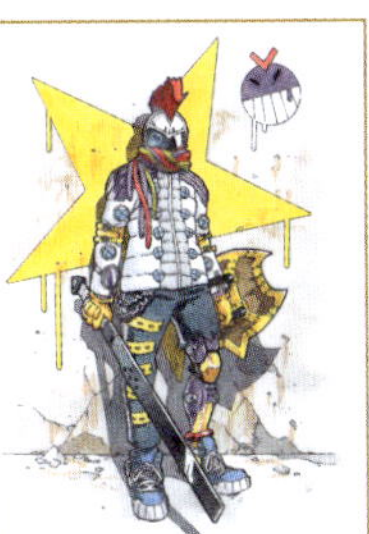

Extra 01 p44~45

Cyber-Gladiator

Ryunosuke & Thomas
12/05/2017

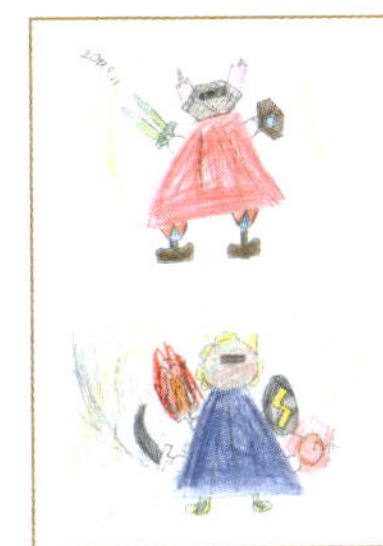
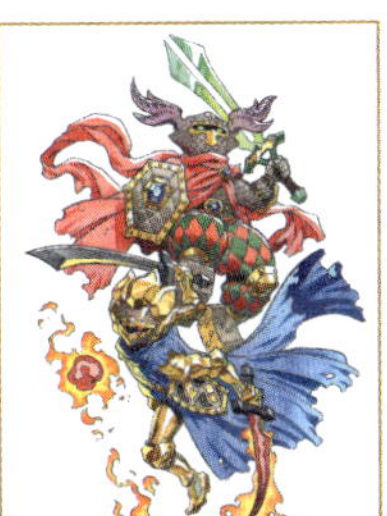

18 p46~47

Zenith and Twilight the Brothers in Arms

Itsuki & Thomas
30/04/2017

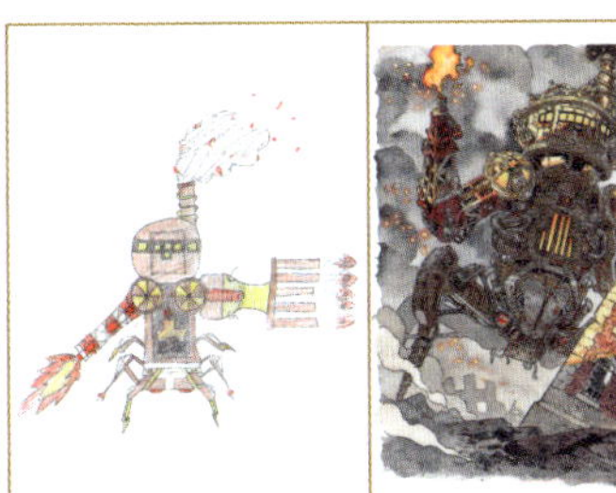

19 p48~49

The War Machine

Ryunosuke & Thomas
07/05/2017

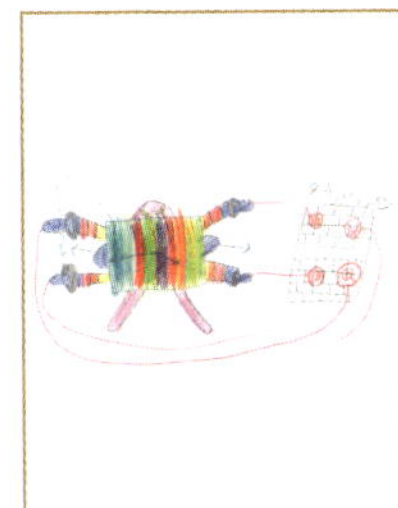
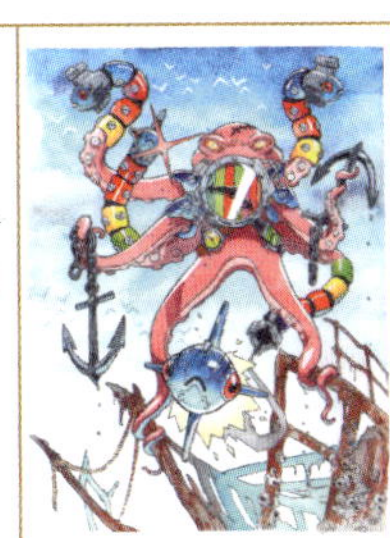

20 p50~51

The Time Octopus

Itsuki & Thomas
17/05/2017

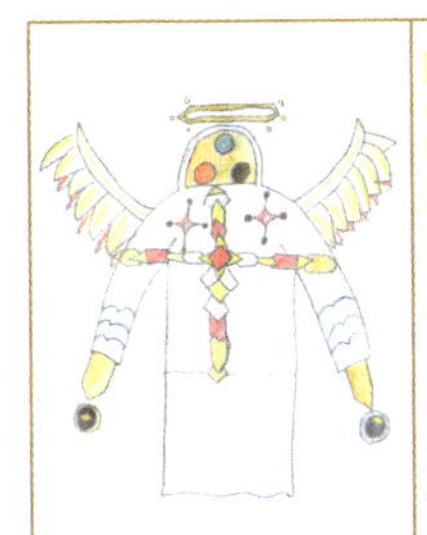
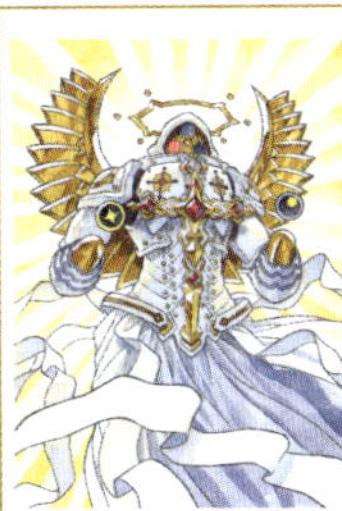

21 p52~53

Lord Wafida

Ryunosuke & Thomas
21/05/2017

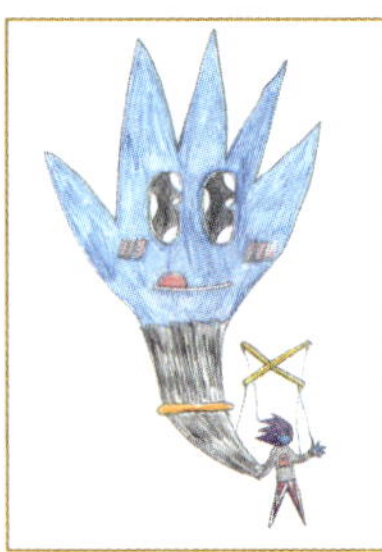

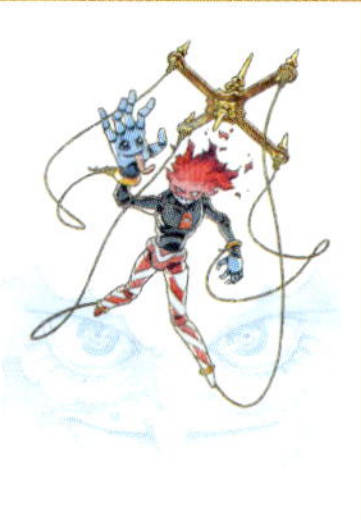

Extra 02 p54~55

The Phantom Marionette

Ryunosuke & Thomas
29/06/2017

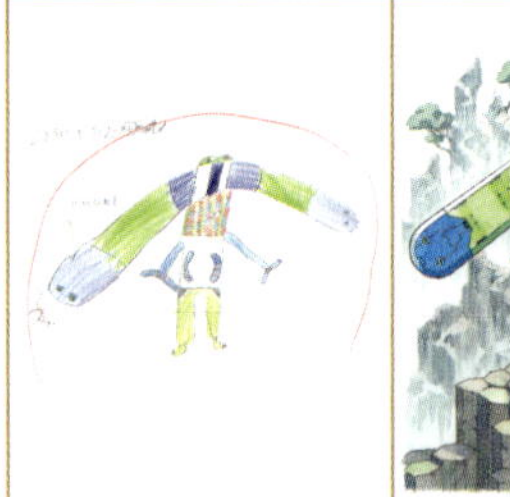

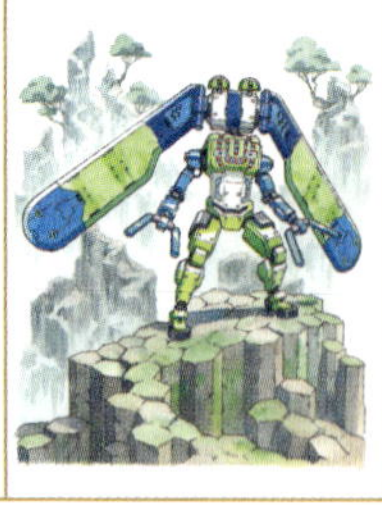

22 p56~57

The Boomerang-bot

Itsuki & Thomas
30/05/2017

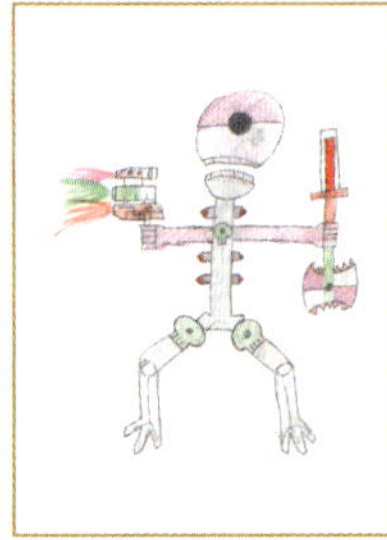

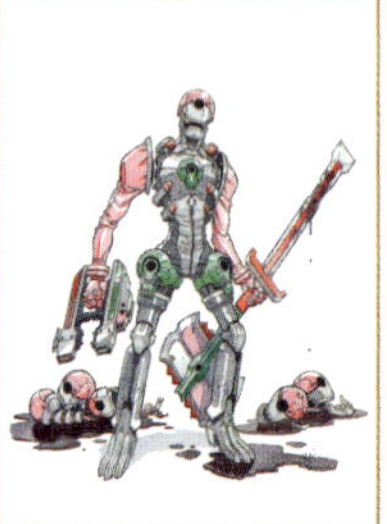

23 p58~59

The Skulloid

Ryunosuke & Thomas
06/06/2017

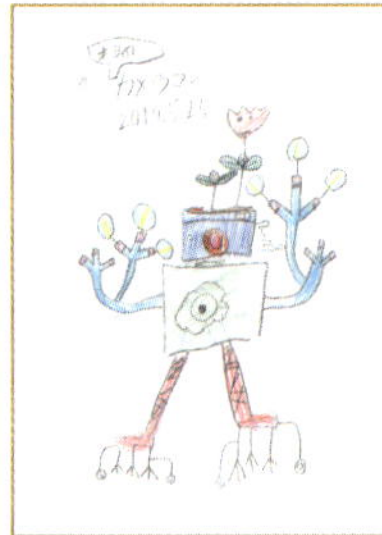

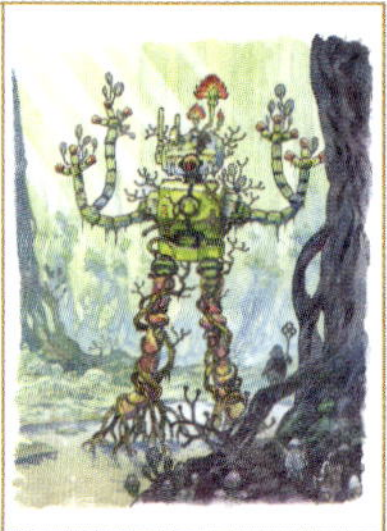

24 p60~61

The Forgotten Giant

Itsuki & Thomas
13/06/2017

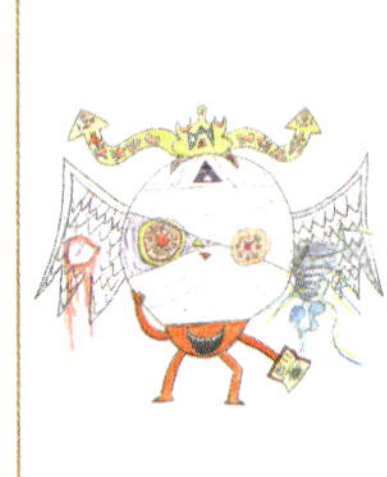

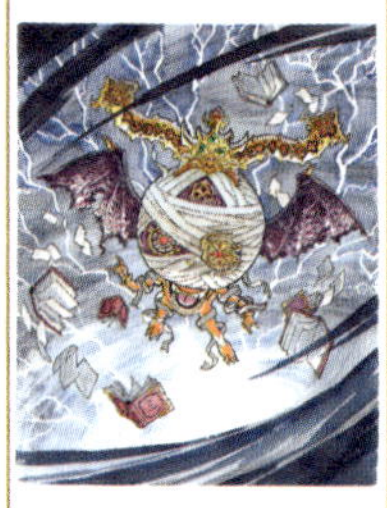

25 p62~63

The Baby Mummydemon

Ryunosuke & Thomas
19/06/2017

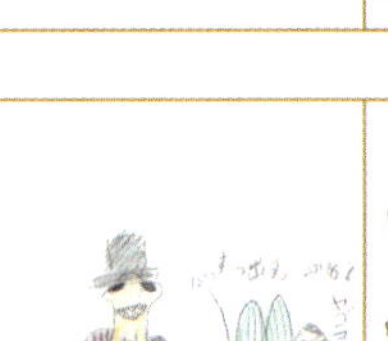

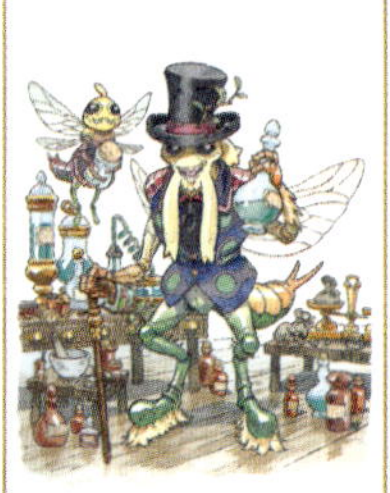

26 p64~65

Yago the Apothecary

Itsuki & Thomas
27/06/2017

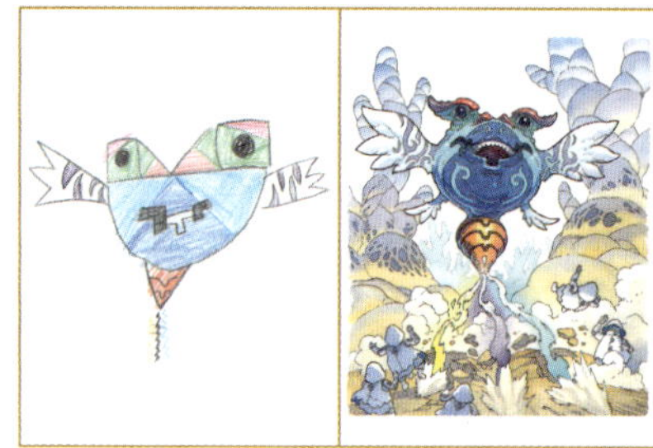

Extra 03 p66~67

The Mantamoth

Itsuki & Thomas
07/09/2017

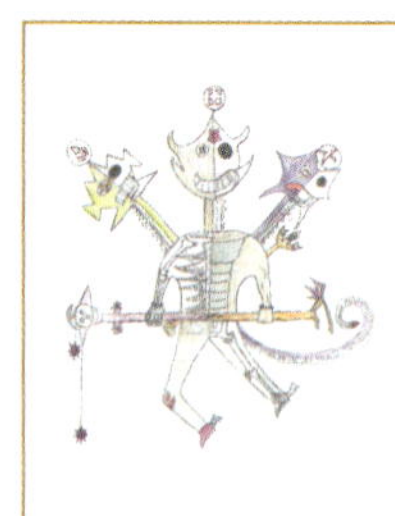

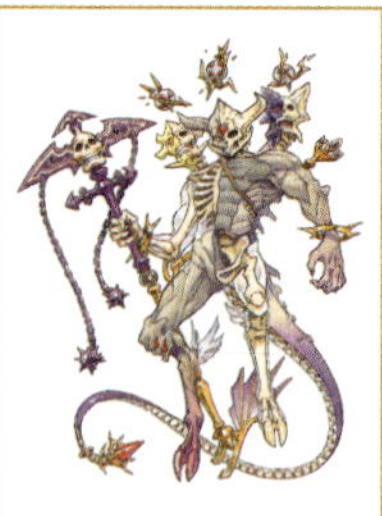

27 p68~69

The Demon Lord of the Half-Dead

Ryunosuke & Thomas
03/07/2017

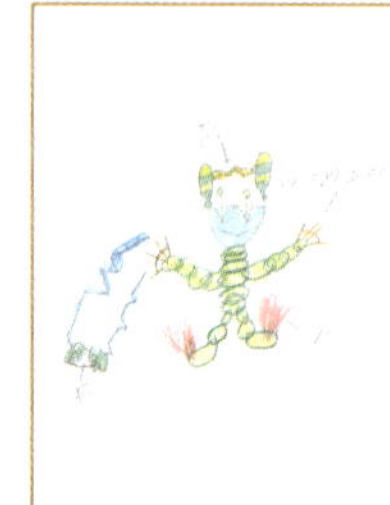

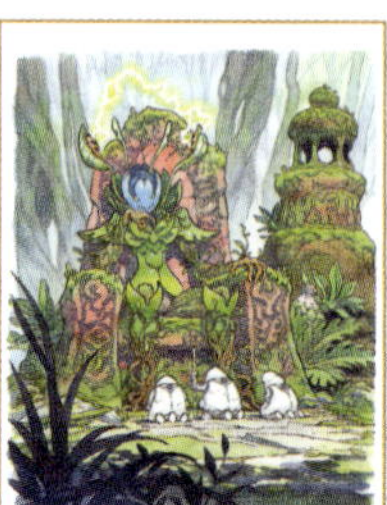

28 p70~71

Sylveria Guardian of the Woods

Itsuki & Thomas
10/07/2017

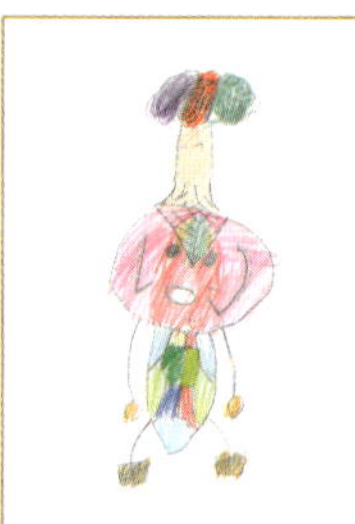

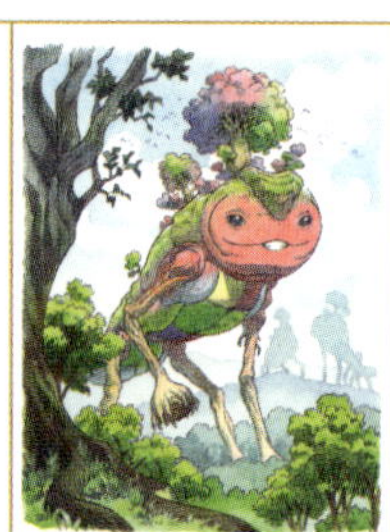

Extra 04 p72~73

The Wandering Forest

Itsuki & Thomas
03/10/2017

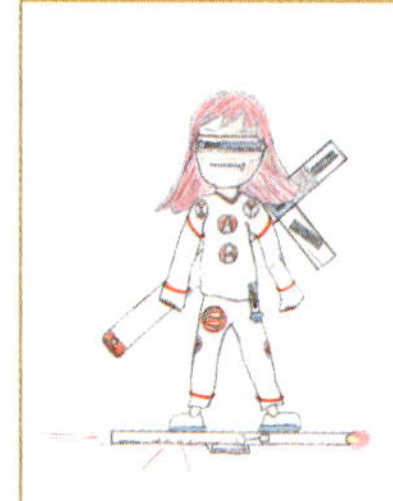

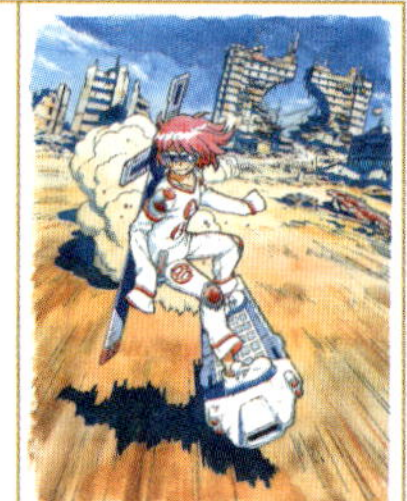

29 p74~75

Justice

Ryunosuke & Thomas
17/07/2017

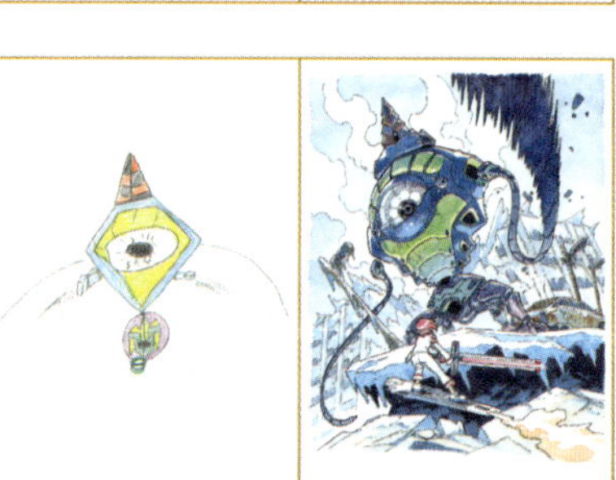

30 p76~77

The Eye of Ice

Itsuki & Thomas
24/07/2017

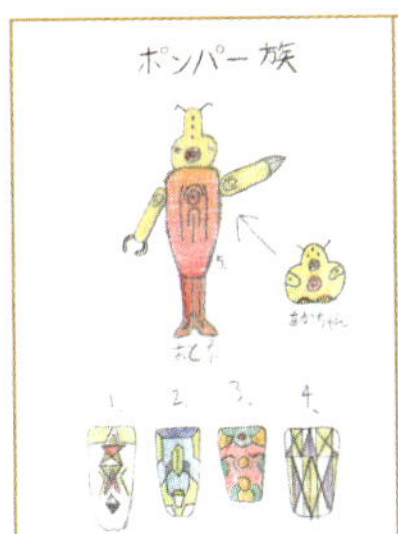

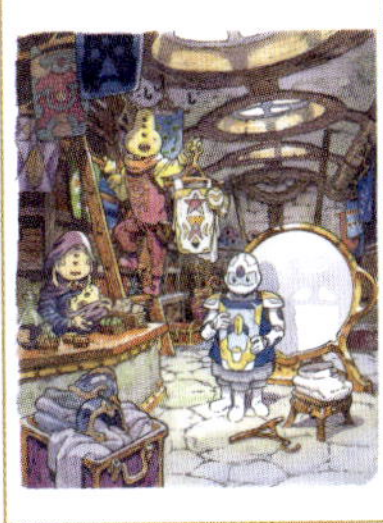

31 p78~79

The Pompaa's Boutique

Ryunosuke & Thomas
01/08/2017

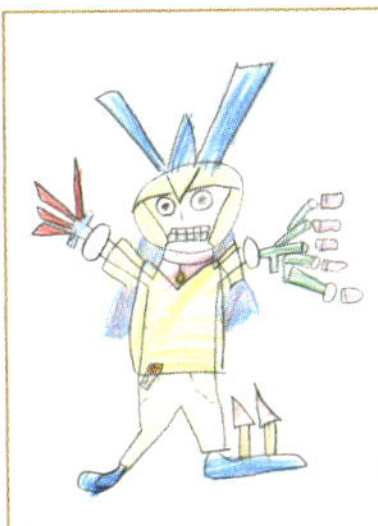
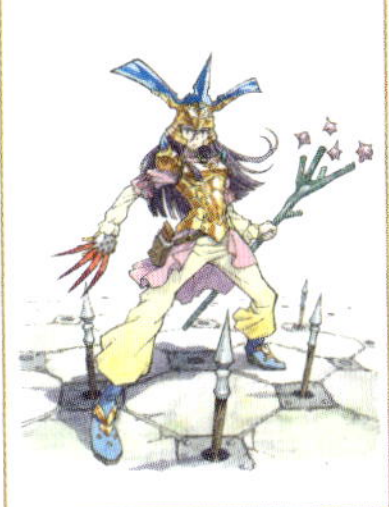

32 p80~81

Tomoe

Itsuki & Thomas
06/08/2017

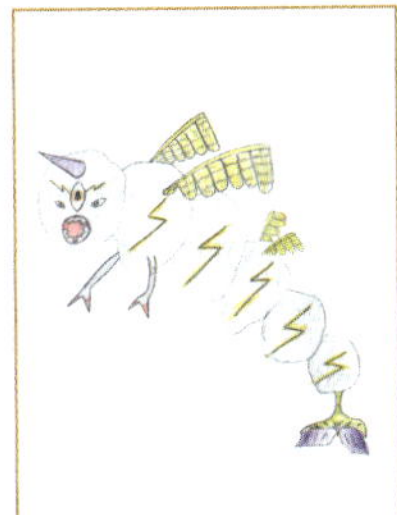
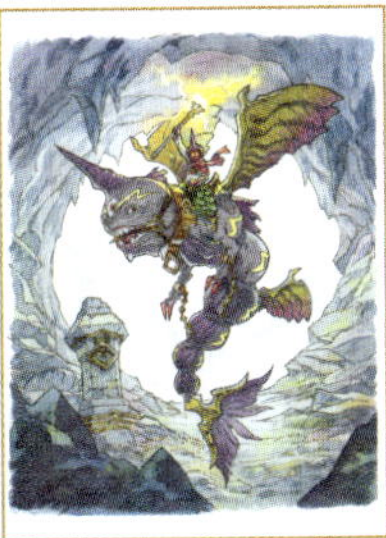

33 p82~83

Narwhagon

Ryunosuke & Thomas
13/08/2017

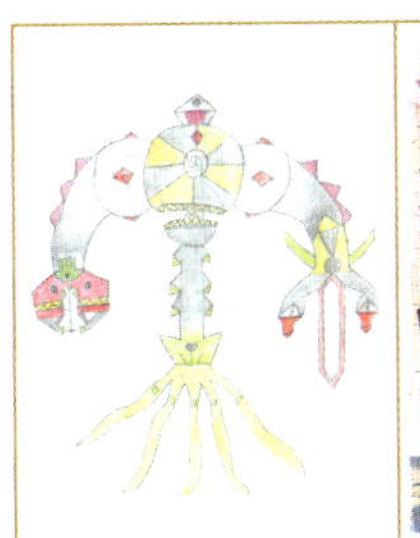
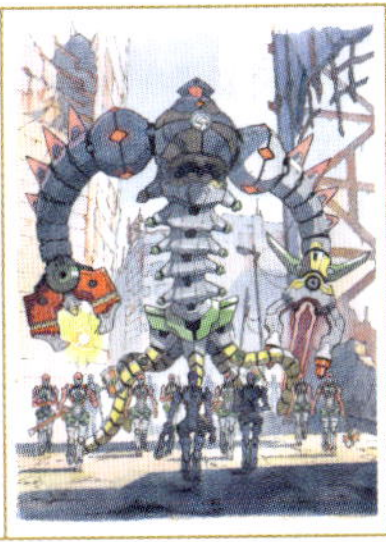

Extra 05 p84~85

Heavy Combat Unit SK-02

Ryunosuke & Thomas
08/11/2017

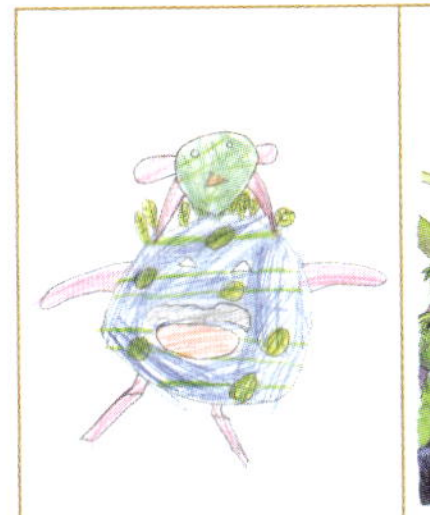
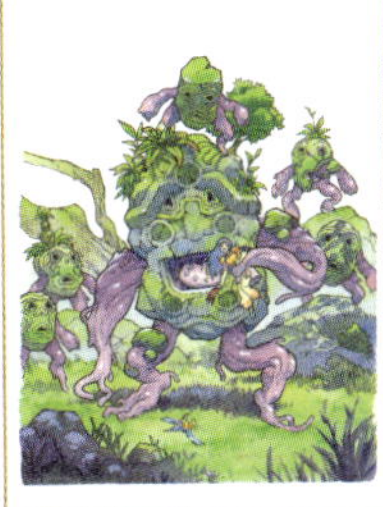

34 p86~87

The Rockthieves

Itsuki & Thomas
20/08/2017

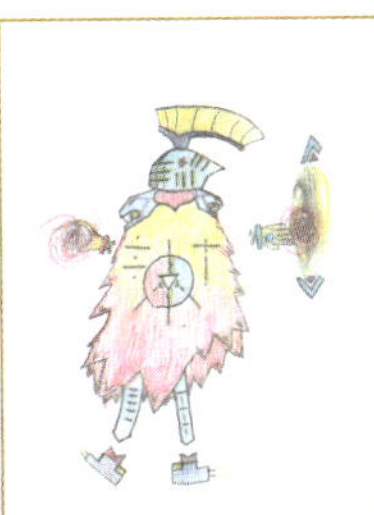
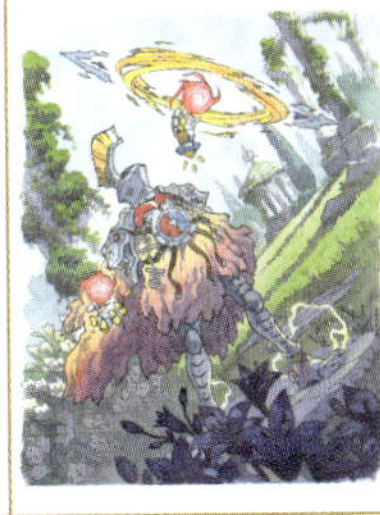

35 p88~89

Knight of the Royal Garden

Ryunosuke & Thomas
31/08/2017

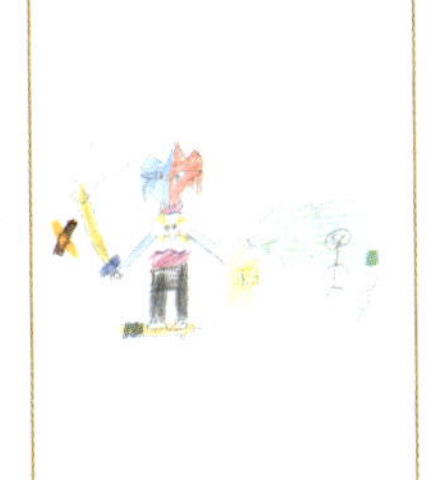
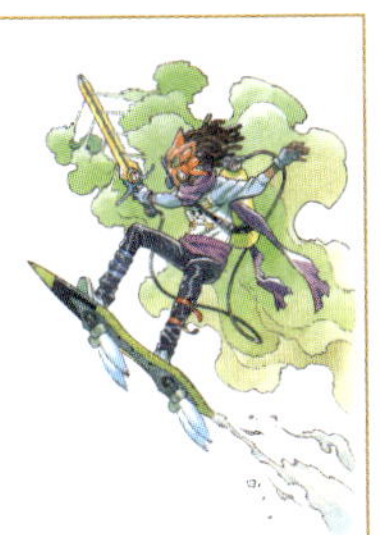

36 p90~91

Noah the Toxic Surfer

Itsuki & Thomas
12/09/2017

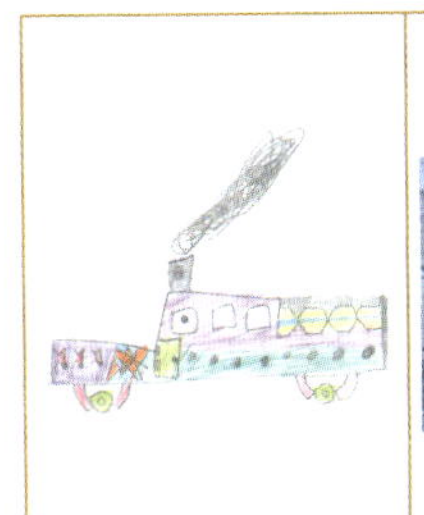
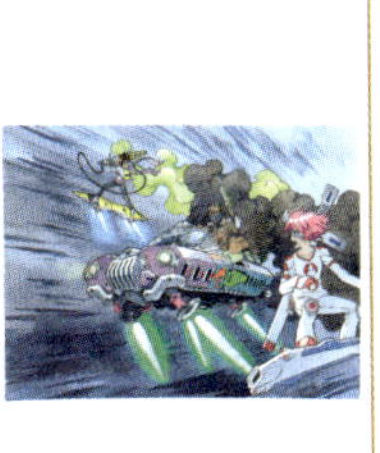

Extra 06 p92~93

Cyber Pursuit

Itsuki & Thomas
08/12/2017

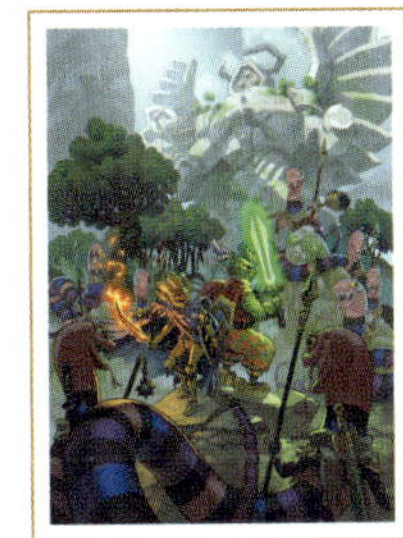

p107

Digital Illustration

Thomas
07/2017

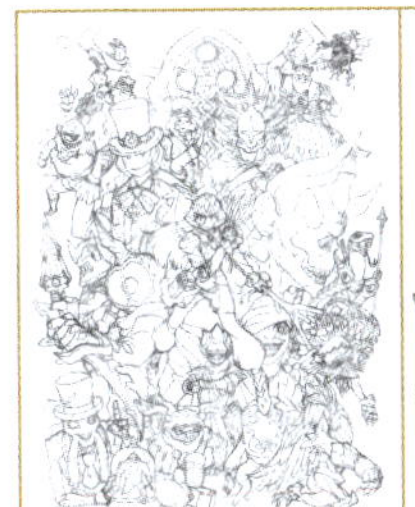
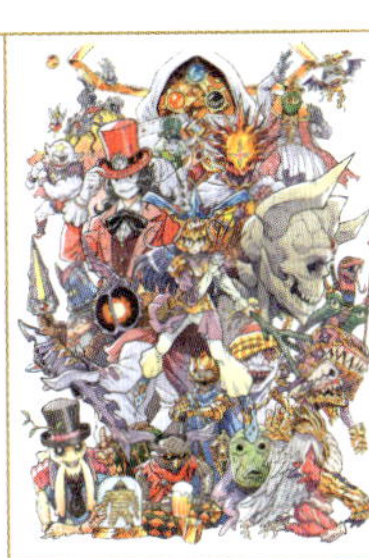

p108~109

Anniversary Illustration

Thomas
01/2018

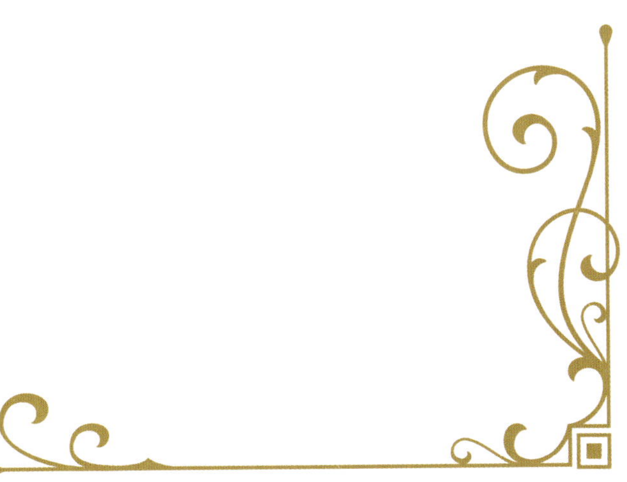

Biography

Thomas Romain was born in Besançon in 1977. In place of inheriting the drawing gene, he was gifted a large dose of love by his parents.

As a child he spent many a day watching the cartoons of the *Club Dorothée* programming block, as well as sitting in front of his *Atari ST* computer. In his teen years he much preferred spending his free time playing his *Super Nintendo* rather than flirting with the fairer sex. After moving to the Parisian region, he became fascinated by the 1992 Dream Team and traded his velvet pants for a tracksuit and a pair of *Reebok* pumps. Between training sessions, he always found the time to draw. It was this passion that led him to discover the works of Enki Bilal and Katsuhiro Otomo, both of whom left their mark on him, as well as the worlds of JRPGs such as *Secret of Mana* and *Final Fantasy VI.*

1996 proved a major turning point in his life. An injury cut his modest pro-basketball ambitions short, and he turned his back on the Faculty of Science he had been frequenting with little to no conviction. He gave drawing his all, using the manga artists and anime directors he so admired as models, at a time when Japanese pop culture began to flood the French market.

Two years later, Thomas enrolled at the Gobelins, the prestigious Parisian school of animation. In his class he rubbed shoulders with Riad Sattouf and Jérémie Périn, future greats of the French creative scene. The animated short he produced with his classmates caught the eye of French production house *Antéfilms* and would later become known as the famous series *Code Lyoko.* However, Thomas wished to consecrate himself to another project, one that represented for him the dream of the land of the rising sun: *Oban Star-Racers.*

Born from a chance meeting with animated series writer/director Savin Yeatman-Eiffel (yup, a descendant of the guy who built the tower), *Oban Star-Racers* was heavily influenced by all things anime, which both creators were huge fans of. Thanks to their perseverance - but also to their meeting with Japanese partners who believed in them - the series became a Franco-Japanese co-production. Along with their colleague Stanislas Brunet, they took a one-way trip to Tokyo with their project clutched in hand. Thomas created the characters, supervised the artistic direction and co-directed the series. In 2006, ten years after its creation, *Oban Star-Racers* was successfully broadcast in over 120 countries.

In 2006, pushed by Japanese studios which sniffed out his talent, Thomas made the decision to stay and work in Japan. He then got to express his talents as background designer on a 100% Japanese anime: *Kissdum.* However, that was not the only reason behind his expatriation. The charm of the French *gaijins* was very much in play and Thomas soon found himself married. His wife, Keiko, was shortly expecting their first child: Ryunosuke. A few years later, in 2008, Itsuki would show up to enlarge their family unit.

Inspired by his experiences on the hardwood courts, he began to dream of a project based on basketball in a sci-fi setting. Shoji Kawamori, the famous Japanese mecha designer, known for creating the *Odysseus* from *Ulysses 31* and *Optimus Prime* from *Transformers,* as well as the iconic Valkyries, the shape-shifting jets from the *Macross* saga, proposed that they develop a series together around that idea - with the condition of adding in giant robots. Convinced by Shoji Kowamori's idea, Thomas accepted and started drawing for the first Japanese anime co-created by a Frenchman,

Basquash!, later recognized for the quality of its artistic direction. To develop the rich universe of the series, from 2007 to 2009, Thomas surrounded himself with a dozen or so young talents from France. Thanks to this, the community of French animators in Japan underwent a boom. A few years later he decided to deepen the ties of his peers by creating the *Furansujin Connection* association. Considered indispensable today, its goal is to promote the Japanese animation job market, and to help foreigners, notably the French, integrate into the field.

Achieving the power of an overseer as well as a character designer and director, domains usually reserved for the most talented and experienced of Japanese creators, he gained the post of background and mecha designer on works produced by studio Satelight : *Aquarion Evol* (2010), *Croisée in a Foreign Labyrinth* (2011), *Symphogear* (2012), *Bodacious Space Pirates* (2012), *AKB0048* (2012), *Nobunaga the Fool* (2014), and *Macross Delta* (2016). He supervised the *France Team*, a group of French artists integrated into the Tokyo studio, a notable exception to a milieu which rarely opens its doors to foreign talents. He was then solicited by other studios for projects such as *Space Dandy* (2014), in which he created the space ships. He also made visual contributions to videogames such as the *Persona 2* remake (Atlus), *Gyrozetter* (Square-Enix) and even *Dai Gyakuten Saiban* and *Dai Gyakuten Saiban 2*, the *Phoenix Wright* spin-offs (Capcom). He also designed the poster for the 2016 Tokyo animation festival (*Tokyo Anime Award Festival*).

His work was noticed beyond the borders of the island. He was contacted to become the character designer for the American project *Cannon Busters* for *Netflix*. In 2015, he was also invited to *Anime Expo*, the yearly pilgrimage of American otaku in Los Angeles. For the occasion, he put out *"Lost in Anime"*, an artbook collecting ten years' worth of drawings, illustrations and designs.

In 2017, he threw himself in a brand-new initiative. Inspired by his sons' drawings, he began to reinterpret them in the form of hand-painted illustrations, which he posted weekly on social media. The growing success of these adaptations led him to launch his own *YouTube* channel, which blew up in popularity on an international level. Pushed by his passion for drawing, creation, and his desire to share, he found there a platform perfect to reach a larger audience.

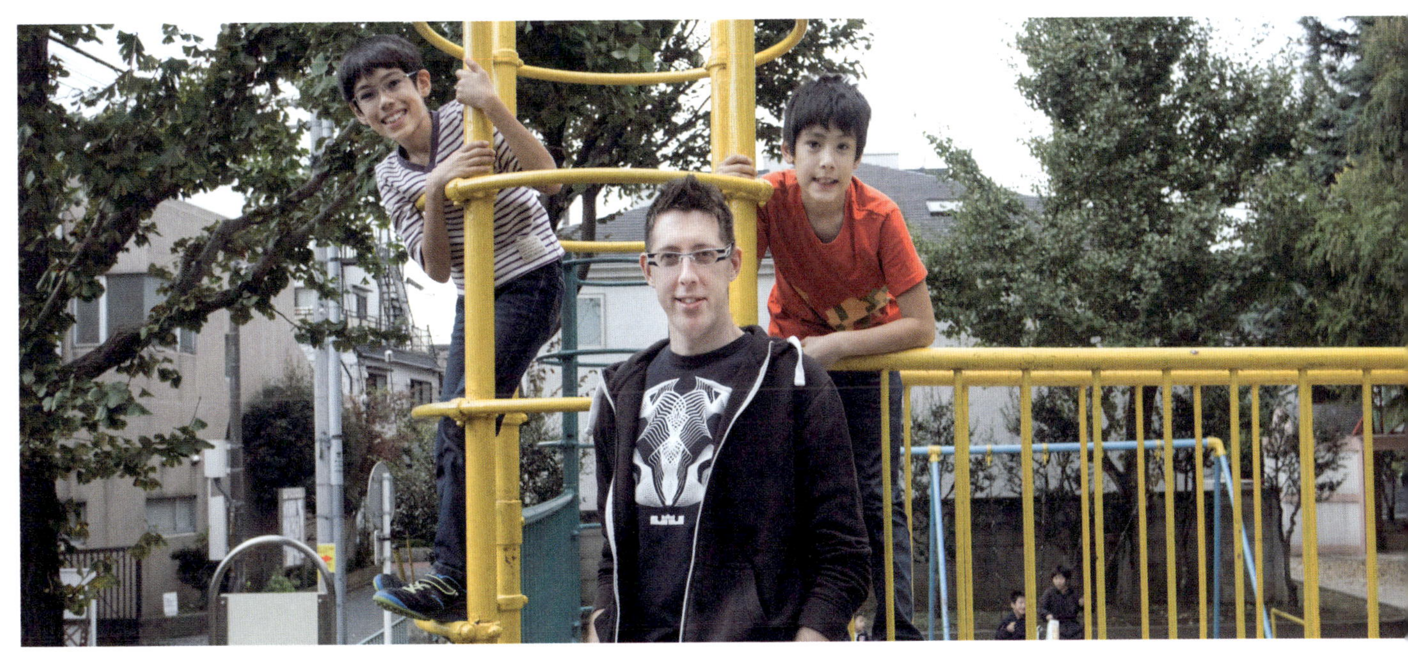

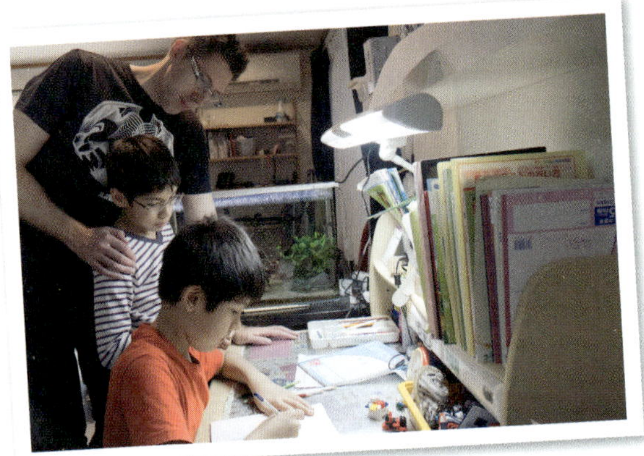

Our thanks to

Keiko, wife and mother, without whom we would be nothing.
Marie-Paule and Roland, Yoko and Takashi, parents, in-laws, and exceptional grandparents.

Stanislas Brunet, for having launched this project by offering a set of watercolors to Itsuki.
Christophe Ferreira, Vincent Nghiem, and all the members of the France Team, for their lasting friendship.
Grégoire Hellot, Fabien Vautrin, and Kurokawa Editions, for believing in us and making this wonderful book.
Shoko Iwamoto, for her precious advice.

All the generous people who have followed us, and still follow us, on Patreon.
All of you who have welcomed our illustrations on social media with an extraordinary enthusiasm.

Find us on social media:
Twitter : @thomasintokyo | Instagram : @thomasintokyo | YouTube : Thomas Romain

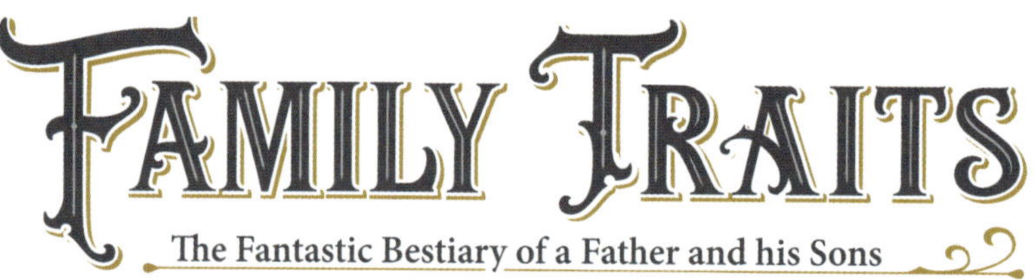

FRENCH EDITION CREDITS
Work published under the direction of Grégoire Hellot
Artistic Direction: Fabien Vautrin
Scans: Madame Kei
Photography: Aude Boyer

ENGLISH EDITION CREDITS
Project Editor: Matt Moylan
English Translation: David Lumsdon
Associate Editor: M. Chandler

UDON STAFF
Chief of Operations: ERIK KO
Director of Publishing: MATT MOYLAN
VP of Sales: JOHN SHABLESKI
Senior Producer: LONG VO
Marketing Manager: JENNY MYUNG
Japanese Liaisons: STEVEN CUMMINGS
ANNA KAWASHIMA

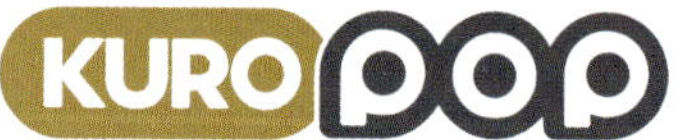

Published in English by UDON Entertainment Corp.
118 Tower Hill Road, C1, PO Box 20008
Richmond Hill, Ontario, L4K 0K0 CANADA.

www.UDONentertainment.com

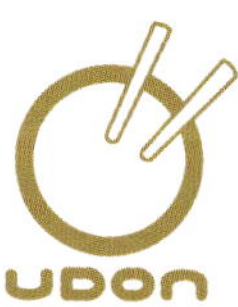

First Printing: February 2019
ISBN-13: 978-1-77294-092-3
ISBN-10: 1-77294-092-5

Printed in China